STUDIES IN ARCHITECTURE

EDITED BY ANTHONY BLUNT AND RUDOLF WITTKOWER

VOLUME III

BURGUNDIAN GOTHIC ARCHITECTURE

ROBERT BRANNER

BURGUNDIAN GOTHIC ARCHITECTURE

ROBERT BRANNER

DEPARTMENT OF ART HISTORY AND ARCHAEOLOGY
COLUMBIA UNIVERSITY, NEW YORK

1960

A. ZWEMMER LTD

LONDON

© 1960

A. ZWEMMER LTD, 76–80 CHARING CROSS ROAD, LONDON WC2

MADE AND PRINTED IN GREAT BRITAIN

BLOCKS ETCHED BY W. F. SEDGWICK LTD, LONDON SE1

TEXT AND ILLUSTRATIONS

PRINTED BY PERCY LUND, HUMPHRIES AND CO. LTD, BRADFORD

BOUND BY KEY AND WHITING LTD, LONDON N1

Contents

List of Plates

List of Text Illustrations

Table of Abbreviations

Guillaume	A. Guillaume, *La Côte-d'Or. Guide du touriste, de l'archéologue et du naturaliste*, Dijon, 1954.
Hautecœur	L. Hautecœur, *La Bourgogne. L'architecture (Les richesses d'art de la France)*, 3 vols., Paris-Brussels, 1929.
Hubert (1952)	J. Hubert, *L'architecture religieuse du haut moyen âge en France (École pratique des Hautes-Etudes, Section des sciences religieuses, Collection chrétienne et byzantine)*, Paris, 1952.
Jantzen	H. Jantzen, *Burgundische Gotik (Sitzungsberichte der Bayerischen Akademie der Wissenschaften, Ph.-Hist. Kl.*, 1948, 5), Munich, 1948.
Laurent-Claudon	J. Laurent – F. Claudon, *Abbayes et prieurés de l'ancienne France*, vol. 12: *Province ecclésiastique de Lyon*, pt. 3: *Diocèses de Langres et de Dijon (Archives de la France monastique*, vol. 45), Ligugé–Paris, 1941.
Lebeuf	J. Lebeuf, *Mémorial concernant l'histoire civile et ecclésiastique d'Auxerre et de son ancien diocèse . . .*, ed. Quantin-Challe, 4 vols., Auxerre, 1848–1855.
Longnon, *Lyon*	A. Longnon, *Pouillés de la province de Lyon (Recueil des historiens de la France, Pouillés*, vol. 1), Paris, 1904.
Longnon, *Sens*	A. Longnon, *Pouillés de la province de Sens (ibid.*, vol. 4), Paris, 1904.
Mém. com. C.-d'Or	*Mémoires, Commission des antiquités du département de la Côte-d'Or.*
Petit	E. Petit, *Histoire des ducs de Bourgogne de la race capétienne (Société bourguignonne de géographie et d'histoire. Publications)*, 9 vols., Dijon, 1885–1905.
PM	*Petites monographies des grands édifices de la France.*
Philippe	A. Philippe, "L'architecture religieuse aux XIe et XIIe siècles dans l'ancien diocèse d'Auxerre", *Bulletin monumental*, 66, 1904, 43–92.
Quantin I, II	M. Quantin, *Cartulaire générale de l'Yonne*, 2 vols., Auxerre, 1854–1860.
Quantin III	M. Quantin, *Recueil de pièces pour faire suite au cartulaire générale de l'Yonne*, Auxerre 1873.
Quantin, *Rép.*	M. Quantin, *Yonne (Comité des travaux historiques. Collection de documents inédits . . .*, s. 7, pt. 7, *Répertoire archéologique de la France*, vol. 8), Paris, 1868.

Roserot   A. Roserot, *Dictionnaire topographique du département de la Côte-d'Or (Comité des travaux historiques . . .)*, Paris, 1924.

Soultrait, *Rép.*   J. H. G. R. de Soultrait, *Nièvre (Comité des travaux historiques, Collection de documents inédits . . ., s. 7, pt. 7. Répertoire archéologique de la France*, vol. 4), Paris, 1875.

von Veltheim   H. H. von Veltheim, *Burgundische Kleinkirche bis zum Jahre 1200*, Munich, 1913.

ACKNOWLEDGEMENTS

Permission to reproduce the following photographs is gratefully acknowledged to the Archives Photographiques for Plates 1, 2, 3, 4a, 6b, 7, 8a, 9b, 10, 13a, 14, 15, 18, 20, 23b, 25b, 26a, 27a, 29b, 32, 33, 34, 36a and 37b; to the Bibliothèque Nationale for Plates 30a and 38a; to the Dean and Chapter of Canterbury Cathedral for Plate 11a; to the Musée d'Art et d'Histoire de la Ville de Genève for Plate 11b; to M. Francis Salet for Fig. 97; to Mr. Carl F. Barnes II for Plate 45b.

Preface

THE present book grew from an investigation of the impact of High Gothic architecture – that of Chartres Cathedral and its immediate followers in the first decades of the thirteenth century – on the various regions of France. It had been my original intention to reassess this short but important phase of Gothic style from the point of view of the provinces and to determine whether the dissemination of Gothic in France, and by extension in Europe at large, could have been due to the particular qualities of the Chartrain group. The architectural situation in the early thirteenth century turned out to be complex, however, and it seemed more valuable at the present time to dissect this complexity than to attempt the formulation of a general theory.

Burgundy is of course famous as one of the major centres of Roman-esque architecture, the early "international" style of the Middle Ages. In the thirteenth century it was also the scene of a highly developed regional Gothic style. Gothic had no deep roots there, however, and the forms of this style vanished almost as rapidly as they had appeared, so that by 1300 Burgundian Gothic was virtually extinct. Chartres made itself felt at the very start of the movement, but in succeeding decades it was the newer designs of the Ile de France, themselves innovations upon the Chartrain formula, that formed a source of inspiration for Burgundian architects. No attempt has been made here to isolate pecu-liarly local types among the parts of the church, such as the façade or the porch, largely because I do not believe such types existed, at least in their simplest forms. The façade of Notre Dame at Dijon, for instance, is virtually unique, and if the porch there inspired the later ones at Beaune, St Père sous Vézelay and Semur, these differ fundamentally from Dijon in being "extrusive", and they also differ amongst themselves. A Catalogue of monuments, with summary descriptions and biblio-graphies, is provided at the end of the volume. I have not intended this as a complete archaeological repertory but have included only the buildings discussed in the text, a scattering of small priories and parishes and some famous destroyed churches.

This study could not have been completed without the advice and criticism of Professors Jean Bony, of the Institut Français de Londres, and Rudolf Wittkower, of Columbia University in the City of New York. To MM. Kenneth John Conant, Professor Emeritus of Harvard University; Jean Troubat, proprietor of the former abbey of Flavigny; Jacques Palet, Director of the Musée Archéologique at Nevers; Robert Gauchery, sometime Architecte des Bâtiments de France at Bourges; René Louis, Director of the Musée Archéologique at Auxerre; Louis Blondel, Archéologue Cantonal at Geneva; Pierre Gras, Director of the Bibliothèque Publique at Dijon; Pierre Quarré, Director of the Musée de Dijon, and his gracious wife, Mme. Madeleine Oursel-Quarré, Adjunct Librarian at Dijon, are due my profound thanks for their assistance in making available little-known information and in solving problems all too often raised by ignorance of the local idiom. The Direction de l'Architecture of the Commission des Monuments Historiques de France, and especially M. André Lapeyre, Adjunct Director, benevolently undertook to provide introductions to local authorities, and the various guardians and beadles were most helpful in facilitating the close examination of the monuments. In the United States, I must acknowledge my debt to the students of my seminars in the Faculty of Philosophy at Columbia University, Miss Sheila M. Edmunds, Mrs. Meredith Lillich and MM. William Carney, Bertrand Davezac, Dawson Kiang, Joshua Kind and Damie Stillman, for their collaboration in sorting out the materials of this study; and to the Librarian of the Avery Memorial Library of Architecture, Professor James Grote Van Derpool, and his efficient staff, especially Mr. Adolf K. Placzek, to Miss Mary Chamberlin and the staff of the Fine Arts Library, and to the Reference Staff of Butler Library, all at Columbia. Travel grants were provided by a Watkins Faculty Scholarship from the University of Kansas at Lawrence (1956) and by the Council on Research in the Humanities at Columbia University (1958).

New York, November, 1959   ROBERT BRANNER

CHAPTER I

Historical

"La Bourgogne historique a un centre, mais
point de frontières visibles ni fixes."[1]

THE descendants of the ancient Senones lived in a vast region of eastern France that is remarkable for its geographical variation. From the plateau of Langres to the cliffs of the Morvan and the rolling hills of the Charollais, Burgundy comprises a series of separate landscapes penetrated or flanked by major rivers, the Saône, the Loire and the Seine.[2] In the early Middle Ages, the political landscape was also disunited. The duchy of Burgundy, largely an inheritance of the Frankish kingdom, was acquired by the Capetian family about 1015,[3] and during the next two hundred years the dukes often followed the separatist policy of the crown's major vassals. They nevertheless grew steadily in stature and strength, to become one of the king's staunchest allies at Bouvines. They sometimes had to cope with formidable internal problems, such as the rebellious house of Vergy that nearly dispossessed them until Eudes III "reduced" it by marriage,[4] and relations with their immediate neighbours were seldom calm. The count of Champagne was constantly ready to receive the homage of any lord living on the northern edge of Burgundy and even entered into an anti-Burgundian alliance with

1. H. Drouot–J. Calmette, *Histoire de Bourgogne* (*Les vieilles provinces de France*), Paris, 1928, p. 1. Cf. M. Chaume, *Les origines du duché de Bourgogne*, II, Dijon, 1927, pp. 48 ff. The Saône was a political boundary from 843 (Drouot–Calmette, pp. 75–76; cf. J. Richard, "Passages de Saône aux XIIe et XIIIe siècles", *Annales de Bourgogne*, 22, 1950, pp. 245–274). See also J. Richard, "Le 'conduit' des routes et la fixation des limites entre mouvances féodales. La frontière bourguignonne dans le comté de Bar-sur-Seine (XIe–XIIIe siècles)", *Annales de Bourgogne*, 24, 1952, pp. 85–101.
2. See G. Chabot, *La Bourgogne* (*Collection A. Colin, Section de géographie*, 233), Paris, 1941; A. Déléage, *La vie rurale en Bourgogne jusqu'au début du XIe siècle*, Mâcon, 1941; and E. Jarry, *La formation territoriale de la Bourgogne. Essai de géographie historique* (*Provinces et pays de France*, III: *Monographies provinciales*), Paris, 1948.
3. E. Petit, *passim*; J. Richard, *Les ducs de Bourgogne et la formation du duché du XIe au XIVe siècle* (*Publications de l'université de Dijon*, 12), Paris, 1954, with bibliography.
4. Petit, vol. 3, chs. XIX and XXII.

the count of Nevers,[5] the duke's vassal for a large western portion of the duchy.[6] A similar absence of unity was imposed on Burgundy by ecclesiastical boundaries. There had been no bishop residing in the duke's capital at Dijon since the late ninth century, when the Bishop of Langres, who sought refuge there during the invasions, returned to his proper seat.[7] Langres and the southern bishops, at Chalon sur Saône, Autun and Mâcon, were suffragans of Lyon, while Sens was the superior of Auxerre and Nevers.

This lack of unity was undoubtedly more apparent than real in the late twelfth century, for with the general increase in population and the rise of commerce, communications were ameliorated over large portions of France and the more disruptive features of feudalism gradually subsided. The density of population in Burgundy, from the closely placed cities of the south to the isolated and distant communities of the north-east, was altered by the founding of *villeneuves* and by the numerous tracts of land put into cultivation, especially by the Cistercians.[8] North-eastern Burgundy was still rural as late as 1250, however, and Dijon itself remained a small agricultural centre that consumed most of its own produce.[9] Cloth was manufactured and exported by Sens, Auxerre and the Cistercian monasteries of the Yonne Valley, where the rivers and streams pushed more than an occasional fulling mill.[10] This area grew particularly

5. Petit, vol. 2, *passim*. R. de Lespinasse (*Le Nivernais et les comtes de Nevers*, Paris, 1909–1914, vol. 1 (to 1200), p. 214) suggests the anti-Burgundian feeling of Nevers may have dated from the early eleventh century, when Count Lanfry was affianced to the daughter of Robert the Pious.

6. "Burgundia inferior" comprised the counties of Auxerre, Nevers, Autun, Chalon, Mâcon, Langres, Troyes and Sens in 1054 (Petit, vol. 2, pp. viii–ix), when the count of Nevers and Auxerre had already added to his titles that of Tonnerre (Lespinasse, vol. 1, p. 227).

7. P. Gras, "Le séjour à Dijon des évêques de Langres du Ve au IXe siècle. Ses conséquences sur l'histoire de la ville", *Recueil de travaux offert à M. Clovis Brunel* (*Société de l'Ecole des Chartes, Mémoires et documents*, 12), Paris, 1955, vol. 1, pp. 550–561.

8. Jarry, pp. 197 ff., largely from Chaume, vol. 2, pp. 478–479.

9. M. Oursel-Quarré, "Les origines de la commune de Dijon", *Mémoires de la Société pour l'histoire du droit et des institutions des anciens pays bourguignons, comtois et romands*, 6, 1939, pp. 5–112 and 7, 1940–1941, pp. 5–94, and offprint, Dijon, (194–), esp. pp. 169 ff.

10. For Sens, see F. Bourquelot, *Etudes sur les foires de Champagne* (*Mémoires présentés . . . à l'Académie des inscriptions et belles-lettres*, s. 2, 5, pts. 1–2), Paris, 1865, vol. 1, pp. 230, 242 and 280; E. Chapin, *Les villes des foires de Champagne* (*Bibliothèque de l'Ecole des Hautes-Etudes, Sciences historiques et philologiques*, 268), Paris, 1937, pp. 96 and 111, n. 22; and M. Quantin, III, p. 345. For Auxerre, see J. Lebeuf, vol. 4, pp. 76, 89–91, 107 and 141. *Viridus* of Auxerre was worn by Herbert

wealthy as an exporter of wine, which was floated down the Yonne and Seine Rivers to Paris and even to Rouen, whence it was shipped to England.[11] Salt was another commodity, mined across the Saône in the Imperial County of Burgundy and transported overland to the barges at Auxerre.[12] Yet none of this was comparable to the industry of Flanders or to the commerce of Champagne, with its four great fair cities.[13] The fair at Chalon was the biggest Burgundy could offer, but it attained a secure place as an international centre only late in the thirteenth century, when the Champagne fairs had begun to decline.[14]

Despite their middling character, the rising levels of economy and population in Burgundy had important repercussions in the twelfth and early thirteenth centuries. One of these was the frequent granting of communes – to Dijon in 1183 and again in 1187, to Sens finally in 1189 and to Auxerre in 1194[15] – and another the enormous increase in building.

of Boseham, secretary of Thomas à Becket (O. Lehmann-Brockhaus, *Lateinische Schriftquellen zur Kunst in England . . .*, vol. 3, Munich, 1956, no. 6480). For the fulling mills, see Quantin, II, pp. 115, 147, 233–234 and 443, and Quantin III, p. 118; Petit, vol. 4, pp. 161, 359 and 360; and Dom U. Plancher, *Histoire générale et particulière de Bourgogne*, Dijon, vol. 1, 1739, p. 341.

11. See J. B. Biot in the *Journal des Savants*, 1851, p. 672. Cf. A. L. Simon, *History of the wine trade in England*, vol. 1, London, 1906, pp. 60, 74–76 and 97; the chronicle of Salimbene, ed. Holder-Egger, *Monumenta Germaniae Historica, Scriptores*, vol. 32, p. 218, and R. Dion, "Le commerce des vins de Beaune au moyen âge", *Revue historique*, 79 (214), 1955, pp. 209–221. The Cistercians also sold wine at Troyes, Provins and Bar-sur-Seine (Quantin II, p. 426 and III, p. 143)

12. J. Richard, 1950, pp. 248 ff; Lebeuf, vol. 3, p. 134 and *Ordonnances des rois de France*, IX, pp. 280–281 and 290 (1204 charter, on which see *Réglemens sur les arts et métiers de Paris* (Et. Boileau), ed. G. B. Depping (*Collection de documents inédits sur l'histoire de France*, 4), Paris, 1837, pp. xxviii–xxix).

13. See Chapin, p. 193, and H. Laurent, *Un grand commerce d'exportation au moyen âge. La draperie des Pays-Bas en France et dans les pays méditeranéens, XIIe-XIVe siècles*, Paris, 1935.

14. P. Toussaint, *Les foires de Chalon-sur-Saône* (*Collection d'études sur l'histoire du droit de la Bourgogne*, 22), Dijon, 1910, and Laurent, pp. 166–168, although drapers from Troyes and Provins went there in the early thirteenth century (Chapin, pp. 73, n. 85 and 96). Cf. in addition A. Parat, "Les foires anciennes dans l'Avallonnais", *Bulletin de la Société des sciences de l'Yonne*, 71, 1917, pp. 393–404; J. Mouton, "Foires et marchés d'Auxerre", *ibid.*, 83, 1935, pp. 35–42; E. Collette, *Les foires et marchés à Dijon* (*Collection d'études d'histoire du droit et des institutions de la Bourgogne*, 2), Dijon, 1905, and M. Henriot, "Les foires de Semur-en-Auxois", *Annales de Bourgogne*, 6, 1934, pp. 371–380.

15. J. Garnier, *Chartes de communes et affranchissements en Bourgogne*, 3 vols., Dijon, 1867–1877 and *Introduction* (completed by E. Champeaux), Dijon, 1908. See also M. Oursel-Quarré, p. 193 (Dijon), G. Bourgin, *La commune de Soissons et le groupe communal soissonnais* (*Bibliothèque de l'Ecole des Hautes Etudes, Sciences historiques et philologiques*, 167), Paris, 1908, pp. 315 ff. (Sens), and Lespinasse, vol. 1, p. 405 (Auxerre).

In the eleventh and early twelfth centuries, most of the new churches erected were in the southern part of the region, but after 1150 the emphasis shifted. Not only was a considerably larger number of churches founded or rebuilt at this time, but they were most often situated in the north and in the neighbouring portion of Champagne. Greater wealth provided the means, and more people the necessity, for this increase. Bishop Guillaume de Seignelay actually stated he was founding three new parish churches at La Charité sur Loire *crescente multitudine plebis*, in 1209,[16] and the chronicler of the *Gesta Pontificum* of Auxerre wrote a few years later: ". . . the piety of the people far and wide waxed hot for the new construction of churches . . ."[17] By 1250, however, the saturation point seems to have been reached. The "agricultural frontier" had virtually ceased to exist, the population was at a relatively stable level and fewer and fewer major campaigns of construction were undertaken, until, by the mid-fourteenth century, work came almost to a standstill. The Black Death and the Hundred Years' War merely provided the finishing touch to this situation.

One would like to know more about how the considerable number of twelfth and thirteenth-century churches in Burgundy were built – who decided upon and approved the projects, who paid for them, and, most important of all, who actually did the work. Documents furnishing specific information of this sort are rare, and more often than not, when a text has been preserved, the building to which it refers has not. But the documents occasionally do cast some light on the procedures by which an edifice came into being. In 1265, for instance, the collegiate chapter of St Julien du Sault founded a new parish church that was to be built with funds left by a certain Jean Henri, probably a canon, and a curate was appointed to the parish; but the actual construction was overseen by a canon of the metropolitan chapter of Sens, who was the archbishop's

16. *Gallia christiana*, vol. 12, *Instrumenta*, c. 150.

17. A. St.-Paul, "Mélanges", *L'Année archéologique*, 1879, p. 136 (*devotio = de novo* in *Gesta pontificum Autissiodorensium*, ed. L.-M. Duru (*Bibliothèque historique de l'Yonne*), vol. 1, Paris, 1850, p. 474); cf. Lebeuf, vol. 1, p. 389 and *Patrologia latina*, ed. Migne, vol. 215, cc. 1308–1309.

bailiff and who undoubtedly hired the workmen.[18] If a layman sponsored a project, the rate of execution might vary considerably. Hervé de Donzy, Count of Nevers, for instance, founded three monasteries in the early thirteenth century, in return for the papal sanction of his marriage, and in at least one case, as his interest flagged, so construction slowed down or stopped entirely.[19] The situation was often no better when the church was sponsor, although in this case it was usually a sudden fluctuation in income or a sharp rise in cost that had an adverse effect on the work.

The patron and the architect both seem to have played major roles in the formation of the programme and in the design of a church. Master Elias of Dereham, a canon of Salisbury in the early thirteenth century who often acted as a patron's agent in the arranging of commissions and the overseeing of their execution, was well versed in technical matters and had a "keen understanding of artistic questions" and a "sympathy with artistic movements."[20] He may of course have been somewhat unusual in this respect. It is probable that the average patron – a dean, prior or curate – found a particular building to his liking and hired a mason from its workshop to design and execute his own church. While the men of the twelfth and thirteenth centuries rarely left comments on beauty in writing – there was as yet no language in which to express a detailed aesthetic appreciation, and the very concept of beauty was intimately bound up with philosophical and theological matters – this does not mean they were unaware of it. And architects were no exception, for the first recorded statement of acclaim was made not by a patron but by the mason Villard de Honnecourt, about 1235.[21] The success of a new design sometimes even started a local vogue, and this in turn could make possible an important architectural development. The Burgundian Gothic style seems to have begun in this way with the Cathedral of Auxerre.

18. Quantin III, p. 620.
19. See Charrault under Bellary, in the Catalogue, esp. pp. 546–547.
20. A. H. Thompson, "Master Elias of Dereham and the King's works", *Archaeological Journal*, 98, 1941, pp. 1–35.
21. H. R. Hahnloser, *Villard de Honnecourt*, Vienna, 1935, pp. 49–55 and pl. 18.

Many of the smaller thirteenth-century churches in Burgundy, however, were undoubtedly erected by men who scarcely merit the title of architect or master-mason.[22] They seem to have moved about the hinterland with their fellows, like bands of country-builders, accepting work where they could find it. This accounts for the dissemination of "provincial" designs which frequently kept forms alive and fundamentally unaltered for generations after their original creation. The larger monuments were of course major projects that necessitated careful preparation, both by the administrators and the executants. Here an architect was certainly in charge, at least in the thirteenth century, most often with assistants, and labour was divided into specific tasks performed by quarriers, hewers, layers, and so on. It would seem that the masons, in particular, were accustomed to working for different masters, for only in this way can one explain such phenomena as a striking similarity of capitals in two otherwise totally unrelated monuments. In some cases, the architect apparently took the masons with him, and one can occasionally infer that an assistant in a workshop became the director in another, that he graduated, as it were, to the highest rank of his profession. Only the faintest glimmerings of these movements appear in mediaeval texts – even the very detailed exposition of Gervasius of Canterbury on the two Williams is frustratingly incomplete on their earlier and later activities, and Continental sources are usually less numerous and precise. One must supplement them with the archaeological study of the monuments. In this way it is possible to reconstruct at least a fragmentary picture of how Gothic architecture was made.

The architecture of the first half of the thirteenth century in Burgundy has long fascinated architects as well as historians. Vauban is reported to have admired the vaults of Notre Dame at Dijon and to have remarked that it only needed "une boîte pour le conserver", and Soufflot had a

22. Cf. J. H. Harvey, "The architects of English parish churches", *Archaeological Journal*, 105, 1948, pp. 14–26. Some of the many groups outlined by Mr. Harvey do not seem to hold for the Continent.

model of it constructed in wood.[23] For Pierre Patte, the editor of J. F. Blondel's *Cours d'architecture*, it was "des plus reccommandables par la légéreté de son exécution",[24] and for E.-E. Viollet-le-Duc, in the nineteenth century, the Cathedral of Auxerre was "plus légère encore".[25] But Dijon and Auxerre are more than simply the work of engineers, as all these men considered them. They are the creations of visionaries, in which structure, space and sculptural effects, the primary elements of architecture, are indissolubly united in a very special manner. This can easily be seen at Auxerre (Pl. 1). The structure of the wall, for instance, has been bared so that the relationship of the support to the part supported is clearly visible. This was done by piercing the walls with passages that both lessen the mass of stonework and form slots of space, altering the solid boundaries of a normal Gothic interior and isolating the supports both before and behind. And it must not be forgotten that these supports are of stone and have a weight and mass of their own. They are formed into series of colonnettes, many of which are detached, free-standing shafts, which contribute a distinct sculptural effect to the overall design, a complex rhythm of tubes, like a permanent scaffolding, that helps to organize and to unify the interior.

Burgundian style also forms a particular expression of the illusion that is fundamental to all Gothic architecture. The various ribs and shafts are normally taken to represent the delineation, on the surface of the masonry, of the thrusts and pressures that are exerted within it – or, to be entirely accurate, those that existed when the building was first put up. In other words, one has the illusion of reading the internal structure on the very surface. The Burgundian architect went a step further. He designed a support that appears to have normal parts, such as a capital, an impost and the departure of the ribs directly above. But in reality the true functions of the several stones often do not correspond at all with the apparent ones. Such concealment is the sign of the virtuoso designer

23. For both Vauban and Soufflot, see Courtépée, 2, p. 104.
24. J. F. Blondel, *Cours d'architecture*, vol. 6 (ed. J. Patte), Paris, 1777, p. 218.
25. E.-E. Viollet-le-Duc, *Dictionnaire raisonné de l'architecture française*, vol. 4, Paris, 1875, p. 147.

and it marks the presence of a very complex and highly mannered point of view.

All this is in sharp contrast to contemporary High Gothic architecture, that of Chartres Cathedral and its immediate following in the early thirteenth century, where clarity and straightforwardness are stressed. The High Gothic elevation has three stories, two almost equally tall, the arcades at the ground and the large clerestory windows above, and a short, dark triforium passage in between. In the Burgundian edifice (Auxerre is exceptional in this respect), the arcades are normally as tall as both upper stories combined, and each of the latter has approximately the same height. The proportions of High Gothic are tall, and if the relation of width to height is in balance at Chartres, it becomes exaggerated and towering at Reims and Amiens. In Burgundy, the constant, rather low and wide proportions have a "slow" feeling about them, to which the active and tense walls are almost in opposition. And finally each bay of Chartres, the unit both of structure and design, is essentially flat, for the triforium openings are small and the clerestory replaces solid wall with acres of glass, an equally finite limit for the interior volumes. Burgundian style, by recessing the walls, reduced their impact on both the volumes and the design of the bay.

Burgundian Gothic was not the product of a long, local tradition, although certain fundamental elements, such as the general proportions, were rooted in the region. It was rather the last in a series of waves that moved south across the region in successive generations from about 1150 on. The history of Gothic architecture in Burgundy is to a certain degree the history of these importations and it becomes a case in point for the dissemination of Gothic style on the Continent. In the first half of the thirteenth century, what is here called "Burgundian Gothic" was itself related to a vast international family stretching from Canterbury to Switzerland, the history of which has recently been traced by M. Jean Bony.[26] The character of the Burgundian branch of this family is nonetheless sufficiently distinct from its immediate relatives to merit special

26. J. Bony (1958).

attention. It is moreover marked by an extraordinary success throughout the furthermost reaches of the province, from Auxerre to Nevers and from Dijon to Cluny. It was perhaps a quirk of fate that it should have had a very short historical life, so short, in fact, that there is some question as to whether it can legitimately be called a style. After the middle of the thirteenth century, a final wave from the north, this time from the Ile de France and representing the designs favoured by Saint Louis and the court patrons of the mid-century, overwhelmed Burgundy as it did other regions of France. Local taste had changed and despite a brief revival at the end of the century, the Burgundian style ceased to be one of the living forms of Gothic architecture.

CHAPTER II

The Twelfth Century

The Romanesque Landscape

B Y the middle of the twelfth century, the architects of Burgundy
had created a notable group of Romanesque monuments. Two
distinct architectural personalities, the groin-vaulted basilica and
the Cluniac style, had already emerged before 1100,[1] and still another,
the style of the Cistercians, was to be formed within less than half a
century.

The originality of the groin-vaulted church lay not in the development
of a particular plan on the ground or in an unusual composition of the
exterior masses of the edifice, but in the creation of strongly defined
compartments of space in the interior. Each bay of the nave is bounded
by vigorous piers and is capped by an individual vault. Such a "parti",
to use the convenient French term for the disposition of the major architectural elements, has the technical advantage of concentrating the weight
of the stone cover on the piers alone, and as if in response, the latter bear
pilasters and colonnettes that rise without interruption to support the
arches separating the vaults. The nave therefore appears to be formed by a
series of independent units. This was perfectly expressed in the small
eleventh-century nave of Anzy le Duc, with its two stories, the main
arcade and the vault lunette, the latter pierced with windows to
form a clerestory (Pl. 2a). And the parti remained unusually constant
throughout the developments of the next hundred years. By the early
twelfth century, a veritable family of groined-basilicas had formed
around Anzy in the Brionnais[2] and a few years later there appeared in

1. C. Oursel, *L'art roman de Bourgogne*, Dijon-Boston, 1928, chapters 2 and 3.
2. See R. and A.-M. Oursel, *Les églises romanes de l'Autunois et du Brionnais*, Mâcon, 1956, pp. 110–
113 and 122–126.

the north a second group, largely in the archdeaconry of Avallon, that persisted well into the second half of the century.[3] The Avallonnais group, probably inaugurated at Vézelay shortly after 1120, reveals a number of refinements: not only a more consistent use of the pointed arch, which emphasizes the vertical movement of the bay, but more elaborate sculptural effects, such as mouldings on some of the arch soffits. The spread of the parti into the Yonne Valley is of especial interest, since this area was to play an important role in the initial reception of elements of Gothic style in Burgundy.

The architecture of Cluny and its followers differed from the groin-vaulted basilica both in conception and development (Pl. 2b). It, too, was fully formed at the very start, in the gigantic and richly adorned third church at Cluny (1088 ff.).[4] But the shop assembled by Saint Hugh was international in character[5] and seems to have been drawn as much from the stations of the pilgrimage roads which Cluny had fostered, as from the surrounding region. The major impact of Cluny was also international, and its local following at first consisted of reduced versions of the mother church, such as Paray le Monial. Nearly a full generation passed before the style of Cluny penetrated the spirit of Burgundy and then it was with accommodations to local taste, as is indicated by the various ground plans. At Cluny, the plan was highly articulated, with two transepts, an ambulatory with radiating chapels, and five aisles in the nave. One by one, these features vanished, in the reduced "copies" and in the progressive assimilation of the style by local shops. The minor

3. Avallon: St Lazare and St Martin du Bourg (nave); Pontaubert; Sacy (nave); Vézelay: Madeleine, St Etienne and St Pierre le Haut (only the west bay of St Pierre survives, as a garage and fire-station; St Etienne is now occupied by a bakery; see V. Petit, *Description des villes et campagnes du département de l'Yonne* (arrondissement d'Avallon), Auxerre, 1870, figs. 251–255); and the Cistercian abbeys of Pontigny (first chevet and transept) and Reigny (according to an eighteenth-century plan published by l'Abbé M. Terre, *L'abbaye de Reigny*, Semur en Auxois, 1954, pp. 18–19, despite M. Aubert in *Cong. arch.* (Auxerre), 116, 1958, 271–274). There are other groined vaults in the west, at Donzy, Lurcy le Bourg and the transepts of St Martin at Nevers and Cervon (M. Anfray, *L'architecture religieuse du nivernais au moyen âge*, Paris, 1951, pp. 106, 148 and 185. See also J. Vallery-Radot in *Cong. arch.* (Auxerre), 116, 1958, 16).
4. K. J. Conant, "Mediaeval Academy excavations at Cluny", *Speculum*, 29, 1954, pp. 1–43.
5. K. J. Conant, as cited by R. Oursel, "La Bourgogne dans l'art roman. Essai de mise au point", *Revue du moyen âge latin*, 6, 1956, pp. 347–354.

transept was dropped everywhere except at Souvigny, the additional aisles after La Charité sur Loire, and finally, during the second decade of the twelfth century, the ambulatory and radiating chapels were replaced, at Chalon, Autun, and probably also Moûtiers St Jean, by three simple apses.[6] A similar action can be noted in the proportions of the nave, which became progressively shorter and squatter, as if influenced by the taste for wide, low spaces that was periodically to characterize Burgundian architecture throughout the twelfth and thirteenth centuries.

What persisted from Cluny and formed the hallmarks of the later edifices of the group, were the barrel vault, the three-story elevation with triforium and clerestory, and the eleborate design of the wall surface. The barrel vault required continuous support along its entire length, and the piercing of windows directly below the vault, without the additional support of tribunes, testifies to the daring of these architects. At Cluny itself, however, the great vault collapsed in 1125 and was at once rebuilt with a complex system of weights designed to minimize the lateral thrust.[7] But great height was an imperious requirement in the eyes of the designers of Cluny and it was achieved by the use of the three-story elevation, with tall, pointed main arcades and a triforium almost the same height as the clerestory. All three were united by a grid design that emphasized the flatness of the surface. Pilasters replaced colonnettes on the nave side of the piers, forming continuations of the rectangular arches beneath the vault, and smaller pilasters separated the arcades of the triforium. Intersecting these verticals were three prominent string-courses, at the vault springer and above and below the triforium. The wall, like the vault, was treated as a continuous plane, and the bays were merely delineated on the flat surface. The interior of the nave formed a long

---

6. The destroyed abbey church of Moûtiers Saint Jean probably was in the Cluniac style, as is suggested by the three clerestory windows in the seventeenth-century bird's-eye view (*Monasticon Gallicanum*, no. 41). See also A. Vittenet, *L'abbaye de Moutier-Saint-Jean*, Mâcon, 1938, esp. pp. 101–105; Laurent-Claudon (1941), pp. 262–270; and M. Aubert-M. Beaulieu, *Description raisonnée des sculptures du moyen âge . . . (Musée du Louvre)*, 1, Paris, 1950, nos. 25–26.

7. K. J. Conant, "Observations on the vaulting problems of the period 1088–1211", *Gazette des Beaux-arts*, s. 6, vol. 26 (86), 1944, pp. 127–134.

tunnel, the sanctuary a screen of thin columns silhouetted against the shallow ambulatory.

The vitality of this architecture, with its tall, pointed arches and vigorous massing, is shown by its acceptance in twelfth-century Burgundy. In the nearby Saône Valley at Chalon and Beaune, in the more distant Bourbonnais at Souvigny, and even at Vézelay, Cluniac design radiated and intermingled with local traditions. It appeared as far north as Bar sur Aube, with ribbed vaults, and it was still alive at Semur en Brionnais, although in a vastly different context and considerably weakened, toward the end of the century.

The architecture of Cluny and the groin-vaulted basilica amply testify to the creativeness and power of assimilation of Burgundy at the start of the twelfth century. As if this were not sufficient, however, still another, totally new Romanesque personality was to emerge before Saint Bernard preached the Second Crusade at Vézelay in 1147. The early architecture of the Cistercians, although anti-Cluniac in theory, did not lack refinement, and although austere, represents perhaps the clearest manifestation of coordination and balance in Romanesque Burgundy (Pl. 3a).[8]

The first Cistercian churches were remarkably similar to each other in conception, almost as if their design had been prescribed by code. Such a code must be understood as conformation to the spirit of the Order, rather than as specifications for the parts of the building, and it was undoubtedly strengthened by the personal influence of Saint Bernard, whose name has recently been given to the early chevet plans.[9] In a revival of the letter of Saint Benedict's rule, the church was conceived

8. See M. Aubert, "Existe-t-il une architecture cistercienne?", *Cahiers de civilisation médiévale*, I, 1958, pp. 153–158; H. Hahn, *Die frühe Kirchenbaukunst de Zisterzienser* (*Frankfurter Forschung zur Architekturgeschichte*, I), Berlin, 1957; F. Bucher, *Notre-Dame de Bonmont* (*Berner Schrift zur Kunst*, 7), Bern, 1957; for a different analysis, see O. von Simson, *The Gothic Cathedral* (*Bollingen series*, 48), New York, 1956, chapters 2 and 4.

9. K.-H. Esser, "Der Kirchenbau des heiligen Bernard von Clairvaux", *Archiv für mittelrheinische Kirchengeschichte*, 5, 1953, pp. 195 ff.; and H.-P. Eydoux, "Les fouilles de l'abbatiale de Himmerod et la notion d'un 'plan bernardin'", *Bull. mon.*, 111, 1953, pp. 29–36.

as a "workshop for prayer", and was purged of all features considered unessential to this ideal. A number of altars was required for the celebration of masses, but they were clustered around the projecting transept rather than the sanctuary as at Cluny. The sanctuary itself remained small and simple. The vaulted naves were low and acoustically good, and they received dim but diffused light from windows in the terminal walls, complementing the monastic rule permitting the use of only five candles in the interior. The design of piers and wall surfaces displays a strong antipathy to the elaborate decoration of Cluny, for they are clear and clean, with a minimum of added ornament. It was here that the Cistercian architect exercised his ingenuity, however, for he planned the interior of the building with great economy, combining proportions, plastic shapes and surface decoration with a profound sense of elegance.

Of the Cistercian churches built before 1150, less than a handful, among them Fontenay, have survived. But since the Cistercian Order was internationally-minded from its inception, the same architectural spirit prevailed in its various houses despite their distance from Burgundy. And when the Cistercians adopted the ribbed vault, as early as 1150, they performed an act of major importance for Gothic architecture by disseminating it across Europe. If they were quick to adopt the rib, however, they were slow to explore its possibilities and to alter the general conception of the monument in its behalf. Like Cluny, the Cistercians had a strong impact on Burgundian architects, and their "rib-vaulted Romanesque" style helped to create a resistance to Gothic until the early years of the thirteenth century.

The Acquisition of the Rib

Although early Gothic architecture cannot be summed up simply as the use of the ribbed vault, the adoption of the rib was often a prelude to more important developments. This was the case in the vast area stretching east of Paris into the dusty plain of Champagne, and south from the Valley of the Marne to that of the Saône (Fig. 1). In the course of the

second half of the twelfth century, the rib appeared sporadically throughout this area: as early as the 1140's at Châlons sur Marne, in the 1150's in
the Yonne Valley and north-eastern Burgundy, and then in the 1160's

Fig. 1. Map of eastern France and the Yonne Valley.

and '70's in the Saône Valley as far south as Mâcon and to the west at Cluny and La Bénissons Dieu.[10]

There was no architectural frontier between the northern zone of Burgundy and Champagne in this period. Although they owed allegiance to different feudal lords, the cities of Bar sur Aube, Langres and Dijon, for instance, participated in the same stylistic movement. Nor did the ecclesiastical boundaries have an effect on the geography of forms.[11] The bishops of Auxerre and Nevers were suffragans of Sens, but the immediate sphere of influence of Sens Cathedral, the lone major Gothic foyer in the west prior to about 1180, extended northward in the direction of Provins.[12] A royal citadel, and the seat of an archbishop whose suffragans included the eminently royal cities of Paris, Chartres and Orléans, Sens was not at this time a funnel to the south but an outpost of the Ile de France.

The ribbed vault was first employed in the Yonne Valley by the Cistercians.[13] Shortly before the middle of the century, the abbey church of Pontigny was begun as a larger and somewhat simpler version of the groined basilica (Pl. 3b). Two details normally found in the Avallonnais are missing in the early parts of this edifice: the wall-rib, that masks and strengthens the joint of vault and wall, and the pilaster behind the colonnette of the pier, that gives visual support to the corners of the vault and accentuates the individuality of the spatial compartments. But about 1150

10. E. g., at Châlons sur Marne: in the towers of Notre Dame en Vaux (L. Demaison, in *Cong. arch.* (Reims), 78, 1911, pt. 1, pp. 473–496); and in the north tower of the cathedral, with an Anglo-Norman profile (E. Maillart, *La cathédrale de Châlons-sur-Marne*, Paris, 1946, and view in *Les Monuments historiques de la France*, n.s., 3, 1957, p. 185); at Mâcon, a similar rib was added under the groined-vault of the narthex in the second half of the twelfth century (Fig. 66); at Belleville sur Saône, in the chevet built between 1168 and 1179 (J. Vallery-Radot, in *Cong. arch.* (Lyon and Mâcon), 98, 1935, pp. 334–356); in the eastern bay of the narthex at Cluny III (Fig. 50); and at La Bénissons Dieu (Aubert, *Arch. cist.*, 1, p. 246 and fig., p. 269). In the Franche Comté, the rib was introduced by the Cistercians and remained in their hands for well over a generation (R. Tournier, *Les Eglises comtoises*, Paris, 1954, p. 109).

11. See the maps in F. Fossier, "La fondation de Clairvaux et la famille de Saint Bernard", and H. Beis, "La place prise par l'abbaye de Clairvaux . . .", both in *Mélanges Saint Bernard* (*XXIV Congrès de l'association bourguignonne des sociétés savantes*), Dijon, 1953, pp. 21 and 31.

12. See de Maillé, *Provins*, Paris, 1939, 1, *passim*.

13. See H. Rose, *Die Baukunst der Cisterzienser*, Munich, 1916, pp. 13–25 and C. Oursel, *L'art en Bourgogne*, Paris–Grenoble (1953), pp. 79–80.

both reappear in the nave, together with the ribbed vault, as it were emphasizing the basic affinities of the groined parti to the articulated space of Gothic design. Yet the nave of Pontigny can hardly be called Gothic, so dominant is the parti of the groined basilica and so omnipresent the solid wall surfaces of Romanesque style. Toward the end of the work, in the western bay (about 1155), the rectangular pilaster was replaced by colonnettes, as if, to hold for a moment to the functional theory of the nineteenth century, the ogive were acting upon and altering the form of the pier. In this bay there also appeared a new rib profile, the first Burgundian example of a design that was to be widely employed during the next forty years (Fig. 2).

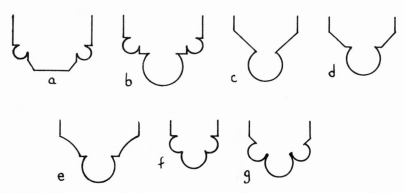

Fig. 2. Rib profiles: a. Pontigny, nave; b. Pontigny, nave, western bay; c. Bléneau, crossing and Sementron; d. Ligny le Châtel; e. St Sauveur; f. Vézelay, narthex and Avallon, St Martin du Bourg; g. Vaux (schematic).

After about 1150 the rib was used with increasing frequency in two particular parts of Yonne Valley edifices, the sanctuary and the crossing. The decorative quality of the ribbed vault seems to have made it especially fitting for the sanctuary of the church, and probably the oldest such vaults after Pontigny are those in the upper story of the narthex at Vézelay, where the chapel of Saint Michael was located. Only a year or so later a similar vault was placed over the rectangular apse of St Martin du Bourg at Avallon. Within the next fifteen years, no less than eight apses were covered with ribs,[14] and this pattern continued to be repeated in many of the small buildings of Burgundy in the thirteenth century. But the structural quality of the ribbed vault also seems to have impressed a few Yonne Valley masters, who used it to reinforce the lower stories of towers in the manner widely practised throughout western Europe in the late eleventh and early twelfth centuries. Such are the vaults beneath the crossing towers at Ligny le Châtel and Bléneau. Vézelay and Ligny were perhaps the "têtes de série" among those early vaults and the technique of construction is often similar: they are domed even though the side arches are pointed, the latter perhaps a legacy of local Romanesque style.[15] In the central vault of the Vézelay narthex, however, only the lateral webs slope, and at Pontigny the ridge lines are almost horizontal in both directions, foreshadowing at the very outset the final solution of the great thirteenth-century naves.

The next extensive use of the rib can be traced only evanescently, in the annexes to churches. Among the oldest is the chapter house at Fontenay, about 1155 (Pl. 4a). In plan, this building originally had nine slightly rectangular bays, and in elevation all the vaults were at the same level. In such conditions, the design of the vaults takes on a particular interest. All the arches and ribs are round-headed, and it is apparent that the vaults would be quite domed if some adjustment had not been made. This included stilting the arches on the short sides of the rectangles and using less than full semicircles for the ogives. The result was to provide horizontal ridges and to open up the various volumes so that a true hall, rather than a succession of independent spaces, was formed. The mutual abuttment of the vaults of course reduced the need to direct their thrust downward as much as possible, one of the qualities inherent in the pointed arch that was to be exploited in later decades, but the absence of the latter is noteworthy. It was old and familiar in the Yonne Valley

14. Bléneau, Chemilly, Montréal (the priory of Saint Bernard), Quenne, St Cyr les Colons, St Sauveur, Sementron and Vaux.

15. M. Aubert, "Les plus anciennes croisées d'ogives", *Bull. mon.*, 93, 1934, pp. 5–67 and 137–237, esp. p. 191.

and was present in the early ribbed vaults mentioned above. In the chapter house at Fontenay, and in the one at Vézelay, about 1161–1164, the round-headed arch reigned, even though considerable calculation and manipulation were involved in producing the same general result as at Pontigny. It was probably non-technical reasons, such as the proximity of the vaults to the ground and their consequent "visibility", as well as the predominantly non-ceremonial uses for which this and other halls were built, that determined the choice of the round-headed arch. The sacristy of Auxerre Cathedral was constructed on this pattern, as were the cellars of Clairvaux and Pontigny and the "hostelry" at Quincy, ranging from about 1160 to the end of the century. With these structures, the Cistercians and the Yonne Valley architects revealed their ability to control the technique of vaulting with ribs and their desire to expand the uses of the vault to include the annexes of the church proper.

Two other churches in the Yonne Valley with interesting ribbed-vault programmes have survived from this period, at Chablis and Montréal. In both, ribs were used only over the main vessel, while the aisles were covered by groined vaults. At St Pierre in Chablis, about 1165, the spatial concept of the Romanesque groined parti persisted, although the forms changed (Pl. 6a). The pier, for instance, is a massive cross, with colonnettes both on the faces and in the angles. Yet one can hardly speak of a wall-respond here, since the very pier itself does not rise as high as the summit of the arcades. The latter are even more out of scale for this small edifice than the heavy, projecting piers. And since the blind upper story is eaten into by the arcades, one has the impression that the whole upper story, as well as the piers, was pushed down over the great arcades, as if to crowd the compartments of nave and aisles into a compact form that could then be covered by a single roof.

By comparison, the collegial church of Montréal is clarity itself and represents the meeting of the rich design of the Romanesque Avallonnais and the simplicity of the Cistercians (Pl. 6b). The ground-plan of Montréal, with transept and with two square chapels flanking the square apse, was familiar to both.[16] The interior is enlivened by a certain amount of decoration, such as the volutes at the departures of the ribs, and the capitals, wall-ribs and imposts girdling the piers are Avallonnais features as well. But the corbelled responds, the rose flanked by colonnettes and the rib profiles are distinctly Cistercian. The ogives are supported by pilasters without capitals, except at the crossing and in the western bay (about 1195).

The irregular, often groping use of the ribbed vault in the Yonne Valley during the period 1150–1180 was roughly analogous to that in certain areas near Paris, such as the Soissonnais, a decade or so earlier. The Aisne basin seems in fact to have been the immediate source of the southern experiments, for many features are common to both, such as the square apse or the group of two or three lancets in the terminal wall and the smooth roll around the window, and it is not astonishing to find close, and in some cases, identical rib profiles in both regions.[17]

The relationship of the Yonne Valley to the north in the second third of the century is confirmed by the small parish church of Vermenton (Fig. 3). Begun about 1170, it originally had ribbed vaults only over the nave, the scheme of Chablis and Montréal that was also common in the area between Sens and Provins.[18] The supports are alternately compound piers and twin columns. The four-part vaults rest on the strong piers,

16. Cf. St Martin du Bourg at Avallon; and also St Savinien at Sens, in the eleventh century (von Veltheim, pp. 44–46), St Verain (*ibid.*, *passim* and M. Anfray, *Nivernais*, pp. 135–167, *passim*), Sermaize (R. Crozet, "Les églises romanes des environs de Vitry-le-François", *Bull. mon.*, 86, 1927, pp. 269–320) and Goailles in the Franche Comté (dedicated 1202; Tournier, *Eglises comtoises*, p. 139 and fig. 116). Cistercian edifices: La Bussière (dedicated 1172; Dimier, pl. 58) or Les Pierres (A. Buhot de Kersers, *Histoire et statistique monumental du département du Cher*, III, Bourges, 1885, pp. 253–256 and pl. III. 7; M. Robert Gauchery, of Bourges, has kindly confirmed for me the presence of the two square chapels flanking the apse, which are not clear in the published plan).

17. Cf. especially the Pontigny type (west bay) at Aizy, Berzy le Sec or St Bandry; the Vézelay type at Marolles or Vauxrezis; and the Ligny-St Sauveur type (Norman) at Bruyères, Pernant or Veuilly la Poterie, in E. Lefèvre-Pontalis, *L'architecture religieuse dans l'ancien diocèse de Soissons*, 2, Paris, 1896, *passim*. For the window roll, see Lefèvre-Pontalis in *Bull. mon.*, 70, 1906, pp. 27–29.

18. One groined vault is still extant in the north aisle at Vermenton. The same parti has been suggested for St Quiriace at Provins and is found in a number of nearby edifices (Maillé, *Provins*, 1, pp. 86–87), as well as originally at Notre Dame en Vaux at Châlons sur Marne (Demaison, in *Cong. arch.*, *loc. cit.*, p. 486 and L. Hubert, *Notre-Dame-en-Vaux de Châlons-sur-Marne*, Epernay, 1941, pp. 54–55).

Fig. 3. Vermenton, elevation of the nave.

with the result that oversized compartments are formed, each of which is flanked by two main arcades with a single clerestory unit above. This system of alternation, although it occurs within the important regional context of Sens, Provins, Troyes and even Châlons sur Marne, is actually quite special, since the compartment is cubical and capped by a single vault. Moreover it should not be considered merely an extension of the *schemate longobardino* of the Rheinland and Alsace, although this may have been its ultimate source.[19] It belongs properly to a small group of churches – Bellefontaine, Voulton and St Loup de Naud [20] – that is strung out in a line between the Yonne Valley and the Soissonnais.

The archaeological links between the members of this group are not always close, and certainly the same builders did not erect them all. But the men who carved the capitals at the eastern end of Vermenton, for instance, worked in a style that was used at Sens and Provins and was elaborated throughout the area between in the 1160's.[21] In several instances, striking analogies exist with the capitals at Bellefontaine and in the western bays of St Loup, and even the cusped capital of Anglo-Norman fame appears in a later part of Vermenton, possibly from the vicinity of Noyon.[22] There are further links with the area just north-east of Paris. The rib with a zigzag on the soffit, for instance, that was used in one bay of Vermenton and part of another (where it was

19. P. Rolland, "Schemate longobardino", *Les cahiers techniques de l'art*, 3, 1954, pp. 21–38; Avesnières, near Laval in the Maine, often mentioned in this context, seems essentially unrelated to Vermenton.

20. For Bellefontaine, see E. Lefèvre-Pontalis, *Soissons*, 2, pp. 4–8, where a date of 1125 is advanced (probably incorrectly); for Voulton, F. Salet, "Voulton", *Bull. mon.*, 102, 1943–1944, pp. 91–115; for St Loup, Salet, "Saint-Loup-de-Naud", *ibid.*, 92, 1933, pp. 129–169. Two other examples from the end of the century are Arcy Ste Restitue, with tribunes, however (Lefèvre-Pontalis, *loc. cit.*, 2, pp. 116–119), and Champigny (F. Deshoulières, "Champigny-sur-Marne", *Cong. arch.* (Ile de France), 103, 1944, pp. 9–17).

21. Maillé, *Provins*, 1, pp. 163–173.

22. See L. Hautecœur, *La Bourgogne. L'architecture (Les richesses d'art de la France)*, Paris-Brussels, 1929, vol. 2, pl. 103. The cusped capital also appears once at Pontigny (G. Fontaine, *Pontigny (Etudes d'art et d'archéologie publiées sous la direction d'Henri Focillon)*, Paris, 1928, fig. 89), but it is not as close in design to Vermenton as one at Noyon (C. Seymour, Jr., *Notre Dame of Noyon (Yale Historical Publications, History of Art*, 1), New Haven, 1939, fig. 101). The western piers of Vermenton use the pilaster-respond and the "twisted" capital of Pontigny (Pl. 4b) (C. Enlart, *Manuel d'archéologie française*, 3d ed., Paris, 1929, p.485, n. 2). See also J. Vallery-Radot in *Cong. arch.* (Auxerre), 116, 1958, 19.

abandoned for a better-known profile) (Pl. 4b), is found at Acy en Multien, and the respond of three intersecting colonnettes was rather widely used in the Soissonnais in the 1150's.[23] Then, too, the short twin columns, which do not appear in the immediate family of Vermenton, are like those in small buildings at the very end of the century – Arcy, Champeaux, Deuil and Gonesse, the last three in the neighbourhood of Paris.[24] Thus Vermenton is very much a case in point for the movement from the north to the Yonne Valley in the later twelfth century.[25]

Cluniac and Cistercian Gothic

As was the case in the Yonne Valley, north-eastern Burgundy in the second half of the twelfth century was in certain respects closely related to neighbouring Champagne. The countryside from Laignes and Epoisses, near Montréal, to Pichanges and Orgeux, is studded with small rib-vaulted buildings similar to those in the Yonne Valley, but which were all erected a few years later, from about 1175 on, and which reveal the slow movement of the new technique across the hinterland. The Cistercians were of course the first to employ the ogive in major programmes here, for example at Clairvaux (1154 ff.). Most of their edifices have unfortunately been destroyed and their exact value is therefore difficult to determine. But this is not the case with another group of monuments at Bar, Langres and probably Dijon – where the rib was also used from about 1160 on, in a context parallel, but antithetical, to the spirit of Cistercian style.

23. See Bony (1949), p. 5, n. 5, for the respond. The zigzag on the soffit is also found at Guarbecques (Nord); see P. Héliot, *Les églises du moyen âge dans le Pas-de-Calais* (*Mémoires, Commission départementale des monuments historiques du Pas-de-Calais*, VII), Arras, 1951, pl. II and pp. 143 (and n. 21) and 144, n. 42. Cf. the chapter-house at Bristol (G. Webb, *Architecture in Britain. The middle ages*, London, 1956, pl. 57).

24. For Champeaux, see J. Messelet in *Bull. mon.*, 84, 1925, pp. 253–282; for Gonesse, M. Aubert in *id.*, 109, 1951, pp. 424–428; for Deuil, A. Lapeyre in *id.*, 97, 1938, pp. 392–423, all with bibliography.

25. A similar relationship is indicated by the twelfth-century capital at Rosnay (J. Thirion, "Notre-Dame de Rosnay", *Cong. arch.* (Troyes), 113, 1955, pp. 236–257, which belongs to the Arras-St Leu d'Esserent series (Bony (1949), p. 8 and n. 4).

The church of St Maclou, in the former château of the Counts of Champagne at Bar sur Aube, was begun shortly after 1159. The simple plan comprises a three-bay nave, a non-projecting transept, a choir and an apse flanked by smaller bays and oriented chapels (Fig. 4). The elevation is unmistakably Cluniac, with its wide, pointed main arcades, a flat,

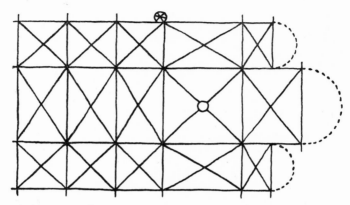

Fig. 4. Bar sur Aube, St Maclou, ground plan with suggested original eastern termination.

blind triforium with fluted pilasters, and clerestory (Pl. 7b).[26] Yet the church reveals an advanced technique, for it was planned from the start with ribbed vaults over both nave and aisles, although the ribs end in inverted cones that are not supported by articulations of the piers (Pl. 5b). The present nave vaults, as well as the arches of the triforium, were constructed at a later date on a different pattern, and it is possible that they were originally planned with sloping lateral webs, as at the Cathedral of Langres.

Many relations, technical and otherwise, existed between Langres and the nearby Cistercian abbey of Morimond, both of which were begun about 1160. But a noticeable difference, almost an opposition between these two monuments, lay in the association of Langres with the Cluniac tradition (Pl. 7a). The elevation contains three stories with a blind triforium

26. The triforium pilasters are not flanked by smaller orders, as in the older Cluniac designs, so that it is not certain whether they were intended to support a string-course or arcades.

and a hemicycle covered by a half-dome, all of distinctly Cluniac type. The piers are basically square, with pilasters on the faces and colonnettes sunken into the corners. The design of the Cluniac clerestory was of course altered to permit the use of ribbed vaults, but the very narrow, *barlong* vaults slope sharply on the sides, so that the interior space is

Fig. 5. Pier plans: a. Dijon, St Bénigne (after Chomton); b. Irancy; c. Bar sur Aube, St Maclou (not in scale).

actually closer in shape and feeling to the one formed by the Romanesque barrel than by the groin vault. This is emphasized by the absence of strong verticals down the walls.

The form of the piers at Bar and Langres is of especial interest, since it permits us to include in the Cluniac group the destroyed twelfth-century nave of St Bénigne at Dijon (Fig. 5).[27] The precise form and

27. The Langres rib and a fluted, rectangular trumeau are indications that the former narthex of the destroyed abbey church of St Pierre at Flavigny probably belongs in this group (Pl. 39b, d). I am profoundly indebted to M. Jean Troubat, proprietor of the site of the destroyed abbey, for his gracious permission to study and photograph portions of the church.

date of this nave have frequently been a bone of contention among archaeologists, but its existence is strongly suggested by the base of a pier unearthed some eighty years ago. Each face of the square core bears two sunken, literally half-circle colonnettes at the angles and a pilaster in the centre. The pilaster suggests Cluniac design, as at Langres, and the corner colonnettes are almost identical with those at Bar. Of course the pier of St Maclou has a colonnette on the major face instead of a pilaster and the core is cruciform, but the wall-respond above includes the corner colonnettes as well as a little of the returning faces, once again as at Langres. This detail is very close to the respond at Irancy (about 1190), in the Yonne Valley, where the core of the pier is square. But since the vaults of Irancy were replaced in the eighteenth century, they cannot help us reconstitute the twelfth-century parti of St Bénigne.

The reconstruction of St Bénigne is generally dated immediately after the fire that consumed the city of Dijon in 1137, and it is assumed to have been finished for the dedication ceremony of 1147. In addition to the pier base, the extant remains of the period include fragments of the west portal. The study of the profiles of the bases of these parts, the only precisely datable evidence, indicates that they could scarcely have been cut before 1160, and probably not before 1170 (Fig. 6). It may therefore have been the eastern end of the church (the apse and choir) that was consecrated in 1147, while the nave formed a second campaign which would have been inaugurated after 1160 and completed in about a decade. The pier has been interpreted as evidence for the existence of both ribbed vaults and groined vaults over the nave.[28] If this part of the edifice was actually built around 1160–1170, it is not unlikely that the vaults were ribbed: Bar and Langres, alone, prove that ribs were used in the region

28. L. Chomton (1900) favoured ribbed vaults; V. Flipo (1928) and M. Aubert favour groined vaults. It has recently been suggested that the pier form had been used in the eleventh-century nave of St Bénigne as well, and evidence is adduced from the terminal responds in the early Romanesque chevet, as recorded in Dom Plancher's plans (A. S. Wethey). But the difference between these responds (or the intermediate piers in the choir of Vignory, which are also brought into Mrs. Wethey's argument) and the piers at Bar, Irancy, and twelfth-century St Bénigne lies precisely in the unusual *half-circle* colonnette of the latter. If Mrs. Wethey's argument is correct, the piers at Langres would be better comparative evidence.

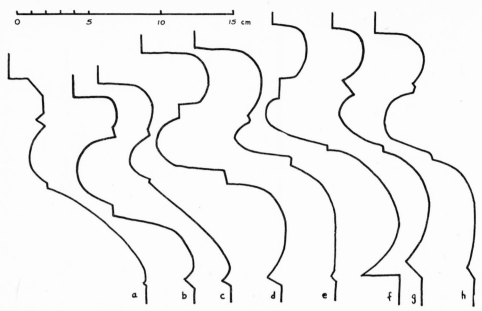

Fig. 6. Base profiles: a. Chablis, St Pierre, crossing pier; b. Montréal, collegiate church, crossing pier; c. Bar sur Aube, St Maclou, crossing pier; d. Langres Cathedral, axial chapel; e. Langres Cathedral, ambulatory; f. Dijon, St Bénigne, XII c. nave (after Chomton); g. Dijon, St Philibert (not measured); h. Flavigny, St Pierre, narthex trumeau.

at this time,[29] over the aisles as well as the nave, and the pier plans show they were related to St Bénigne. The plan of the twelfth-century church of St Bénigne, in so far as it can be imagined, may in fact have been similar to Bar.

Dijon, Langres and Bar represent the ultimate stage of Cluniac design. If their architects adopted Cistercian solutions to technical problems,

29. The presence of groin-vaulted St Philibert at Dijon, literally a few feet from St Bénigne, and built at precisely the same time, does not pose an insoluble problem in this respect. It may be explained by the newness of both the ribbed and the groined partis to Dijon, as well as by the cost and prestige of the different programmes. The mother church of the abbey was unquestionably more elaborate, the parish church simpler, as is evident in the treatment of the western portals. Groin-vaulted naves were rare in eastern Burgundy. One was perhaps planned at St Marcel lès Chalon and another at nearby St Loup de la Salle, where the present vaults are on corbels. Barrel vaults were much more traditional in the area: at Til Châtel, about 1150 (J. Tillet, in *Cong. arch.* (Dijon), 91, 1928, pp. 465–473), and as late as the last quarter of the century at Pernand.

however, the basilica of Cluny itself seems to have influenced the new Cistercian chevet of the later twelfth century.

Immediately after the death of Saint Bernard in 1153, a campaign was inaugurated to enlarge the chevet of Clairvaux. Ready in 1174, the structure replaced the square apse and adjacent chapels of the older church with a hemicycle, an ambulatory and nine radiating chapels, the latter contiguous along the periphery as if hollowed out of a very thick wall. The design represents the importation of a formula developed in the extreme north of France, probably at Thérouanne.[30] Here, the semi-circular chapels were like so many niches in the outer wall. The plan was repeated, probably about the middle of the century, at the Cathedral of Reims,[31] and at the same time nearer to Thérouanne, at Dommartin (dedicated in 1163).[32]

From Clairvaux, the new chevet spread to Pontigny (about 1186), perhaps also to Quincy, and on a rectilinear pattern to Morimond and Cîteaux (dedicated in 1193). Within the next twenty years, it appeared in various Cistercian houses across western Europe, and in non-monastic buildings as well, such as the Cathedral of Avila.[33] But this rapid expansion was not uniform. In the early thirteenth-century chevet of the priory of St Pierre at Bar sur Aube, an obvious imitation of the Cistercian formula, ambulatory and chapels are covered by a single roof (Pl. 5a), as was probably the case in the north French examples. At Pontigny, the ambulatory rises above the chapels only enough to break the roof line. But at Cîteaux, and probably also at Morimond and Clairvaux, chapels,

30. The plan is in Enlart, *Manuel*, p. 255. This was presumably the church dedicated in 1134, although Enlart elsewhere noted features more characteristic of the later twelfth century (*Villes mortes du moyen âge*, Paris, 1920, pp. 15–29). The hemicycle was rebuilt in the thirteenth century (pp. 23–24). P. Héliot ("Le chevet de la cathédrale de Thérouanne", *Bull. mon.*, 108, 1950, pp. 103–116) follows H. Rheinhardt ("Hypothèse sur l'origine des premiers déambulatoires en Picardie", *ibid.*, 88, 1929, pp. 269–288) in assuming Thérouanne had three separate masses, even though they do not appear in the sixteenth-century view published by Enlart (*Villes mortes*, plate following p. 14).

31. See the excavation plan in H. Deneux, "Dix ans de fouilles dans la cathédrale de Reims, 1919–1930", *Société des amis du vieux Reims*, Reims, 1944.

32. C. Enlart, *Monuments religieux de l'architecture romane et de transition dans la région picarde* (*Mémoires de la société des antiquaires de Picardie*), Amiens-Paris, 1895, pp. 104–122.

33. E. Lambert, *L'art gothique en Espagne*, Paris, 1931, pp. 53–59.

ambulatory and hemicycle formed three separate masses on the exterior of the edifice. This was precisely the massing of Cluny III and of Paray le Monial, and there can be little question that the three tiers of the Cistercians represented the revival of a Cluniac form nearly a century old.

The chevet of Pontigny is the only Cistercian church structure surviving in Burgundy from the later twelfth century (Pl. 10). Although simple almost to the point of plainness, it exemplifies the Cistercian gift for elegance. The elevation has two stories, the main arcades separated from the clerestory by an even taller expanse of flat wall than in the nave. But the piers, responds and ribs are finer and in closer *rapport*, giving an effect of thinness not found in the earlier campaigns here. The clarity of the ground-plan and volumes is brought to a rhythmic conclusion in the vaults – in the ten-part vault that seems to hover above the polygonal hemicycle, and in the five and six-part vaults covering the ambulatory and chapels. This is an unwonted luxuriousness for the Cistercians. Although the hexagonal chapels may have seemed to require a six-part vault, the extra ribs in the ambulatory are corbelled above the keystones of the arches leading to the chapels and are structurally unnecessary.

In reality, neither Cistercians nor Cluniacs were very successful in creating a Gothic style. The restraint of the one, which barred such "unnecessary" features as a middle story or the voiding of the wall with complex windows and passages, counterbalanced the archaism of the other, which retained the monumental but rigid Romanesque elevation and refused to reorganize the interior volumes. Although both were active locally in the dissemination of the rib, they went no further than this, and the next important step toward a fully Gothic design was left to the builders of the Yonne Valley.

The Sens Revival

At the end of the twelfth century, some of the Yonne Valley masters continued to repeat the work of earlier generations, with modifications only in the garb of the edifice. At Pont sur Yonne, for instance, about 1190, the low chapels flanking the apse were still groin-vaulted, and the later two-story nave is broad and low, the upper story eaten into by the main arcades in the manner of St Pierre at Chablis. Alternation and six-part vaults are the only concession to contemporary taste, and the weak piers themselves are merely thinner versions of those in the nave of Pontigny.

One movement alone, by its reference to the Cathedral of Sens, represents a sharp departure from this continuum. The chevet of Sens was dedicated in 1164, and was certainly complete at this time, although work continued on the nave and west façade until the turn of the century. The elevation contains wide main arcades, a triforium opening on the aisle roofs and a clerestory that was originally much shorter than it is at present (Pl. 8a). The hallmark of Sens is the triforium, which, unlike the normal middle story of the Ile de France at mid-century, is composed of *two* units per bay. Each unit consists of a large relieving arch surmounting two smaller arches, a design known from Normandy (Mont St Michel) and England (St Albans)[34] in the eleventh century. It was also employed in the Romanesque narthex at Cluny, at almost the same time as at Sens. At Sens, however, it takes on a new meaning as one of the earliest Gothic "band" triforia, linking the wide bays together. The Sens triforium never had more than a limited success on the Continent, although it continued to recur at widely scattered sites for over a hundred years.[35] Its appearance in no less than three local buildings in the last quarter of the twelfth century is therefore remarkable and constitutes a veritable revival of the forty-year-old formula.

Begun about 1185, the new chevet of the Madeleine at Vézelay was completed some twenty-five years later (Pl. 9b). Although the design seems to have been altered rather frequently during the course of construction, as will shortly become clear, the original plan of the triforium

34. See G. Webb, *Architecture in Britain* (1956), pl. 22a. It was also found in the naves of Gloucester and Hereford and, later, at Canterbury, whence it seems to have become one of the standard designs in thirteenth-century English Gothic (Webb, plates 28, 34 and 64 a).

35. E.g., Joinville (Hte Marne); Appoigny, nave; Boiscommun (Pl. 40a); and the eastern bay of the nave of Blécourt (Pl. 40b). The Norman version of this form (e.g., in the ambulatory of Le Mans cathedral), deriving from England, must be kept separate; Amiens would appear to belong to this group.

called for two units above the wide main arcades of the choir, as at Sens. In the hemicycle, only a single triforium unit was placed in each bay, quickening the slow, regular rhythm of the choir in the same manner as at St Germain des Prés in Paris. The Sens triforium also inspired the nave of St Eusèbe at Auxerre, in a campaign probably inaugurated after the city fire of 1188 but making considerable use of the fabric of earlier campaigns (Pl. 9a). The twin arches of each bay rest on heavy octagonal piers, while slim colonnettes support the smaller arches. Finally, at St Martin at Chablis, begun perhaps in 1212, the triforium appears in a reduced version of one unit per bay (Pl. 8b). Its Sénonais origin is apparent both in the generally heavy sculptural effects and in details, such as the impost that links the units behind the wall-respond. The reduction in the number of units may have been due to the small size of the edifice.[36]

Many differences distinguish these monuments from one another. At Auxerre, there is an obvious archaism for which the earlier campaigns, that produced the Romanesque piers and the groined aisles, were only partly responsible. The large triforium piers suggest a certain hesitation in piercing the wall, but they also maintain the heavy scale of the older parts. The progress toward Gothic here is limited largely to the triforium that represents an early stage in the introduction of new ideas to the Yonne Valley, but one that had already been superseded by the Madeleine at Vézelay. At Chablis, the triforium has a longitudinal passage,[37] and flying buttresses counteract the thrust of the main vaults. Despite these up-to-date features, however, the alternating piers and six-part vaults betray an almost servile dependence on the cathedral of Sens, and the parti loses much of its dignity in the modest size of the monument.

At Vézelay, the lightness of the triforium is stressed by its thin supports, a detail symptomatic of the whole conception of the chevet. The sense

36. In the straight bay of the hemicycle, which is as long as each section of the double bays to the west, the two arched openings do not touch each other and they are not subdivided by arcades. This design also appears in the transepts of Vézelay.

37. Salet (*Cong. arch.* (Auxerre), 116, 1958, 204) says the rear wall is brick and the central story originally opened into the aisle roofs.

of point-support is everywhere heightened by the effects of the real and the apparent thinness of the masonry – the absence of a wall above the dado between the chapels, the reduction of solid areas in the clerestory and triforium, the flat wall-responds and the general use of detached shafts of a dark hue against the light masonry. Far more clearly than Chablis or Pontigny, the chevet of the Madeleine reveals an ingenious and inventive mind experimenting with structure, sculptural effects and light in a mature Gothic manner. It marks the end of "rib-vaulted Romanesque" in major programmes in Burgundy and the turning-point toward a fully Gothic style.

The Affirmation of Axes

Both Chablis and Vézelay, however, contain a strong dose of non-local elements. In the plan of St Martin, the ambulatory without chapels, the five-part vaults and the respond on axis are very close to two buildings near Paris – Gonesse, built only a few years before, and Deuil.[38] And the original plan of the Madeleine was drawn from the Ile de France – Noyon, St Germain des Prés and the destroyed abbey of St Martin at Pontoise all have certain similarities to Vézelay. But the various changes of plan at the Madeleine also bear a distinct resemblance to the destroyed cathedral of Arras, which was under construction in 1160.

From the plans and views of Arras that have come down to us, it is quite clear that the chevet was not constructed all of a piece, as M. Bony has pointed out.[39] This is particularly noticeable in the choir bays (Fig. 7). There were more main piers here than there were responds on the aisle

38. See M. Aubert, "L'église de Gonesse (Seine-et-Oise)", *Bull. mon.*, 109, 1951, pp. 424–428 and A. Lapeyre, "Les chapiteaux historiés de l'église de Deuil (Seine-et-Oise)", *ibid.*, 97, 1938, pp. 392–423, both with bibliography.

39. Bony's observation is cited by Héliot, "Les œuvres capitales du gothique français primitif et l'influence de l'architecture anglaise", *Wallraf-Richartz Jahrbuch*, 20, 1958, pp. 85–114, esp. pp. 98–99 and fig. 59. See also J. Lestocquoy, "L'ancienne cathédrale d'Arras", *Revue belge d'archéologie et d'histoire de l'art*, 9, 1939, pp. 97–107, and Héliot, "Les anciennes cathédrales d'Arras", *Bulletin, Commission royale des monuments et sites* (Brussels), 4, 1953, pp. 11–109. Were it not in fact for the interior views made before the destruction, which show five four-part vaults, and which I have used in my reconstruction, it would be possible almost to superimpose the Vézelay vault plan on Arras.

walls, and the four-part vaults must have been extremely narrow and cramped. Furthermore the openings of the main arcades resulted in an off-axis, mannered rhythm when seen against the periphery. Each bay was identical in elevation, or nearly so, those of the choir being made to resemble as nearly as possible the ones in the hemicycle. It takes but a

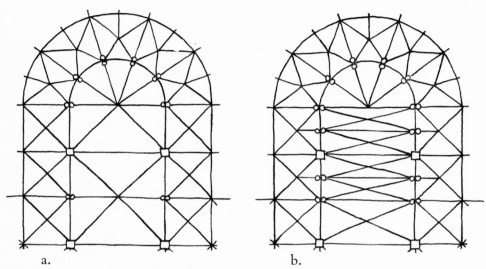

a.   b.

Fig. 7. Arras Cathedral, chevet plans: a. suggested original plan; b. suggested plan as executed.

moment's thought to realize that this disposition could hardly have been original, that the choir bays must first have been planned to be considerably wider than those in the hemicycle and the whole covered by two large vaults. A similar alteration, the subdivision of the wide choir bays, has long been recognized as having taken place at Vézelay during the course of construction. That the new design of Arras lay at the base of this change of plan is strongly suggested by the use of thin twin columns on the north side of the choir (unfortunately not visible in the plate) and by the reversed five-part vaults over the aisles here and on the south. Another northern feature at Vézelay is the contrast of colours in the masonry. The juxtaposition of dark brown and light, almost pinkish stone, was of course used in earlier campaigns and had become a tradition

at the Madeleine. But in the ambulatory and triforium, the dark stone was used only for the detached shafts, while the pink was largely relegated to the solid masonry. This slight shift relates Vézelay once more to Arras, where similar contrasts were used,[40] and in turn to an experiment both with detached shafts and with colour that originated in north-eastern France and of which the outstanding example is Canterbury.[41]

The appearance of such elements from the far north is related to the importations that have already been noted, both of details, as at Vermenton, and of the whole plan, as at Clairvaux. This was not simply the expansion of the Ile de France style that M. Pradel discerned some years ago in the Bourbonnais,[42] for instance, but a much vaster movement embracing the transfer of many elements in many directions. Thus the Thérouanne-Clairvaux plan appeared at Basle independently of Burgundian intermediaries, in the 1180's.[43] M. Bony has recently shown that the campaign of the 1190's on the chevet of Lyon cathedral was directly inspired from the region of Cambrai and that the compressed six-part vault, which occurred at Vézelay about 1205–1210, must be related to the same plan in a wide variety of places such as Geneva and St Albans.[44]

One of the clearest examples of such migrations is represented by the church of the Madeleine at Troyes (Pl. 12a). This small building, begun about 1195 as a parish in the suburb of Troyes where the fair was held, is clearly an intruder in Champagne. The elevation contains two features that cannot be found earlier in the region: a triforium with deep niches, and a clerestory housing an interior passage, which has since been walled in. The clerestory, which occupies the lunette of the vault and is completely open toward the interior, at once suggests a Norman or English source, and this may be confirmed by the passageless triforium, which resembles

40. See the 1623 description cited by Héliot, "Arras", (1953), p. 35, n. 3.

41. J. Bony (1949), p. 9. It is also recorded at St Trond between 1169 and 1180 (J. Helbig, *La sculpture au pays de Liège*, 2d ed., Bruges, 1890, p. 26). The presence of coloured stone sometimes gave rise to the name of a building ("Chronique de l'abbaye de Signy", ed. L. Delisle, *Bibliothèque de l'école des chartes*, 55, 1894, pp. 644–660, esp. p. 651).

42. P. Pradel, "L'apparition de l'art gothique en Bourbonnais", *Bull. mon.*, 95, 1936, pp. 405–432.

43. H. Reinhardt, *Das Basler Münster*, Basel, 1949, pp. 19–21.

44. J. Bony (1958).

the twelfth-century Norman church of St Georges de Boscherville, as well, perhaps, as certain English designs. It is important to note that the triforium is contemporary with the one in the west bay of Sens cathedral (Pl. 12b), probably the first triforium-passage in the whole area, but that it is relatively tall, having almost the same height as the clerestory. This feature makes the Madeleine at Troyes particularly noteworthy, since it becomes one of the three earliest examples of the "tall triforium" that was to be a fundamental part of thirteenth-century Burgundian style. The first was probably the chevet at St Amé at Douai (1191?–1198),[45] unfortunately destroyed, but where the relative height of the central story is suggested by the abrupt inclination of the aisle roof in the surviving model. The other is the former Cathedral of Geneva, where, about 1195, the triforium was raised a few inches in the choir (Pl. 11b). Geneva, with its two superimposed passages, belongs to the Lausanne-Canterbury axis isolated by M. Bony, and Douai, which was situated to become the source of the tall band-triforium of Picardy and Flanders, very probably also had a passage at this level. In this respect, the absence of the passage at Troyes must be considered a revival of older Norman forms, although the elevation was in the latest manner and foretokened the proportions of the Burgundian style of the thirteenth century.

These rapid transfers across great distances must without doubt be explained in terms of the Champagne fairs and the trade routes that drew merchants to them from north and south. A variety of roads connected Picardy and Flanders with Champagne, while two major routes ran up from the south through Burgundy. Both passed Lyon and the port of Chalon on the Saône, one proceeding overland to Auxerre and the Yonne Valley, the other via Chagny,[46] Dijon and Langres to Troyes and

45. Président Taillier, *Chroniques de Douai*, I, Douai, 1875, p. 209 (1191); G. Espinas, *La vie urbaine de Douai au moyen âge*, vol. 3, Paris, 1913, pp. 4–5 (no. 4) (1198). The height of the central story in the model on the relief-plan of the city (Douai, *Musée de la Ville*) is increased by reason of the scale (1:600 in plan as against 1:400 in elevation). I am indebted to M. Bony for calling Douai to my attention.

46. Cf. the route indicated in Duke Hugh III's concessions to the Genoese merchants (1191), previously conceded to those of Asti, in the *Liber Jurium* (*Historiae patriae monumenta*, VII), Augustae Taurinorum, 1854, cc. 354–355 (cited by M. Oursel–Quarré, *Les origines de la commune de Dijon* (194–), pp. 175–176).

points north. Camille Jullian's description of these roads in Gallo-Roman Burgundy seems equally appropriate for the twelfth and thirteenth centuries: "C'était, sur ces routes, un encombrement continu de soldats, de courriers, de fonctionnaires, de marchands, de touristes, de pèlerins, de charrettes et d'animaux de mille sortes."[47]

The coincidence of routes and architectural geography is in some cases even more specific. The Clunaic style at Chalon and Beaune, and at Dijon, Langres and Bar sur Aube, studded the road to Troyes that was known and used from the Gallo-Roman period on.[48] Vermenton itself was situated on the route from Chalon to Sens,[49] and from Sens it was commonplace, when going north, to pass St Loup de Naud and Provins on the way to Beauvais, for instance, as did the abbot of St Pierre le Vif at Sens in 1120.[50] This is not to say that the existence of such routes controlled or directly influenced the dissemination of architectural forms,[51] but it does suggest something of the mechanics of such transfers. These routes were travelled by abbots, deans and noblemen, the actual and potential patrons of new projects, and it was undoubtedly along the same paths that architects and stonemasons moved from one site to another.

It is clear that the architectural tradition of Burgundy at the turn of the twelfth century was twofold. It comprised, on the one hand, a local

47. C. Jullian, *Histoire de la Gaule*, Paris, 1920, vol. 6, pp. 416–417. It is regrettable that M. Jean Hubert's study of mediaeval routes (in *Les routes de France depuis les origines jusqu'à nos jours* (*Collection colloques. Cahiers de civilisation*), Paris, 1959) appeared too late to be included here.

48. It occurs in the Peutinger Table (E. Desjardins, *Géographie historique et administrative de la Gaule romaine*, vol. 4, Paris, 1893, pl. X; cf. F. Lot, "Itinéraires du XIIIe siècle", *Bulletin philologique et historique*, 1920, pp. 217–219, esp. p. 218) and still was used by the Duke of Burgundy in 1365 (E. Petit, *Itinéraires de Philippe le Hardi et de Jean sans Peur . . . (Collection de documents inédits sur l'histoire de France)*, Paris, 1888, p. 18).

49. A. Grenier, *Archéologie gallo-romaine (Manuel d'archéologie préhistorique, celtique et gallo-romaine*, ed. J. Dechelette, VI), pt. 2, vol. 1, Paris, 1934, fig. 44, p. 116.

50. *Gesta pontificum Autissiodorensium*, ed. L.-M. Duru (*Bibliothèque historique de l'Yonne*), vol. 2, Auxerre, 1863, p. 535; it was still used in the sixteenth century (C. Estienne, *Guide des chemins de France*, ed. J. Bonnerot, vol. 2, Paris, 1936, (*Bibliothèque de l'Ecole des Hautes-Etudes*, 267), p. 353, no. 548.

51. Cf. M. Robert Bautier's recent suggestion that it was not their situation at important cross-roads that determined the choice of the cities in which the Champagne fairs were held, since in fact the crossroads were originally well outside some of them (R. H. Bautier, "Les foires de Champagne", *La Foire*, Brussels, 1953, pp. 97–148).

Romanesque sensitivity, of which the monastic orders were the main repository, and on the other, a repertory of forms compiled from a broad area in the north. If the northern experiments were not part of a coherent, unilinear development, however, so much the greater their apparent disparity in the Burgundy of 1200. Yet less than two decades later, once more under the influence of the north, a homogeneous style that was to enjoy a wide success in the region and that constitutes the Burgundian Gothic style abruptly made its appearance at Auxerre and Clamecy.

CHAPTER III

The Formation of the
Burgundian Gothic Style

GOTHIC architecture came of age in Burgundy in the second decade of the thirteenth century, with the construction of the cathedral of Auxerre, the collegiate church of Clamecy and the parish church of Notre Dame at Dijon. The Burgundian style, as here formed, consists of a particular proportion, space and structure. There are three stories, in the approximate ratio of 2:1:1, a main arcade, a relatively tall triforium and a short clerestory. Both upper stories contain deep interior passages, and even the wall of the side-aisle is pierced, so that the wide main volumes are everywhere bounded by narrower slots of space. The fabric of the building is composed of thin supports, with skins of screen-like wall stretched around them. While the light reaching the interior is rather limited, for the windows are small, it plays upon the screens and passages to create a series of spectacular marginal effects.

Auxerre and Clamecy

The Gothic cathedral of St Etienne at Auxerre was begun under Bishop Guillaume de Seignelay (1207–1220).[1] Guillaume was actively engaged in church building as a means of implementing his mission to the rapidly increasing population of the see, and he took a personal interest in the construction of the cathedral. He seems to have initiated the project himself, contributing £700 of his own money during the first year of work – probably enough to cover the major expenses for the year[2] – and

1. See Lebeuf, vol. 1, pp. 365–396 for Bishop Guillaume, and the *Gesta pontificum Autissiodo-rensium*, ed. L.-M. Duru (*Bibliothèque historique de l'Yonne*, vol. 1), Auxerre-Paris, 1850, pp. 474–486.
2. The first year of work (1231) on the abbey of St Nicaise at Reims cost about £720 (Ch. Givelet, "L'église et l'abbaye de Saint-Nicaise", *Travaux de l'académie de Reims*, 98, pt. 2, 1894–1895, p. 347).

he is said to have given an average of more than £260 each year thereafter, even after his removal to the see of Paris in 1220. He also contri-
buted the fees paid for court judgements and he was undoubtedly the
leader in obtaining funds by other recognized means, such as through
the organization of a confraternity[3] and the circulation of relics both in
and outside the diocese. Guillaume's successor, Henri de Villeneuve
(1220–1234), was perhaps less generous toward the new work, although
he left it £1000 on his death and also donated stained glass for the windows.[4]

The real patron was of course the cathedral chapter, which unquestionably named the overseers of the work and which appointed the profes-
sional architect (*magister operis*) who carried it out. The reconstruction of
St Etienne was begun about 1215 and the chevet was probably completed
shortly before 1234, when Bishop Henri was buried in the choir.[5] In
these nineteen years or less, the entire eastern end of the cathedral was
completed in one campaign, apparently without interruption, although
as we shall see, alterations of design were frequent during the course of
construction (Fig. 32).

A story told by a mediaeval chronicler informs us about the master of
the work, and since it has a bearing on our understanding of the Gothic
monument, it is worth quoting:[6]

Now in the year of our Lord 1217, on the Sunday before Advent in honour of the
Holy Trinity, we were starting the solemn day. There were on either side, in the
old church, two towers of no inconsiderable height and of great thickness (of
wall), one on the south, the other on the north, containing between them the
whole breadth of the choir and the stalls of the canons. These towers began to
crack open when the (roof) beams of the old work, by means of which they
used to stand firm, were removed to make way for the new fabric – the soundness
of their structure having earlier been impaired by a small rift. Yet it was not
foreseen that they would threaten so quick a ruin. On the aforementioned feast,

3. Lebeuf, vol. 4, pp. 84–85 (no. 139).
4. *Gesta*, p. 486; Lebeuf, vol. 1, p. 402 and editor's note *a*; J. Lafond in *Cong. arch.* (Auxerre), 116,
1958, p. 60.
5. Lebeuf, vol. 1, p. 405.
6. Tr. from *Gesta*, pp. 475–476.

therefore, in a solemn manner as is the custom in such things, not only the small but even the great bells were rung; in their progressive clanging, it was feared not without reason that they would fall and crush all those who had gathered at the church in even greater numbers (than usual) on that day, on the pretext of the feast, (to learn) if the bells were thought about to fall. Furthermore, the south tower was opening up in a major fissure. Seeing this, some people began to gather round to discuss it, and word reached the canons. The master of the work was called, hard on the third hour, and was asked if the fall of the towers was imminently to be feared, and if the congregation could safely celebrate the divine offices beneath them. As he affirmed over and again that there was no reason to be afraid, one of his apprentices who was present said it was not safe to remain beneath them for an hour. The master began to object, as if this were pressing an unnecessary fear on the canons, while pointing to some beams extending to the tower, which were keeping the whole apparatus from falling. When he was pressed even more urgently on the question of their security, that he should make no pronouncement except the most certain, as if overcome by the importunity of his questioners, he replied, "I mean nothing is at all certain; I do not know what the future may show." At these words, as if in some presentiment of the spirit, the common feeling of all was that, when the impending procession was over (for it was the third hour) in the church of the Blessed Mary which is among the annexes of the great church, the solemnities of the mass would be celebrated, which was done. Nevertheless all the bells were solemnly rung in the usual manner, as if there were nothing to fear . . . and when the mass was over and the canons were sitting down to dinner together, lo, the south tower fell with a sudden crash against the north one, whose base was crushed deep within.

This brief account casts some light on the character and abilities of the Auxerre Master. He was daring and confident, if not always the best of engineers. His prowess seems to have been put in question again at the end of the thirteenth century, when major elements of the chevet had to be rebuilt or restored, probably because of structural weaknesses. Yet it must be said in his defence that such faults were probably due, not to the overboldness of the original conception, but to the constant enlargement of the chevet during the very course of its construction. A close look at the cross-section of the monument (Fig. 8), as it stands today, reveals that the piers, the base of the triforium and the crowns of the main vaults were one by one raised to higher levels than had at first been

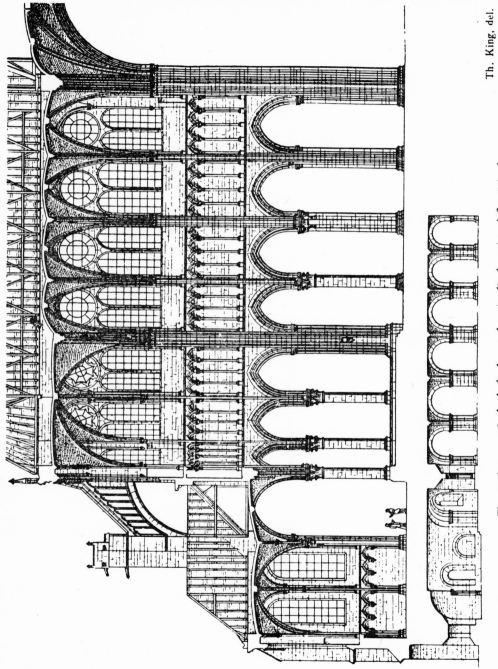

Th. King, del.

Fig. 8. Auxerre Cathedral, chevet, longitudinal section (after King).

planned. This very likely had the result of overtaxing the stability of a structure that would seem at the outset to have been close to the margin of safety. The elevation first planned at Auxerre must have been much lower, resembling those of Clamecy and Notre Dame at Dijon (Fig. 9).

Fig. 9. Auxerre Cathedral, suggested elevation of choir as projected.

The chevet of Auxerre is a masterpiece of Gothic illusion, as can be seen in the side-aisle (Pl. 13a). The wall here consists of a solid dado decorated with blind arcades and, above this, of a series of slender piers backed by strips of masonry that form internal buttresses. These protrude outside the edifice to form the regular wall-buttresses and are joined to one another down the length of the aisle by a thin wall bearing the windows. Most of the "wall", however, is formed by the passage, a void that even penetrates above and behind the vault, where it is covered by slabs. The thin supports seem to defy the weight placed upon them by the vaults and to remain erect despite our expectation of seeing them buckle under such pressure. The effect, heightened by the penetration of the void above the vaults themselves, is of course an illusion, for the slim strips of masonry, situated at precisely the proper places, convey the thrust of the stone covers to the exterior buttresses.

The isolated columns in front of the chapel are even clearer examples of the deception of this design (Figs. 10, 11). Each column supports four ribs – two small arches crossing the entrance and two larger ogives (E, D). The figure shows how the ogive spanning the ambulatory (B–D), and the stilts for the small arches (F, G) are all independent stones, the former in horizontal beds and the latter detached shafts, so that the vault-departure on three sides in reality forms a continuation of the vertical column, although the ambulatory ogive is curved all the way down to the impost (A). Now the thrust of the small arches and the ambulatory ogive actually meet well above the impost, at the point where the structure changes to the normal complex of voussoirs and webbing (C, D), and they are maintained on the rear side by the web over the chapel ogive (E). But the vault *seems* to depart from the impost itself, which is at the level of the other major supports in the ambulatory. This technique, known in French as the *tas-de-charge*,[7] was a recent development in Gothic methods of construction, and it had never before been employed above free-standing elements such as these. The balancing, as it were, of the four different arches on the small summer of a slender column is striking evidence of the architect's inventiveness and of his ability to maintain the illusion of weightlessness created in the aisle walls.

A similar impression is made by the triforium and clerestory, although later restorations have added strengthening masonry here (Pl. 15). The supports once again are slender shafts, yet the wall of the triforium is reinforced on the rear (and invisible) side by heavy longitudinal arches. And in the clerestory, the passage is only partly covered by slabs, while

7. See J. A. Brutails, *Précis d'archéologie du moyen âge*, 3d ed., Toulouse–Paris, 1936, p. 300.

the larger and most visible portion is surmounted by segmental arches. The arches link and stabilize the vertical supports in this topmost region of the building. Both they and the hidden triforium arches are unusual in Burgundy at this time and probably reveal a certain hesitation on the part of the Auxerre Master in relying entirely on thin supports, while extending the stories upward above their original positions. The overall

Fig. 10. Auxerre Cathedral, entrance to chapel.

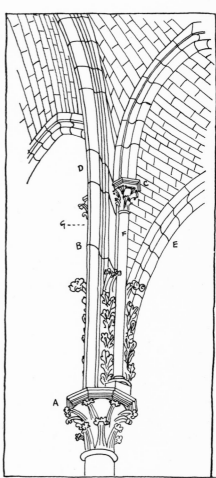

Fig. 11. Auxerre Cathedral, detail of entrance to chapel (after Viollet-le-Duc).

effect of the chevet is nevertheless one of lightness and spaciousness, in which the real functions of the structure are deliberately and systematically concealed from the viewer.

Six-part vaults were first planned in the western bays of the choir, although only the alternating piers had been erected when the design was altered to carry the present four-part vaults (Pl. 1). The piers here were built about 1220–1225, the date of the first alteration toward greater height, and both reveal the influence of High Gothic design on the Auxerre Master. The *pilier cantonné*, a column flanked by four shafts, is distinctly Chartrain, with a slight advance in the design of the capital, and the raising of the aisle vaults and main arcades is symptomatic of the desire, more clearly expressed in the upper parts of Auxerre, to imitate the verticality of Chartres. The clerestory window, a great rosette over two short lancets, is clearly an importation from Chartres, and it is an ill-digested one at that, since the monumentality of the design seems to contradict the apparent thinness of the window wall and its shape is not adapted to the height of the story, leaving ungainly panels of wall beneath. This is not true of the last Chartrain element at Auxerre, the monolithic struts between the upper and lower courses of the flying buttresses (Pl. 14). Here the spokes of Chartres have been straightened up, thinned and elongated in a manner that recalls the triforium supports in the hemicycle. The presence of flying buttresses may have been considered a necessity at Auxerre, in view of the new height of the vaults. But they are in fact in contradiction with the sophisticated structure of the walls, where the buttresses are drawn in between the two sheaths. The superfluousness of the flying buttress is particularly clear, however, in smaller buildings such as Clamecy and Notre Dame at Dijon.

The volumes at Auxerre were to have been dominated by an open lantern tower over the crossing.[8] They are broad at present and they must have been massive, indeed, had the original short clerestory and six-part vaults been executed. The recollection of the cathedral of Sens

8. This is indicated by the central colonnette on the eastern crossing piers, which rises above the present vault and was to have supported an ogive.

is unmistakable in the protruding responds that bound the hemicycle, and similar markers may in the original plans have been intended for the strong piers of the choir, to reproduce the majestic double bays of Sens (Fig. 9). As it is, the choir bays are smooth and continuous, and the proportions of the volume more nearly resemble those of the side-aisle. The limits of the interior spaces at Auxerre are largely imaginary, since they consist of fine screens outlining or drawn across the smaller voids of the passages. The wall of the elevation has in fact ceased to exist as a tangible surface – it is fragmented and recessed, and the result is what Herr Jantzen has aptly termed "diaphanous architecture".[9] The diaphanous effect is not the result of real dimensions – the triforium, for instance, is a constant feature of the great monuments of the first half of the thirteenth century, and at Auxerre it does not differ greatly in actual height from the one at Chartres[10] – but it is the direct outcome of the proportions and the handling of stone with a view to its sculptural effects. The triforium at Auxerre seems much vaster than at Chartres because the supports are thinner, the arcading is lighter and the full depth of the passage is illuminated and visible.

The presence of important subsidiary volumes at Auxerre brings into sharp relief the sculptural effects of the structure. The illusion of the screen is maintained even in the completely open clerestory, where the sharp wall-rib and responds underline the distinctness of the two spaces, or in the aisle, where the smaller space penetrates above the vault. Seen against the smooth, unornamented outer walls, the supports bearing the weight of the structure are entirely isolated by void. Yet the screens and tube-like shafts would be austere without sculpture. The capitals, with rather heavy imposts, are covered by spiny crockets that cast deep shadows, and every arcade, in the triforium and dado, bears a sculpted head or a single, tall crocket that reaches out from the wall and seems to activate the surrounding space. These diversions punctuate the overall design and underline the rhythm of the structure. Their effect in

9. H. Jantzen, *Über den gotischen Kirchenraum* . . . (reprint, Berlin, 1951), pp. 7–20.
10. At Auxerre, it is about 4m. 80; at Chartres, about 4m. 60.

Fig. 12. Clamecy, St Martin, interior.

accentuating the differing heights of the vault-departures in the ambulatory is especially noticeable.

The cathedral of Auxerre, as it stands today, is less pure an example of Burgundian Gothic style than the collegiate church of St Martin at Clamecy (Fig. 12). St Martin is a much smaller building, in which the structural system was not strained to the limit and then trussed up to insure stability, and in which the various parts are in a more categoric relationship to each other. When the subsidiary voids were enlarged, as in the clerestory of Auxerre, or later at Semur, the effect of the open screens on the main volumes was weakened. At Clamecy, they are limited in size but clearly defined, and the play of small volumes against large is distinctly enhanced.

St Martin was begun at almost precisely the same time as Auxerre, although it took longer to complete, as was often the case with small and unevenly financed buildings, and the western end was finished only in the sixteenth century. The plan, a seven-bay nave with aisles and a

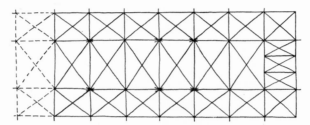

Fig. 13. Clamecy, St Martin, plan with restored western end.

rectangular ambulatory across the eastern end, while unusual, was not unique (Fig. 13). It was used again at Champeaux around 1250,[11] and may originally have derived from England.[12] The phases of construction at Clamecy are easily discerned and seem to have followed an oblique pattern from east to west. The Chartrain pier was first used about 1225, toward the end of the first campaign, and alternating piers were introduced about 1240, although six-part vaulting does not seem to have been planned above them. The initial work at Clamecy, the ambulatory, is characterized by a wall-passage covered by arches and an extensive use of detached shafts, or colonnettes *en délit*, set into the niches of masonry cores (Pl. 13b). After about 1220, however, all *délit* was abandoned and the passages, betraying an influence from Auxerre, were slab-covered and made to rise about the vaults.

11. J. Messelet, "La collégiale Saint-Martin de Champeaux", *Bull. mon.*, 84, 1925, pp. 253–282.
12. For instance, Byland or York (A. W. Clapham, *English Romanesque architecture after the Conquest*, Oxford, 1934, figs. 27 and 29).

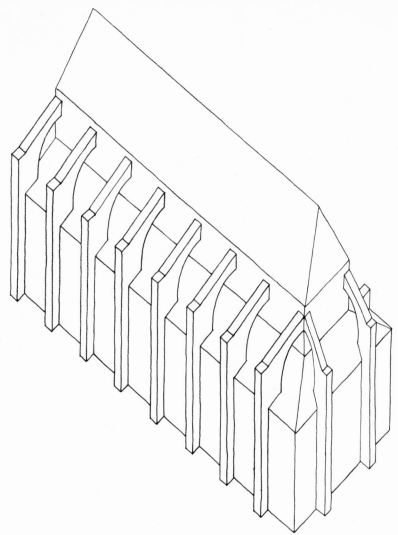

Fig. 14. Clamecy, St Martin, exterior massing as projected.

The massing at Clamecy recalls the rectilinear solids of twelfth-century Cistercian chevets (Fig. 14). Since the various wall-passages are all internal, the outer surfaces of the building are smooth and flat. Only the flying buttresses create a half-open, aerated mass in the upper story, and these are in fact structurally unnecessary because the edifice is not large and the vaults could be stayed by the wall-buttresses and by the strips of masonry concealed within the thickness of the passages. As at St Martin at Chablis, the flying buttresses represent the aesthetic success of a recent device that had already become part of the modern exterior by the early thirteenth century.

Clamecy and Auxerre were the first *foyers* of Burgundian Gothic style, yet neither was built by a local workshop and the Gothic acquisitions of Burgundy in 1215 can scarcely be said to have prepared them. As was the case during the preceding fifty years, the forms and the parti were imported, and it is to their sources that we must now turn our attention.

The Sources

The Masters of Clamecy and Auxerre participated in the development of an architectural style that very nearly became the "standard" we now associate with the High Gothic design of Chartres or Reims. Rooted in the same area of north-eastern France that produced Chartres, this vast "anti" or "para-Chartrain" style, as M. Jean Bony has made us realize,[13] developed along an axis extending from England to Switzerland, embracing Flanders on one side and Burgundy on the other. The dominant feature, the one that came most clearly into conflict with Chartrain design after 1220, was the elevation with a tall triforium and a short clerestory. Other than this the style had little uniformity, for the Flemish parti contained an external clerestory passage that was very often screened, and the triforium was less deep and spacious than in Burgundy. The Burgundian monuments were the first fully developed statement of the para-Chartrain style in the thirteenth century, and at the same time they expressed a particular regional spirit.

The outstanding characteristic of Burgundian Gothic, the superimposed interior passages, was first employed in the cathedral of Canterbury (Pl. 11a)[14] and immediately after at Lausanne[15] and Geneva.[16] The Swiss

13. Bony (1958).
14. R. Willis, *The architectural history of Canterbury cathedral*, London, 1845, and Bony (1949).
15. E. Bach, L. Blondel, A. Bovy, *La cathédrale de Lausanne* (*Les monuments d'art et d'histoire de la Suisse*, 16), Basel, 1944.
16. C. Martin, *Saint-Pierre. Ancienne cathédrale de Genève*, Geneva (1910).

campaigns, begun respectively about 1190 and 1195, were largely terminated by 1210–1215, precisely at the time the parti appeared in the
Yonne Valley, and certain features are common to both, such as the tall
triforium (at Geneva) and the string-course with an undulated upper
side.[17] There can be little question that Lausanne and Geneva played an
important role in the design of Auxerre and Clamecy.

On the other hand many details of the Burgundian edifices derived,
not from Switzerland, but from a variety of monuments that were
themselves formative for the para-Chartrain style. This is the case of
the passage in the side-aisle wall. It was first used in the axial chapel of
St Remi at Reims, about 1170–1175,[18] and should therefore be called the
Rémois rather than the Champenois passage, as M. Bony has made
clear.[19] It was employed again about 1200 in the small south transept
chapel of St Etienne at Caen,[20] and after 1210 it took on two distinct
forms. One is represented by the cathedral of Reims and is distinguished
by a small sculpted frieze that runs across the pilaster, from the respond
to the window wall, as well as by the consistent use of an arched cover.
This form appears in edifices definitely related to Reims cathedral, such
as Rieux, Toul and Trier. The other has no such frieze and is sometimes
covered by slabs, and it is found in a group of monuments that parallels
but does not derive from the cathedral of Reims, among which are Caen,
Clamecy and Auxerre. Caen may have acted as an intermediary between
St Remi and Burgundy, for the narrow space rises above the vault in
the manner of Auxerre. And one must not forget that an older relationship existed between the Yonne Valley and Normandy, between

17. E.g., Martin, figs. 14, 15 and 17.

18. L. Demaison, "Eglise Saint-Remi", *Cong. arch.* (Reims), 78, 1911, pt. 1, pp. 57–106, esp.
p. 87.

19. Bony (1958), p. 43. The term, "Champenois", was put into vogue by E. Lefèvre-Pontalis
("Les caractères distinctifs des églises gothiques de la Champagne et de la Bourgogne", *Cong. arch.*
(Avallon), 74, 1907, pp. 546–558), who failed to differentiate between the various thirteenth-
century types.

20. L. Serbat, "Eglise Saint-Etienne et abbaye aux hommes", *Cong. arch.* (Caen), 75, 1908,
pt. 1, pp. 21–64, esp. pp. 36–38, with interior view following p. 36. A passage may also have been
used at the destroyed church of St Symphorien at Reims, which is said to have been a copy of
St Remi built about 1209 (L. Demaison in *Bull. mon.*, 85, 1926, p. 72).

Vézelay and Caen,[21] that was apparently still alive at Clamecy, where the Norman circular impost was used. The importance of the small chapel at Caen must not be overemphasized, however, since the Rémois passage was undoubtedly available to all architects working in para-Chartrain shops.

The impact of St Remi was nevertheless far-reaching. The ambulatory, for instance, was the source of the isolated columns screening the chapel entrance at Auxerre. This plan had a certain local success in the north, at Soissons (the south transept chapel of the cathedral[22]) and Châlons sur Marne (Notre Dame en Vaux[23]), and it reappeared about 1215 at St Quentin, at exactly the same time as at Auxerre. The structure of the departures at Auxerre is of course more sophisticated than the older, twelfth-century designs at St Remi or Soissons, and the presence of the *tas-de-charge* over a single column at the chapel entrance of St Pierre at Bourges (about 1220–1225) reveals the loose but persistent influence of St Remi on the para-Chartrain development. This seems to be confirmed by the repetition, in the ambulatory of Auxerre, of the six-part vault plan in the tribune of St Remi.

The colonnette clusters in the ambulatory and triforium at Auxerre are another example of the migration of forms within the vast movement in which Burgundy participated at this time. Almost identical clusters, also in hard stone, were used by both Williams in the triforium of Canterbury cathedral. The form appears in the south for the first time about 1195–1200, in the wall of the north tower at Sens (Pl. 12b). Here, the earlier triforium was modernized and the masonry piers were replaced by the cluster of detached shafts, while a passage was introduced behind them. Sens was not the source for this form at Auxerre, but it indicates that the design was not simply a revival of the Canterbury design more than three decades later. At Auxerre, furthermore, the clusters are bearing parts of the structure, and this was an old Burgundian technique that

21. E. Lambert, *Caen roman et gothique*, Caen, 1935, pp. 48–50.
22. E. Lefèvre-Pontalis, *L'architecture religieuse dans l'ancien diocèse de Soissons*, vol. 2, Paris, 1896, pp. 183–192.
23. L. Demaison, "Eglise Notre-Dame", *Cong. arch.* (Reims), 78, 1911, pt. 1, pp. 473–496.

ranged from the large, monolithic columns at St Etienne at Nevers and St Révérien[24] to the short but sturdy shafts at Bois Ste Marie and the cloister at Fontenay. Thus the standard explanation of Auxerre, to wit, that the use of detached shafts was made possible by the very hard stone of Tonnerre, must be re-examined. The reliance on such clusters for support is fundamentally different from the decorative display of colonnettes at Vézelay, an early Gothic technique probably also imported from the north.[25] The structural tradition of Burgundy here seems to have coincided with and prepared the reception of the form from Canterbury.

One element in the design of Auxerre, the rounded pilaster instead of the normal square one to back the engaged colonnette, seems, however, to have been a recent Burgundian acquisition. It originated in the south transept of Soissons and passed at once to Vézelay and then to St Seine (1205–1209 ff.). Its presence in the narthex of Noyon Cathedral, about 1215,[26] must be noted, for there also appears there the same style of capital sculpture as in the earliest phases of Clamecy and Auxerre. This style developed from Soissons and was current in Brie after 1200, forming a rough crescent to the east of Paris,[27] and it may be our best indication of the area in which the two Burgundian masters hired their masons, and where they themselves probably worked prior to 1215. In this context, it is revealing that an interior clerestory passage should have been used in the narthex of Noyon itself, although in a fundamentally High Gothic elevation. Furthermore some details, such as the smooth window-wall and the twin lancets, bear a strong resemblance to their Burgundian counterparts. The narthex of Noyon almost certainly was not under way before Auxerre and Clamecy, but the

24. Crosnier, communication to the *Bulletin, Société nivernaise des sciences, lettres et arts*, 1, 1854, p. 47.

25. See Bony (1949), p. 9, n. 7. See the analysis of Ch. Seymour, Jr., *Notre Dame of Noyon*, New Haven, 1939, pp. 156–157. Detached shafts were also used in a decorative manner in the Avallonnais in the twelfth century (e.g., St Lazare at Avallon), but here they were closer to other Romanesque systems, such as that in Provence.

26. Seymour, *Noyon*, ch. 5. Corbels under the bases indicate that it was probably not begun as early as 1210. The west façade was largely terminated by 1231 (pp. 66–67).

27. In the second campaign at Meaux cathedral (nave), at Champeaux (nave), and so on.

background and the ideas of the architect were remarkably similar to those of the Burgundians.

The Masters of Auxerre and Clamecy were highly competent at organizing structure, volumes and sculptural effects into coherent architectural entities, and their edifices must seem, from this point of view, to escape archaeological dismemberment. It is nevertheless amply clear that both monuments were not completed without revisions, sometimes profound ones, and further that they were not isolated phenomena springing wholly formed, like Athena, from the minds of their creators. Their Burgundian character is affirmed both by the regional details they embody and by their immediate local success. And yet, although they were clear statements of the new design, they did not serve as the exclusive sources for the region. Their derivation from the north was reiterated at Notre Dame at Dijon, the third formative monument of the Burgundian Gothic style.

Notre Dame at Dijon

The parish of Notre Dame at Dijon was not very old and may have been created only after the fire of 1137,[28] when the faubourgs of the town were encircled by a new wall. To judge from some remains unearthed nearly a century ago, an edifice was built on the site in the 1150's, although nothing is known of its form. The church was reconstructed from east to west in essentially one campaign, from about 1220 to about 1245, with a few changes of parti introduced while the transept was under way (Pl. 18). The building had not yet been dedicated by 1251, but it was sufficiently advanced for the ceremony to be envisaged in that year. The consecration was finally performed only in 1334. At that time the western towers were still unterminated and they remain so today.

Notre Dame is not a large building (Fig. 15). A porch of two bays, open to the west but enclosed on the sides, leads through three portals to the six-bay nave. The projecting transept has two oriented chapels

28. M. Oursel-Quarré, *Les origines de la commune de Dijon*, Dijon (194–), pp. 73, 78 and 125.

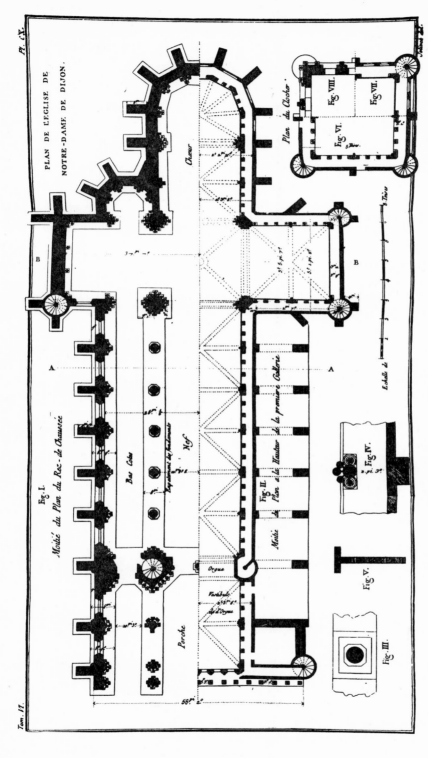

Fig. 15. Dijon, Notre Dame, plans (after Jolivet, 1762): I. ground plan, showing foundations; II. plan at triforium level, showing vaults; III. nave pier; IV. triforium support (strong); V. iron clamp holding detached shafts in triforium; VI–VIII. crossing tower.

flanking a choir that terminates in a simple polygonal apse. All the main vaults except those over the crossing and apse are six-part. The massing forms a simple, large cross with abrupt apsidal shapes at the east that are dominated by the crossing tower. The flying buttresses of the nave do not contribute much to aerating the essentially flat, smooth solids of the walls.

The chevet and eastern walls of the transept of Notre Dame have three stories and as many passages – one over the dado, one in the triforium and one at the base of the clerestory, on the exterior (Pl. 16a). The Rémois passage derived from Auxerre. It is covered by slabs, rising above the arcades to form deep shadows, and in both choir and apse, the supports beneath the minor ribs of the vault are composed of three shafts placed around a heavier monolithic column, precisely as in the triforium at Auxerre. The form is repeated in the triforium at Notre Dame. But the exterior clerestory passage differs from the partis of both Auxerre and Clamecy, recalling instead the structure and massing of the transept chapels at Laon cathedral[29] (about 1175–1180) and the apse of St Yved at Braine.[30]

As all modern historians have pointed out, the whole aspect of the exterior of the apse of Notre Dame seems clearly derived from Braine, one of the major formative monuments of the para-Chartrain style (Fig. 16). The presence of a small buttress atop a larger one, which appears at Dijon, is generally considered a hallmark of St Yved, although it was also used nearby, about 1185–1190, in the south transept chapel of Soissons cathedral.[31] The buttress is in fact merely a leitmotif, as it were helping us to trace the diffusion of forms and the movements of men and ideas, and in the case of Dijon, it certainly points to the north. But the span of years from about 1190 to 1220 is tantamount to a revival in such active milieux as these. The situation at Dijon would be more comprehensible if, as M. Bony has suggested, there were a local intermediary between St

29. Seymour, *Noyon*, pp. 129–131 and fig. 58.4.
30. E. Lefèvre-Pontalis, "Braisne. Eglise Saint-Yved", *Cong. arch.* (Reims), 78, 1911, pt. 1, pp. 428–440.
31. Lefèvre-Pontalis, *Soissons*, vol. 2, Paris, 1894, pp. 185–186.

Yved and Notre Dame. This could have been the destroyed Ste Chapelle of the duke at Dijon, which is famous as one of the replicas of the Braine ground-plan (Fig. 54). The Ste Chapelle may have been begun at the end of the twelfth century or in the early years of the thirteenth, rather

Fig. 16. Dijon, Notre Dame, apse exterior.

than in the 1240's, as is generally assumed, and it may therefore have served as a first contact between Braine and Dijon.

The existence of an intermediary does not lessen the bonds between Notre Dame and St Yved, but their relations were in any case rather limited. The Braine-Soissons buttress was employed only in the apse and chapels at Dijon, and not in the eastern walls of the transept; the crossing tower was originally vaulted at the level of the chevet and nave rather than forming an open lantern as at St Yved, and the interior of the choir and apse was designed on a very different principle. The six-part vault with heavy triangular responds bounding a large volume came from Auxerre, as did the tall, almost square shape of the triforium. And the detailing in the chevet reveals a sensitive elaboration of contemporary Burgundian thought, as for instance in the dado arcade, which seems to stand forth from the wall like a separate screen. One of the most ingenious devices of the Notre Dame Master is the disposition of the lower passage in the western bay of the choir. The passage also runs around the transept chapel that lies immediately behind it. In order to avoid a solid wall where the chapel abutts the choir, the architect prolonged the passage through the bay here, allowing the chapel lancet that would normally be blind in this position to open directly into the choir. The chapel respond thereby becomes a thin, recessed panel of masonry, the emphasis on voids is maintained and the very structure of the edifice seems to be laid bare.

This design has certain historical associations. One of the components may have been the Romanesque device of piercing the wall between choir and chapel above the dado, as at Méobecq[32] and probably also St Seine, and another the type of openings, also above the dado, that are found between the radiating chapels at Vézelay and Caen. Since none of these has a wall-passage, however, the Dijon design could not be exactly formulated earlier. On the other hand, when the Romanesque opening was imitated in later Norman monuments with the Rémois passage, at Rouen and Bayeux, for instance, the passage was not prolonged between the ambulatory and transept chapel, where simple lancets are found. Thus the design at Dijon was a special solution, repeated only at St Urbain at Troyes in the 1260's (Pl. 16b),[33] and in a modified form at St Sulpice de Favières at the end of the century.[34]

32. Between the transept chapels. See F. Deshoulières, "L'église abbatiale de Méobecq (Indre)", *Bull. mon.*, 101, 1942, pp. 277–290.

33. F. Salet, "L'église Saint-Urbain", *Cong. arch.* (Troyes), 113, 1955, pp. 96–122.

34. Y. Sjöberg, "Saint-Sulpice-de-Favières", *Cong. arch.* (Ile de France), 103, 1944, pp. 246–264.

As if to confirm his allegiance to the para-Chartrain style, however, the Notre Dame Master employed an easily recognizable design in the transept (Pl. 17a). The terminal walls have only two stories, both with interior passages, one above the dado and the other at triforium level. The upper story is completely open and contains a large rose window devoid of tracery, as in the smaller transept roses at Canterbury. The lower story has five equally large lancets in the window wall, but only three openings in the inner screen, so that the colonnettes are placed in front of the lancets rather than the mullions. This bizarre and mannered disalignment enhances the effect of the screen across the long end-wall of the transept. It is found earlier in the Canterbury transepts, where the colonnettes cut through the edges of the rose, and it seems to have been considered for the triforium of the north transept at Lausanne, where the colonnette was finally suppressed in front of the windows.[35] But by far the closest parallel to Notre Dame is the rear side of the west façade of St Remi at Reims (Pl. 17b). Here the nave tribunes are connected by an inner passage running through the façade wall, which is divided into three bays. Each of the lateral bays has a single broad lancet in the outer wall, while the inner screen is formed by two arches, with a colon-nette directly before the opening. Once again St Remi takes a major place among the diverse sources of the Burgundian style.

The nave of Notre Dame has often been considered the most pro-digious example of Burgundian Gothic design (Pl. 18). The elevation includes the slab-covered interior clerestory passage that was first employed while the transept was under construction, but the aisle walls are solid and even the dado here is shorn of its blind arcades. The structure of the nave, as Viollet-le-Duc pointed out,[36] is based almost exclusively on colonnette clusters, some of which are held in place by clamps (Fig. 15 V), and the thinness of the structural apparatus is particularly visible above the "weak" supports. It is emphasized by the presence of three equally tall lancets in each clerestory bay, of which the outer two pass

35. Bach, Blondel, Bovy, *Lausanne*, pp. 92–93.
36. Viollet-le-Duc, *Dictionnaire*, vol. 4, pp. 136–146.

above the wall-rib as if to contradict the curve of the arch. The design of the windows actually represents the maximal extension of the openings in order to admit a greater amount of light, and the total surface of the window-wall was employed for this purpose, even though it rises above the hips of the vault.

The columnar piers of Notre Dame mark a resistance to the High Gothic desire to link all the stories together by means of projecting shafts, and a retention of the twelfth-century system in which the ground-story is plastically isolated from those above. There is certainly a sharp contrast between the stories of this nave that recalls the design of a Laon or a Paris, and that is modified only by the tallness of the capitals. The three colonnettes of the strong respond, although flattened against the wall, required an extension of the capital and impost below to support them, and the result is a lop-sided capital looking very much like those at Braine. The non-alternation of the piers beneath the six-part vaults, a combination that the nineteenth century considered an illogicality of the "transitional period" of early Gothic style, was almost a necessity at Dijon: absolute regularity was obviously less important than the envelopment of the largest possible space and the effect of an even greater apparent scale. Thus the double bay of the chevet, massive even in a medium-sized edifice, was here relinquished for a closer relationship between the volumes of nave and aisles, while the six-part vault prevented the dismemberment of the total volume into tall, individual compartments.

The western end of the nave is perhaps the most inventive design of the Notre Dame Master (Fig. 17). While the upper part of the main interior volume is prolonged to the façade, the ground story is hollowed out by an open, three-aisled porch. As an altar was once located here and the twelfth-century building apparently extended at least part-way into the present porch, this may have been considered a ceremonial part of the church. It forms a sort of hall, with all the vaults at the same level. The six-part vault is quite depressed and the lateral vaults take their departure from a high point, so as to avoid excessive stilting (Pl. 19). The double

western piers, which Viollet-le-Duc triumphantly proclaimed a masterpiece of design that drew the buttresses behind the outer wall,[37] in reality
represent only the systematic use of the Burgundian internal buttress
that is found at Clamecy, Auxerre and other parts of Notre Dame itself.

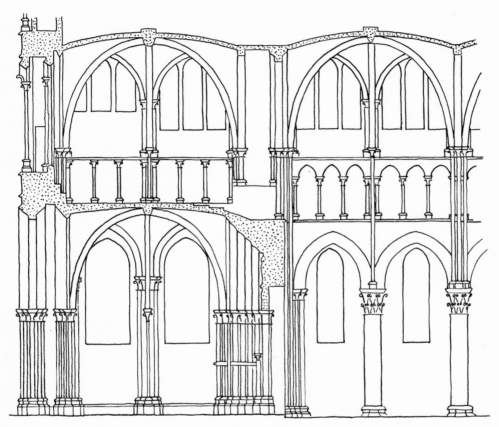

Fig. 17. Dijon, Notre Dame, longitudinal section of western end.

The exterior of the façade, deprived of verticals, becomes a plain wall
covered by two stories of detached blind arcades, a clear rejection of the
harmonic façade well-known in the great north French cathedrals. The
proportions at Dijon are rather tall, however, and to see it as it was

37. Viollet-le-Duc, *Dictionnaire*, vol. 7, pp. 275 ff.

originally planned, one has to add, in his imagination, the two thin towers that would accentuate the height even more.

The western complex of Notre Dame cannot simply be classed as a "Burgundian porch". The examples of Tournus, Vézelay and Paray le Monial, to cite only a few, prove that there was a variety of distinct narthex types in the region. Dijon was probably based upon the final forms at Châtel Montagne and the cathedral of Autun, at both of which, as a result of late twelfth-century additions, there were an open ground-story and a closed upper one that gave onto the nave through a wide arch. The Notre Dame Master made a coherent design from these agglomerations by suppressing the arch and prolonging the volume and the structure of the nave right up to the façade.

Dijon, Clamecy and Auxerre mark the formation of the Burgundian Gothic style. At this very time, however, the creative *élan* of the movement from which they derived began to wane. There was in general little further speculation on structure – the struts in the flying buttresses at Auxerre are perhaps the last important innovation of their kind. The years 1225–1230 saw similar occurrences in the other regions where the para-Chartrain movement had had an effect, particularly in Flanders. Thus the situation had changed: Gothic regionalism, in which recent acquisitions were developed and expanded locally, became a possibility for the first time.[38] In Burgundy, the process took place from 1220 to 1250, and it is to this elaboration that we must now turn our attention.

38. "Il est bien évident que la situation n'est pas la même dans les années 1190 et dans les années 1220 ou 1230: ce qui, en 1190, était le reflet d'un mouvement nouveau, est devenu ensuite pro-vincialisme, après 30 ans d'enracinement . . ." J. Bony, *in litteris*.

CHAPTER IV

The Elaboration of the Burgundian Style

AUXERRE, Clamecy and Dijon set the pace for thirteenth-century Burgundy. The parti spread rapidly after 1220, to Chalon, to Semur and to Nevers, while a reduced version of two stories, in which the triforium was omitted, proved popular in less ambitious projects. Between 1220 and 1250, certain stages of development can also be discerned. The Chartrain pier, visually linking the lower story to the upper ones by means of added shafts, was employed as early as 1220, but more than a decade passed before an effort was made to exploit the possibilities it afforded of reorganizing the surface pattern of the elevation. The designation of each bay as a distinct and equal unit, through the use of one continuous shaft, was first made only in the late 1230's, at Nevers and in the nave of Semur. This rejection of the rhythmic, colossal volumes of the six-part system makes the early work at Auxerre and Dijon look old-fashioned, and it would seem as if the architects of the 1230's were measuring themselves against the early development of the Rayonnant style of the Ile de France. But the fundamental problem of how to adapt the "composed" elevation, that evolved on the flat surfaces of High Gothic monuments, to the passage-ridden Burgundian parti was not to be solved until the early fourteenth century. The *effect* of a screen in front of a deep subsidiary space and the *reality* of a thin, design-bearing surface were two different things. The only compromise lay in foregoing the extreme extension of the clerestory, the very field where composition centred in High Gothic, and in striving for visual balance between the stories both in height and in depth. The Master of Nevers knew this, as we shall see, and so did the Master of Cluny, even though he used an older formula. By the late 1240's, however, the effort to compromise had broken down before the onslaught of the Rayonnant style, the elements of which were simply applied to whatever parts of the Burgundian edifice they would fit.

Chalon and the East

The present apse and choir of St Vincent, the cathedral of Chalon sur Saône, were built shortly after 1230 (Pl. 20). The style of the capitals indicates that some of the masons had in all probability come from Dijon (Pl. 42c), and many details of the design – the rounded pilaster, for instance, and the polygonal impost – are so close to Notre Dame as to suggest that the Chalon Master himself worked on the chevet of the parish church.

The programme of St Vincent was essentially one of renovation. The Romanesque apse was replaced by a Gothic one, the two bays of the choir and the crossing were revaulted and a new, rectangular chapel, originally dedicated to Saint Catherine, was added on the south, immediately east of the semicircular Romanesque chapel (Fig. 45). In elevation the apse has three stories, but the disposition of the passages is the reverse of that at Dijon. The Rémois passage was eschewed in the ground story for a series of simple lancets above a plain dado, while it is the clerestory that bears an interior *chemin de ronde*. The triforium is relatively tall – one must look in the longer straight bays of the choir to appreciate this – and the vault departure is situated above the base of the clerestory, at almost precisely the same point as in the apse at Dijon. It was undoubtedly this difference of level that prompted the fourteenth-century architect of Chalon to add the balustrade that now distorts the original proportions of the stories. The wall-responds in the apse are slim and continuous, but those at the start of the hemicycle, with their seven engaged colonnettes, form triangular masses that project sharply inward. As the large crossing piers are two bays farther west, a single oversized volume like the one at Dijon is formed, although there was apparently never any question of a six-part vault for the choir of St Vincent. The exterior of the apse is less clearly related to Dijon, for the absence of an outer passage in the clerestory reduces the prominence of the buttresses here, and there are no small "Braine buttresses" just below the cornice.

The Catherine chapel at Chalon marks a modification of the Burgundian wall structure and spatial composition that proved particularly successful for smaller monuments. It would have been a *tour-de-force* to employ an interior passage in the small, one-storied chapel, yet the Chalon Master was able to retain the illusion of thinness and translucency here by employing the principle of the semi-detached dado arcade of Notre Dame. He merely recessed the eastern window well behind the wall-rib and supported the latter by detached colonnettes. The window wall is perfectly smooth, as in the clerestory of the apse, and it forms the same thin screen. The space-layer is thus simply reduced in scale to match the size of the chapel. The apparent independence of vault and wall is further maintained by detaching the wall-ribs on the other three sides of the chapel and by placing isolated colonnettes in the responds beneath them, so that these members are everywhere backed by sharp shadows. This design was repeated almost at once at Bèze, where there is some evidence that the lost apse also contained passages (Figs. 38a, b), and it became one of the approved methods of giving small churches an elegant, "modern" look.

The Burgundian parti underwent a further simplification in the mid-1230's, in the apse of the parish church of Auxonne, where it was married to a strong element of late twelfth-century thought (Pl. 23a). Details such as the rectangular impost and the ringed responds reveal the persistence of older design methods that were probably strongly ingrained in the local shops. But the capitals and the rounded pilaster once again indicate a connection with Chalon and with Burgundian *foyers* to the north, and the first thirteenth-century architect of Auxonne had probably worked in one of these larger shops. In his design for the apse, he dropped both the Rémois and the clerestory passages. It is the triforium that speaks strongly in the Burgundian dialect. Squarish in cast, even in the polygonal apse, it is also deep and the arcades are light and open. The small floral ornaments on the arcades especially recall Chalon and Dijon. The master of this chevet seems, however, to have exaggerated the rather low proportions of his models. Although he was restricted as to width and height

by the size of the older crossing, against which he had to build the new
apse, the choice of a six-part division in the hemicycle, with a pier on the
axis, could only have been motivated by the desire to lengthen each bay
and hence to accentuate the broadness of the volume. In sum, his design
represents the provincialization of the Burgundian parti on the very
frontier of the Imperial County.

Semur

The priory of Notre Dame at Semur, on the other hand, which was
begun about 1220–1225, was constructed by a decidedly sophisticated
shop under the guidance of an architect who had the courage to experiment with new ideas (Pl. 21). As the church of the burg of Semur, Notre
Dame undoubtedly had a rather large congregation, and it was probably
this, together with sufficient funds, that prompted the adoption of the
cathedral-like programme. The plan includes a choir of three bays, an
ambulatory, three independent radiating chapels and extra collaterals
running from the transept, all in all a development comparable in complexity to some of the largest Gothic projects of the early thirteenth
century (Fig. 18). Various features of this plan were in fact derived from
well-known cathedrals – the independent chapels from an edifice such
as the cathedral of Rouen, and the combination of the chapels and the
additional collaterals very possibly from the cathedral of Meaux. The

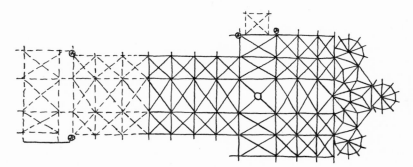

Fig. 18. Semur, Notre Dame, plan with destroyed north transept porch and fourteenth-
century portions.

disposition of the chapels was common coin in the area stretching from Normandy to Flanders, and it is by no means a coincidence that once again, as with Auxerre, Clamecy and Dijon, definite relationships with northern France should be revealed. These are strengthened by the presence of some distinctly non-Burgundian details in the chevet. The corbels that jut out from the capitals to support the wall-ribs were one of the hallmarks of early thirteenth-century Normandy, and the triplet window in the ambulatory of Semur was a favourite form in Picardy and Flanders. It is almost as if the Semur Master had written down for us a list of the places where he had been.

Notre Dame is not a large church, however, and all the parts are re-duced from the colossal scale of the cathedral to miniature size. The elevation has three stories, with a tall and spacious Burgundian triforium. This and other features show that although the Semur Master may have worked at far-distant sites, he had a fundamentally Burgundian vision of forms. What is extraordinary, in this complex of relationships, is his virtually unique clerestory design. It has an interior passage, but unlike the other monuments of the region, it is extremely tall – so tall, in fact, that it is practically equal to both the triforium and the main arcades combined. This cannot have been due to the influence of High Gothic design, for it appeared in none of the great cathedrals, not even Amiens, which was rising from the ground in the 1220's. The verticalism of Semur seems rather to be a direct and voluntary opposition to Burgun-dian traditions and to the regional norm of Gothic design that was in the process of being established in 1225. In this sense the Semur Master left the strong imprint of his personality on the edifice and showed himself a spiritual brother to the Master of Auxerre cathedral. The idea of this clerestory could in fact only have been germinated at Auxerre, where, as we saw in the preceding chapter, the various levels of the building were constantly raised during the course of construction. The "Chartrain" windows in the choir and transept at Semur, and the corbelled arches that frame them, are actually so close to Auxerre as to suggest that the architect had an intimate knowledge of this cathedral. If this were so, it would seem as if he began the priory as a miniature of the great contemporary monuments in the north, and then, like the Auxerre Master and very possibly under his influence, lengthened the clerestory to its present height. Such an interpretation is not ruled out by the archaeological analysis of the phases of construction.

The effect of this towering story at Semur is successful only in the general perspective of the interior. When seen close up, the meaning of the space-layer formed by the passage is so weakened as to be all but lost; the passage is superfluous in the spatial composition since it no longer forms a clearly defined band flanking the main volume. As at Auxerre, the piers still have the traditional columnar form, and the wall-responds, which act as dividers between the bays, terminate at the capitals, leaving the ground-story as a separate and unintegrated part of the design. The retention of this twelfth-century principle may have seemed unimportant to the Semur Master, for in addition to the fact that he probably had already constructed the main arcades before he decided to lengthen the clerestory, he may have realized that the absence of clear divisions in the lowest story would not be very noticeable from the nave of the church.

Yet it must be apparent that the clerestory was too tall, for the west side of the transept and the nave were planned, about 1235, with a ground-story some two metres higher than in the east (Pl. 22b). The main vaults remained at the same level and the tall, narrow proportions of the main vessel were accepted – it would indeed have been difficult to alter these without producing an ungraceful effect in the interior. The triforium was simply pushed up into the clerestory, at the expense of the latter, with a resulting elevation much closer to that of Chartres or Reims. But a final alteration in the nave suppressed the triforium completely – a fragment of it can just be seen next to the crossing pier – so that we now see an elevation of two stories which belongs to the reduced version of the Burgundian parti to be discussed below.

Nevers and Sens
The last major project of the first half of the thirteenth century, the

cathedral of Nevers, is in some ways the most perfect expression of the Burgundian manner. Inaugurated about 1235, the new plan for St Cyr comprised a nave with aisles, a transept and a chevet with radiating chapels, a programme comparable in extent only to the cathedral of Auxerre (Fig. 19). Both edifices are among the largest in Burgundy, although St Cyr is the smaller of the two, and both have the developed eastern end that is also found only at Semur. The St Cyr Master apparently had not worked at Auxerre, however, and it is difficult to say precisely where he had been prior to about 1235, other than at Sens.

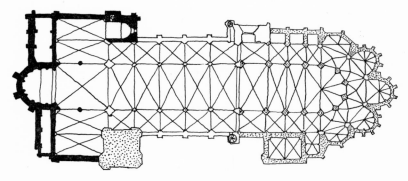

Fig. 19. Nevers Cathedral, plan (after *Congrès archéologique*, 1913).

The link with Sens is made clear by the Rémois passage, of which only two small sections remain in the disfigured aisle walls of St Cyr, but which was also employed in two edifices under construction in the metropolis in the 1230's, the former abbeys of St Jean (Pl. 23b) and St Paul. A curious detail, the arched and moulded lintels crossing the passages in both abbey churches, reappears in the triforium at Nevers, in the dark upper section of the passage. Insignificant as it may seem, this detail is symptomatic of other relationships between Sens and Nevers that seem to have a deeper import. The architecture of Sens in the second and third decades of the thirteenth century, for example Ste Colombe lès Sens, begun in 1218, and St Pierre le Vif, begun in 1219, is almost totally lost to us. By 1240, the city was already in the orbit of the latest

Ile de France style. Yet only a decade earlier, no less than three instances of contact with the para-Chartrain style must be noted: the Rémois passages in St Jean and St Paul, and the Laonnois passage in the Synodal Hall.[1] This may of course have been merely a flirtation, but the existence of Nevers cathedral, with its links to St Jean and St Paul, suggests that Sens may have played a more important role in the development of the Burgundian style than is now possible to reconstruct.

The Rémois passage was not consistently employed in Burgundian edifices – it did not appear, for instance, in the nave of Notre Dame at Dijon, at Semur or in any of the two-storied churches with clerestory passages except Villeneuve sur Yonne. Its virtual reappearance almost simultaneously at Sens and Nevers in the 1230's therefore certainly marks a phase of renewed vigour for the Burgundian parti. At Nevers, this is borne out by the three-storied elevation with triforium and clerestory passages (Pl. 22a). The triforium, with trilobed arcades and small sculpted figures both on the socles and in the spandrels, indicates that the St Cyr Master knew the nave of Bourges cathedral, begun about 1225. But the clerestory, with its slab-covered passage rising above the stilted wall-rib, reveals a profound knowledge of the Burgundian technique as practised at Clamecy and Dijon, in the first flush of the style.

The St Cyr Master's elevation is sophisticated. One shaft of the Chartrain pier rises directly to the vault departure, and it is flanked by an increasing number of colonnettes in the spandrels and the triforium, producing an effect of greater complexity and fineness as the eye mounts upward, in the manner of Amiens. Arcades, triforium and clerestory are decorated by thin rolls that form complexes of lines and shadows, focusing our attention on the arches. The triforium is typical of the care with which the design was worked out, for the slender, monolithic supports are capped by strong imposts with slightly inflected front planes, obviously designed for their elegant silhouette. There is nevertheless a certain relationship in this elevation to the contemporary composed elevation of High Gothic, with its hierarchy of large and small units

1. See Bony (1958), p. 48.

laid out on the flat plane of the wall. The articulated parts of St Cyr are all placed on one thin, forward plane, and the continuous shaft supporting both transverse arch and ogives marks one bay off from the next. The major difference from the northern style lies of course in the short clerestory. Since the vaults spring from the top of the triforium, it was not possible to draw the upper story into the brackets of the wall-responds and to make it function as a significant part of the design of the bay. This is the exact reverse of the situation at Semur and the other Burgundian monuments where the main colonnade is not integrated into the design of the upper stories. And finally the slots of the super-imposed passages and the unadorned outer walls mark the profoundly Burgundian concept of the spaces at St Cyr. It is perhaps as close as a Burgundian architect could come to creating a Rayonnant design, but it remains fundamentally a sister-in-spirit to Notre Dame at Dijon, gayer and less frank, perhaps, but also less ambiguous.

The reduced versions

It is interesting to note the geographical alignment of Gothic shops during the decades 1215–1235 (Fig. 20). The larger projects we have just examined seem to reveal a general division between east and west, as if perpetuating the two major stylistic areas of the later twelfth century. In view of the extraordinary extension and movement of the para-Chartrain style across Europe, this may be seen as the gradual slowing-down, the absorption and digestion of the particular elements that con-stituted Burgundian Gothic. Attrition, as well as the artistic success of certain edifices, which sometimes seems to have been spectacular, must certainly have played roles in the choice of the masters and the approval of the projects.

Little meaning can, however, be read into the geographical diffusion of the two-storied church with clerestory passage. Stretching from Nevers and Villeneuve sur Yonne to St Seine, it represents the ultimate extension of Burgundian Gothic design, penetrating into the heart of the old Romanesque region at Cluny and well past the frontiers of

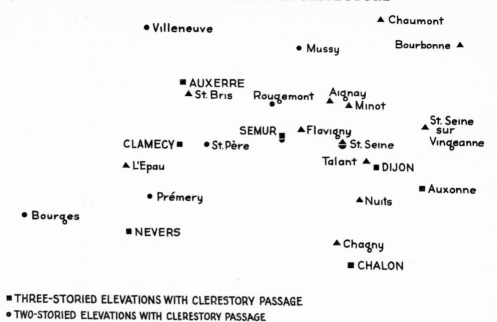

● Villeneuve   ▲ Chaumont

● Mussy   Bourbonne ▲

■ AUXERRE
▲ St. Bris   Rougemont   Aignay
            ●   ▲ ▲ Minot

       SEMUR ■   ▲ Flavigny   ▲ St. Seine
CLAMECY ■   ● St. Père   ♠ St. Seine   ▲ sur
                                  Vingeanne
▲ L'Epau   Talant ▲
                            ■ DIJON

● Prémery   ■ Auxonne

● Bourges   ▲ Nuits

■ NEVERS

                      ▲ Chagny

                     ■ CHALON

■ THREE-STORIED ELEVATIONS WITH CLERESTORY PASSAGE
● TWO-STORIED ELEVATIONS WITH CLERESTORY PASSAGE
▲ TWO-STORIED ELEVATIONS WITH SOLID CLERESTORY   ● Cluny

Fig. 20. Map of XIII c. sites in Burgundy.

Burgundy at Bourges. The two-storied edifice has a history as old as the
Christian church. In addition to the *nefs sans fenêtres*,[2] one version that
persisted throughout the thirteenth century had large panels of solid wall
between the arcades and the clerestory. This parti, which I shall call the
monastic style and for which the chevet of Pontigny may have been one
of the important models, is noteworthy, since it was employed in the
wealthy Benedictine monastery of Flavigny (Pls. 38a, 39a) and even in
the Cistercian house of L'Epau (Pl. 40c). In essence it represents the final
dissolution of the Romanesque groined basilica. The vigorous spatial
compartments have been diluted into a succession of wide but rather
short bays separated by slim, elegant wall-responds, and as often as not,
the naves are covered by six-part vaults. In view of the number of

2. E. Lefèvre-Pontalis, "Les nefs sans fenêtres dans les églises romanes et gothiques", *Bull. mon.*,
81, 1922, pp. 257–309.

buildings with this parti, the two-storied elevation with a passage in front of the clerestory windows marks the profound force of the Burgundian vision of space, as if even in these relatively small monuments the recessed wall could be used to advantage.

The abbey church of St Seine is a special case in point for the relationship of these two partis (Pl. 24c). Begun in the first decade of the century under Abbot Olivier, it was pursued rather slowly until his death in 1226. By this time, the foundations and ground-story of the chevet, transept and most of the nave had been erected. It seems apparent, from the expanse of solid wall and the slim responds here, that the monument was to have had a set of plain clerestory windows in the upper part, in keeping with the elevation of the monastic style. Work was suspended under Abbot Eudes (1228?–1235), however, until the abbey could free itself of debt – it was deeply engaged in borrowing and lending money, not always to its advantage[3] – and about a decade passed before construction was resumed. At this time, with the election of a new abbot, the original design was altered. The length of the unfinished nave was curtailed by two bays, and an interior passage running around the entire edifice was added in the clerestory. It is interesting to find that it bore a screen on the inner side, in the manner of the cathedrals of Lausanne and Geneva, although this is preserved in its original form only in the eastern bay of the chevet. Despite the many restorations St Seine has undergone, the contrast between the light, open clerestory and the massive lower walls is still very much in evidence and brings into sharp relief for us the fundamental aesthetic and structural differences of the Burgundian concept of layered spaces and the plain monastic style.

St Seine was not the first two-storied edifice to have a clerestory passage, however, and the grafting of one design onto another here was an unusual, if not unique occurrence. Projects planned from the start to have an interior *chemin de ronde* above the arcades in all probability represent the *reduction* of the three-storied Burgundian elevation, that is,

3. Cf. for example the abbey acting as guarantor for the debts of the Duchess Alix until 1228 (Petit, 4, p. 237) and of Duke Hugh in 1230 (*ibid.*, 250). The subject has never been fully investigated.

the suppression of the triforium, rather than the amalgamation of two distinct partis. This is indicated by the parish church of St Pierre le Guillard at Bourges (Pl. 24a), which was begun about 1220–1225, during the formative years of the Burgundian style, and which contains several characteristic features of the para-Chartrain movement, such as compressed six-part vaults over the nave.[4] In addition, the isolated column in the centre of the chapel entrance (about 1230–1235), mentioned in the preceding chapter, came from St Remi at Reims, via Auxerre (Pl. 24b). The structure of these columns *en tas-de-charge* is in fact very similar to Auxerre, and the technique was employed throughout St Pierre.

The independent chapels around the ambulatory of the parish church at Bourges were derived from northern France, like those at Semur, although the absence of extra collaterals and of a transept relates St Pierre to an older series of more modest plans such as St Leu d'Esserent and Gonesse (Fig. 43). The western bays of the nave are surmounted by two towers connected by a gallery across the main vessel. In view of these features, St Pierre, like Semur, is a miniature version of a cathedral programme.

Since the vaults spring from points well up in the clerestory, however, there is ample space for a triforium in the elevation of St Pierre. Its absence is surprising in view of the relationships of Bourges with Auxerre and Semur. The latter, for instance, probably suggested the corbels on the main capitals, which also resemble the original Norman type, and the idea of a tall clerestory may well have come from Semur, although an absolute relationship in time is impossible to establish between the two monuments. Yet the fact is, no triforium was built or even contemplated at Bourges, and the church therefore seems more than ever to represent the suppression of this middle story in an otherwise very Burgundian elevation. There can be little question that the elevation of St Pierre is not the "residual" type M. Bony finds at Villeneuve le Comte, at approximately the same date, where the inner side of the

4. Bony (1958), p. 45 and n. 3.

passage is screened by triplet arches, a form deriving from the cathedrals of Lausanne and Geneva. St Pierre marks the establishment, at the very start of the Burgundian style, of a distinct, small-scale variant that was to prosper at the side of the great projects during the ensuing thirty years.

The two stories of the nave at Semur were of course the result of the literal suppression of the triforium, after work had been begun on the nave (around 1235) (Pl. 21). The new proportions of the nave itself were close to those of High Gothic design and the abandonment of the triforium had the effect of drawing the clerestory even farther down in the elevation. But of consequence here is the design of the elevation. In contrast to the plain columnar piers of the chevet, those of the nave are flanked by shafts, and a group of three on the nave-side rises directly to the vault departures. Each bay is thus outlined down to the very pavement, as at Nevers. There is more than a little northern influence in this arrangement, for the three shafts of the wall-respond were among the major elements of early Rayonnant style, of which the outstanding example is St Denis (1231–1236).[5] Coupled with the tall clerestory, the squarish plan of the bays and their four-part vaults, this detail places the nave of Semur in another context. It is one of the first Burgundian examples to reflect the latest Ile de France developments, and only the clerestory passage bears witness to the persistence of local traditions.

The final version of the nave at Semur had a direct impact on the architecture of the vicinity, as is recorded for us in the extant parts of the convent of Rougemont (Pl. 25a). The eastern portion of the abbey church has unfortunately been destroyed, and the nave itself, in construction from about 1245 to about 1265, has been severely damaged. But enough remains to indicate that the architect must have looked on Semur as a model. Not only did he plan somewhat squarish bays with four-part vaulting, but he also adopted the general elevation as well as the details of Semur. The proportions of the nave are quite tall and the clerestory, although it does not have the height of Semur, is nonetheless quite different from the short story of the early years of the century. The

5. S. McK. Crosby, *L'abbaye royale de Saint-Denis.* Paris. 1953.

imposts are situated well up in the story, and whereas at Nevers the main colonnette of the pier supports all the ribs of the great vault while the minor ones help jack up the wall-rib, here each shaft bears an individual rib and the stilt for the wall-rib is placed close to the other colonnettes. Piers, string-course, and even the repetition of the wall-rib on the window wall, are all taken over from Semur and simply executed in a more modern manner. But the Burgundian master could not escape from the impact of the regional tradition. Even though he designed a composed window in the latest fashion, with pierced spandrels and mullions forming a pattern of fine rolls, he was unable to create a composed elevation. The clerestory carries an interior passage that is actually *covered by slabs*, as in the earliest monuments of the style. It is startling to realize to what degree the Burgundian parti had come to dominate the thinking of architects by the middle of the century.

Nevers also had its local circle of two-storied designs. At Prémery, a collegial church founded in 1196 by Bishop Jean de Fontenay, the canons began to construct a permanent edifice about 1220. The broad, low apse of this period, which has two stories of windows in a plain wall, is the work of a provincial shop only slightly cognizant of the Burgundian style that was just emerging at nearby Clamecy. With the second campaign and the construction of the eastern bays of the nave in the late 1230's, however, a definite relationship was established with the cathedral of Nevers (Fig. 21). The clerestory is short and the wall-rib stilted, as at St Cyr, while the piers and wall-responds are almost identical in form. But solids predominate in the nave of Prémery, and both the pervasive voids and the effects of screening, as well as the sophisticated details, were given short shrift. The plenitude of wall surfaces recurs about 1245 at St Gildard, a priory situated near the mediæval city of Nevers and now renowned as the resting-place of Saint Bernadette (Fig. 22). As there are no aisles here, the walls of the two-storied chapel are of necessity solids, but the surfaces are made powerful by the absence of any decoration. The arch over the clerestory passage enhances this aspect of the design, as it does at Prémery, and only the delicate

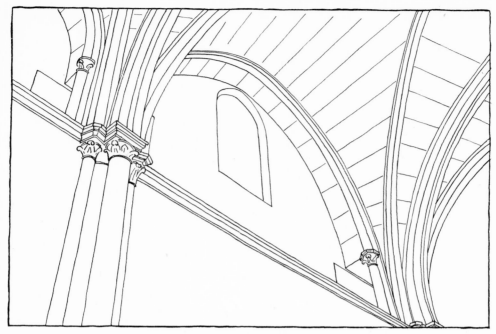

Fig. 21. Prémery, nave, detail.

colonnettes and ribs provide a feeling of lightness within the substantial enclosure.

St Gildard may seem to recall the basic features of twelfth-century Gothic architecture in western France, commonly called the Plantagenet style, for instance the cathedral of Angers, which also has cubical volumes and a clerestory passage above a solid wall. But this is surely a coincidence, since the distance and span of time between these edifices were enormous. Much more likely is some connection with Boult sur Suippe, a small church near Reims, where similar forms were employed about 1225.[6] Yet at Boult, the clerestory occupies only the upper part of the vault zone, as if walls and piers of two different sizes had been forced together. St Gildard marks the clarity and equilibrium that were later achieved in this reduced type, and with Prémery and St Seine it represents the last flourish of the short clerestory in Burgundy.

6. C.-H. Besnard, in *Cong. arch.* (Reims), 78, 1911, pt. 2, pp. 170–185.

The tall clerestory had made its first appearance in Burgundy in
Auxerre cathedral, and directly or indirectly all the later examples of it
that have been mentioned derived from this building. The major exception is also one geographically quite distant from Auxerre: Notre Dame
at Cluny, a parish church that burned in 1233 and was rebuilt at once on
the old foundations. The apse of Cluny, with its single story of tall
lancets, resembles the designs of eastern Champagne and Lorraine a
decade earlier, and the lantern tower may as easily have been inspired
by Laon or Braine as by the projected lantern at Auxerre. This is borne
out by the two-storied nave (Pl. 25b). The *pilier cantonné* is treated as
an entity, the shaft on the nave-side stopping at the capitals rather than
continuing into the wall-respond as at Semur. It is unusual to find this

Fig. 22. Nevers, St Gildard, suggested original disposition (looking west).

Rémois form in southern Burgundy, when other contemporary examples appear far to the north in Brie.[7] And the sculpted frieze running across the pilaster in the clerestory passage seems to have been drawn from Reims cathedral. Only the two-storied porch that once preceded the nave had a counterpart in the family of Auxerre, on the north transept of Semur.

Although these details make Cluny somewhat foreign to Burgundy, the nave is nevertheless a stunning example of the style. Sufficiently tall to permit an adequate development of each story, it has a balance that marks the hand of a master designer. The piers are robust but not squat, the capitals and imposts dense yet finely articulated. The proliferation of mouldings on the main arcades is kept behind the wall-plane, so that the surfaces of the spandrels form a smooth backing for the responds. The movement of these thin, undulated shafts is countered by the sharp string-course, and here for the first time the pattern is visually coherent. The absence of six-part vaults and alternately strong and weak piers is more than compensated for by the regular rhythm of the design. The Master of Notre Dame at Cluny created what the Rougemont Master seemed incapable of: an elevation, with clerestory passage, that appears to be composed.

This is the state to which Burgundian style had evolved by 1240, at Semur as well as at Cluny. In contrast, the last three edifices undertaken before the mid-century represent the resurgence of older ideas. One of these is St Père sous Vézelay, where the chevet was rebuilt in the fourteenth century (Pl. 26a). If in fact St Père were simply a chapel of the Virgin in the thirteenth century, as has been suggested, then the programme must be termed one of extraordinary development. The edifice is very small – nowhere in Burgundy is the clerestory passage so close and visually accessible to the observer – yet it contains a number of the distinctive elements of the style. The short, alternating piers, with the

7. At Donnemarie, Rampillon and Villeneuve le Comte. See de Maillé, "L'église de Donnemarie-en-Montois (S.-et-M.)", *Bull. mon.*, 87, 1928, pp. 3–28 and A. Carlier, *L'Eglise de Rampillon*, Paris, 1930.

extrusive colonnettes on the aisle-side (Fig. 86), were inspired by those in the nave of Clamecy. In both cases, the alternation suggests that six-part vaults were planned, but the rectangular cast of the bays proves this was not so. The alternation therefore seems to have been a revival of the old Norman parti that is represented in Champagne at Châlons sur Marne in the twelfth century and later at Bar sur Aube (St Pierre). The wall-responds at St Père were based upon the Semur design, or one of its descendants, and the support is kept thin in the clerestory. But the monument is too small to accommodate the alternating rhythm, and the elements are not reduced in size to match the overall dimensions – they obtrude upon the eye and the scale of the edifice is jarring.

The second church begun about 1245–1250, at Villeneuve sur Yonne, is considerably larger than St Père and the scale more in keeping with its size. The plan once again is elaborate for a parish church, with an ambulatory and three radiating chapels clustered together at the eastern end (Fig. 98). There is a certain dependence on St Jean at Sens, particularly in the hemicycle piers and the aisle wall. Here the dado is covered with round-headed arches and there is a Rémois passage just above, running clear around the chevet as at St Jean (Pl. 27b). But for the first time the voids are encroached upon by the solids. In a way this repossession of the layered wall by masonry suggests a degeneration of the Burgundian parti, for the small panels of wall are structurally unnecessary at Villeneuve, and they destroy the effect of lightness and thinness for which the Burgundians had always employed the passage. Similarly the opportunity to open the chapels into one another above the dado, which was superbly exploited at Notre Dame in Dijon, was here renounced for solid walls with a simple door giving access from one part of the passage to the other. In the main vessel, in keeping with contemporary Ile de France design, the clerestory is quite tall and the windows are filled with thin, complex tracery, but the choir piers are alternately weak and strong (Pl. 26b). Since they do not project very forcefully into the vessel, however, the recollection of the colossal cubic volumes of Auxerre is indeed dim, and in fact, as at Clamecy and St Père, six-part vaults were probably never planned. Villeneuve lacks the tense look that gives vitality to Cluny, and its calm may perhaps be taken as a sign of the diminishing power of the Burgundian vision.

The last edifice is St Pierre at Varzy, the parish church of a small but ancient town forming part of the *seigneurie* of the bishops of Auxerre. The Gothic church, begun about 1250, seems to have been laid out on virgin land. The plan, with towers above the transept arms and a simple apse, bears some resemblance to the twelfth-century monuments of the Saône Valley (Fig. 95). The apse has a Rémois passage set before a series of very tall lancets, and the dado is decorated with corbelled arcades and crockets, a design inspired by the cathedral of Auxerre and perhaps executed by masons from this older shop. The heaviness of the plastic effects and the impression of solidity and weight are akin to Villeneuve, although the opposition of passage and flat elevation is not very apparent in this single-storied apse.

In looking back over the edifices begun before 1250, the migrations of the various masters and shops can be fairly clearly discerned. Auxerre stands out as the first major foyer from which a number of masters issued, and when Dijon, Semur and probably Sens, in turn became centres of diffusion, it is like the formation of a family-tree. It would be inaccurate to exclude the monuments of the monastic style from this genealogy, since the Master of the nave of Flavigny, for instance, was as much indebted to Semur as was the Rougemont Master. Similarly many of the small country churches were beholden to the larger shops, for if they represent the persistence of the earliest Gothic, and even Romanesque types, with a general inertia toward any development, still elements devised in the major *chantiers* sometimes seeped in. One can imagine the pride of the local curate and congregation in the "modern" look of their renovated sanctuary.

*   *   *

The dominant feature of the Burgundian style in the first half of the thirteenth century was the presence of two subsidiary voids flanking the main volume. It is startling to note that in one other region of France, Normandy, a similar parti was used from about 1230 on.[8] With the chevet of Bayeux cathedral, the three-storied elevation with two interior passages became rather popular along the Channel coast, including the further reaches of Brittany and the area to the south. Bayeux, Lisieux, Norrey, Dol, Quimper, Sées – the list is even longer – all parallel early Burgundian design, with its tall triforium and short clerestory. But there was little exact resemblance and little, if any, direct contact between the two. In Normandy, the plastic effects and profiles are distinctive and much closer to English than to Burgundian or Ile de France design. Then, too, the subsidiary spaces tend to be very shallow and dark, unlike the spacious ones at Auxerre or Nevers. This may be due in part to the form of the openings, for the Norman triforium generally consists of a single relieving arch surmounting two smaller arches, much like the screened opening of a tribune. When the band triforium of regular arcades is employed, as at Norrey, it is comparatively short and the supports are multiplied in depth, obtruding upon the intercolumniation and replacing the lightness of Burgundy with a strong sculptural effect.

It is fascinating to note that the Rémois passage also had a wide dissemination in Normandy, probably starting with Rouen cathedral, and that this area also developed a two-storied elevation with an interior passage. Although the latter was first employed somewhat later than in Burgundy, it, too, originated as a reduced version of the larger elevations and reveals the same persistence of the concept of layered spaces. But the parallelism must not be pushed too far. Interior passages had been a feature of Norman architecture since the eleventh century and their use in the thirteenth was fundamentally a survival of this tradition. In Burgundy, on the other hand, they were a recent acquisition and they serve to underline the degree to which the Burgundians formed a new, regional style.

8. Bony (1958), p. 50.

CHAPTER V

The Dissipation of the Burgundian Style

THE Burgundian style has traditionally been called a "school" of Gothic architecture. This is but a poor generalization for a very complex state of affairs. The Gothic system, in which apprentices were trained by participation, of course tended to perpetuate a particular kind of structure and volume in successive shops, but this does not constitute a school in the formal sense. Moreover in its geographic connotation, the concept of a school overlooks the fundamental mechanism of such a system, that an architect might employ the same design wherever he happened to be engaged. This was demonstrated in the preceding chapters by the "foreign" influences in Burgundy, as well as by the appearance of the Burgundian parti well outside the frontiers of the region, even in its widest possible definition, and we shall shortly examine another example at Lyon.

The regionalism of Burgundy, that is, the stability observable up to 1250, was due in part to the establishment of particular shops in the area, and in part to the artistic success of the monuments they erected, that is, the rapid formation of a new tradition. But it was short-lived. In the thirty years after 1250, the novelty of the Burgundian parti seems to have worn off and Rayonnant design came to dominate the region; while the local shop traditions did not die out, some of the most important commissions were given to architects who either came from the north or were inspired by what they had seen there. After 1280, however, a definite reaction set in and the spatial concept of the early years of the century was revived. Very few major programmes were begun at this time, and even before the cataclysms of the bubonic plague and the Hundred Years' War, construction had virtually come to a standstill in Burgundy. The final stage in the evolution of the style, the extremes of simplicity and elaboration, made their appearance with this revival.

Within a period of about 70 years, no less than four separate designs, each clearly recognizable and deriving from a different source, were employed in the construction of the cathedral of Lyon (Fig. 65). Under Archbishop Guichard (1165–1180), the plan was laid out and the chevet begun on a pattern familiar to the Rhône Valley, with an apse flanked by two rectangular chapels and a transept with towers surmounting each arm. This work was interrupted at the level of the triforium, and when it was taken up again, about 1192, a new architect from north-eastern France was in charge. Jean Bony has shown that his design of the exterior clerestory loggia derived from Cambrai and acted as an intermediary between this cathedral and the Flemish buildings of the second quarter of the century.[1] Yet no later than about 1210, when the eastern wall of the transept was being terminated, a third master replaced the second. He moved the clerestory passage to the interior and abandoned the screen of colonnettes (Fig. 23). The derivation of this parti from Switzerland, where the cathedrals of Geneva and Lausanne were nearly complete, is reinforced by the rhythmic grouping of the triforium arcades, also a Swiss form. And finally, when the foundations and piers of the nave were emplanted, about 1230, a fourth master introduced still another design that affected both the triforium and the clerestory (Pl. 29b). The new triforium is composed of two arched units, each housing two smaller arches, of what I have called the Sens type. This feature, alone, relates the fourth project at Lyon to a very broad movement that included Amiens, Royaumont and Bourges (nave),[2] as well as Joinville and Bois-commun. Moreover in the bays adjoining the crossing, the triforium passage is covered by ribbed vaults (Pl. 29a), even though there is scarcely enough room for the protruding ribs and imposts, and this feature is found again in the north transept of the Madeleine at Troyes and in the

1. Bony (1958), p. 45.
2. For Amiens, see G. Durand, *Monographie de l'église Notre-Dame, cathédrale d'Amiens* (*Mémoires, Société des Antiquaires de Picardie*), Amiens–Paris, 1901–1903, *passim;* for Royaumont, H. Goüin, *L'abbaye de Royaumont,* 2d ed., Paris, 1949; for Bourges, my forthcoming monograph.

chevet of Coutances cathedral, at almost precisely the same date, and later in the upper stories of the north tower at Sens. The last design at Lyon therefore seems to have had very broad affiliations.

It is the clerestory, however, that reveals the origins of this design most clearly. As most of the transept had already been erected when the

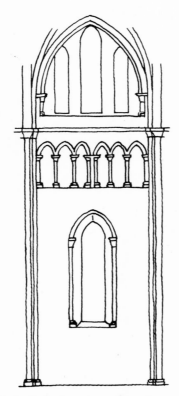

Fig. 23. Lyon Cathedral, elevation of south transept, south bay.

plans were changed, the clerestory could not be altered here. In the still unexecuted nave, however, a full-fledged tall clerestory was created, necessitating the raising of the vault-level and the alteration of the proportions of the main vessel. Yet the interior passage was retained. The result, executed about 1235–1245, is a High Gothic elevation with two tall stories bracketing the short triforium. The nave is covered by six-part vaults and the piers alternate in size, although their difference is kept at a minimum. Together with the form of the piers and the strong wall-responds, these features reveal the fourth Lyon Master's knowledge of the cathedral of Bourges. The High Gothic proportions of the elevation, combined with the interior passages can, however, only be likened to the narthex of Noyon, which was finished before 1231, and to the contemporary nave of Semur, as it was originally planned. The continuous colonnettes of Lyon are precisely contemporary with the first appearance of this detail in Burgundy, at Semur and Nevers. The culture of the fourth Master was very broad, indeed, and his design was somewhat "impure" and eclectic, although it cannot be denied a fundamentally Burgundian inspiration. It was also very modern, if not in the main stream of Gothic development, for the clerestory windows are filled with elaborate tracery and the basic opposition of the Burgundian parti to the composed High Gothic elevation is once again made apparent.

The salient point about Lyon is the relationship of the last three masters to the para-Chartrain movement. Although the first of these, deriving his design from Cambrai, actually set to work before Chartres was begun, his influence was felt in Flanders, one of the regions particularly resistant to Chartrain design in the 1220's and 1230's. The "Swiss Master" was affiliated with the descendants of Canterbury who developed some of the major elements of the Burgundian style. And the fourth Master also had a decided predilection for passages in the Burgundian manner. The cathedral of Lyon seems in fact to have been an established site for various developments of the para-Chartrain tradition and to have attracted architects from very distant regions to this southerly city. But none of the successive designs can be classed in "schools" and even the last, "Burgundian", Master obliges us to reject the concept of the limited geographic diffusion of the Burgundian style.

The Rayonnant Ascendance
As early as 1235 the cities in the lower Yonne Valley began to turn their eyes toward the style that was emerging in the Ile de France and northern

Champagne. The church of Villeneuve sur Yonne, at mid-century, represented a combination of the Burgundian parti and Rayonnant forms, but more than a decade earlier the nearby collegiate chapter of St Julian du Sault had begun a new edifice wholly in the northern style. Although the body of the thirteenth-century church was apparently damaged by the campaigns of the Hundred Years' war and is now badly disfigured by

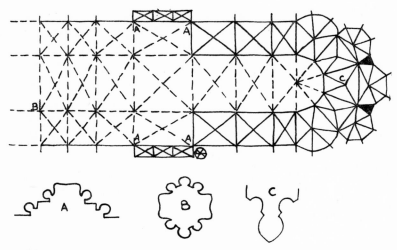

Fig. 24. St Julien du Sault, suggested original ground plan, pier plans, and ambulatory rib profile.

Renaissance work, itself never completed, enough remains of this superb little monument for us to form an idea of its original form.

The ground-plan of St Julien has a ring of five chapels around the ambulatory and a non-projecting transept (Fig. 24). The short transept, although not infrequent in Burgundy, also recalls the twelfth-century work at Notre Dame in Paris and the abbey church of St Denis,[3] and the chevet of St Julien has two other features in common with Suger's basilica: the radiating chapels are progressively deeper toward the east, a feature also found at Nevers, and the western pair are vaulted with the

3. For the unfinished twelfth-century plan of St Denis, see S. McK. Crosby, *L'abbaye royale de Saint-Denis*, Paris, 1953, pp. 49–50 and fig. 20.

ambulatory (Pl. 27a). But here the resemblance ends, and the recollection of the famous abbey, if in fact it were conscious on the part of the architect, was profoundly tempered by his knowledge of contemporary edifices in the north. The shallow, curved chapels are very similar to those at Soissons and Chartres, and the short straight bay just to the west is like the same bay in the cathedral of Reims. The small, vaulted porches screened by columns and set between the transept buttresses, derived from St Nicaise at Reims (1231 ff.), which was the source for a similar disposition on the west façade at Puiseaux, in the Orléanais.[4] The nave of St Julien is unfortunately too badly damaged to permit more to be said than that it was to have had at least four bays. The elevation of the chevet is also disfigured by sixteenth-century work, but here one can still find the original capitals in the vault zone. It very likely had three stories, with a band triforium and a tall clerestory, and almost certainly did not have an interior clerestory passage. There are no detached shafts in the piers at St Julien, but the various colonnettes and string-courses are underlined by deep hollows that accentuate their rectangular, box-like patterns, another similarity to the grid-design of Rayonnant style. The St Julien Master was also responsible for a striking innovation in the transept and nave, where the major faces of the piers are concave, as if a colonnette had been torn out of the pier and those to either side had been merged to fill the gap (Pl. 28b). All these features explain the almost total absence of the Burgundian manner at St Julien. The architect was familiar both with the monuments of the capital and with recent developments in northern Champagne, and his work represents the introduction of new techniques of design and a new conception into the Yonne Valley.

   With St Julien du Sault went the cathedral of Sens. Since the fabric of the edifice here was complete, only relatively minor parts could be modified, and it is clear that the architect engaged to execute the wishes of the metropolitan chapter came from the Ile de France. It is uncertain

4. See H. Deneux, "L'ancienne église de Saint-Nicaise de Reims", *Bull. mon.*, 85, 1926, pp. 117–141; for Puiseaux, see Deneux in *Cong. arch.* (Orléans), 93, 1930, pp. 392–400.

whether the axial chapel he built about 1235–1240 replaced an older one, or whether it was simply an addition (Fig. 25). It corresponds in width and height to a single bay of the ambulatory and is consequently rather spacious. The design of the wall is light and buoyant, with large windows

Fig. 25. Sens Cathedral, axial chapel.

above an arcaded dado. The tracery is flat and all the rolls are kept in a single plane, as in the contemporary windows of Notre Dame in Paris and St Denis. Only the crockets in the dado recall older Burgundian design. The modernization of the clerestory of the cathedral seems to have been motivated by one of the strongest impulses of the 1230's: the desire to admit more light into the frequently dark interiors of the twelfth century. This was the case at Notre Dame in Paris, and the windows there bear a strong resemblance to those at Sens:[5] the pierced spandrels are large and the mullions thin and sober (Fig. 26). The technical problems of creating these windows at Sens was serious, for unlike Paris, where the clerestory was enlarged downward at the expense of the blind third story, the triforium was left intact and the windows were expanded upwards, pushing the lateral webs of the vaults almost to the

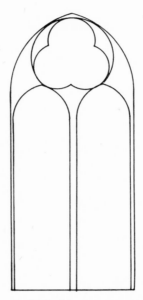

Fig. 26. Sens Cathedral, clerestory tracery (hemicycle).

cornice. The result is horizontal ridges in all directions, and the vaults, now flooded with light, have a distinctly modern form. The tracery is not unlike that of the axial chapel, although it reveals a greater freedom of design, as if the architect now had a regular repertory of forms from which to choose. This is itself one mark of a Rayonnant milieu.

Perhaps the largest project of this period was the reconstruction of the cathedral of St Vincent at Mâcon (Pl. 30a). Begun in the late 1230's, probably by Master Etienne Tondu, the entire body of the church was

5. M. Aubert, *Notre-Dame de Paris et sa place dans l'histoire de l'architecture . . .*, 2d ed., Paris, 1929, pp. 149 ff.

rebuilt in about twenty years, leaving intact only the older crypt and the narthex and towers to the west. It is unfortunate that all the thirteenth-century work should have been destroyed after the French revolution. Only a few fragments of the walls of the side-aisle are preserved, and we must rely on old plans and drawings, themselves often incomplete, for a picture of the edifice.

The main features of the ground-plan of St Vincent were determined by the extensive crypt that was retained from the pre-Gothic edifice (Fig. 66). As with the cathedral and with St Germain at Auxerre, which we will examine below, the crypt was employed as a ready-made foundation for the new construction and consequently the length and width, as well as the flat form of the chevet, must be considered as given. Master Etienne placed walls between the aisles and the main vessel in the easternmost bay of the chevet, thereby creating two chapels and a non-projecting sanctuary. He also divided the "apse" wall into two sections by a central respond and covered the bay with a five-part vault, similar to the one at La Bussière.

If the plan was predetermined in its main outlines, the elevation was not (Fig. 27). The drawings made in 1797 show three stories, with a short triforium and a very tall clerestory, the latter with an exterior passage. There were large rose windows in the transepts and the clerestory windows of both nave and chevet had two mullions apiece, except in the bay preceding the apse, where there were three. But the upper parts of the window design cannot be reconstituted, since the exterior views of the seventeenth and eighteenth centuries do not agree with one another as to their form. Even the form of the triforium is obscure, since it does not appear in any of the known interior views. There were two free-standing supports in each bay, but whether they carried a series of small arches or tracery beneath a large relieving arch, is unknown. The wall-responds seem to have been composed of twin engaged colonnettes, and the shafts of the responds in the aisles (and presumably also the main piers) were separated by deep hollows, giving them an undulated plan.

Despite the many gaps in our knowledge of this destroyed cathedral, it is obvious that Master Etienne's design had no relationship to the cathedral of Lyon and but little to the Burgundian edifices north of Mâcon. The extant bay of the side-aisle, one of the first to be erected, makes this evident and gives us our best picture of the effect of the edifice

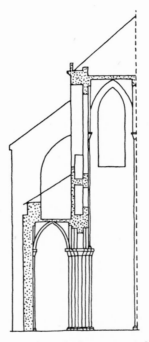

Fig. 27. Mâcon, former Cathedral, section (after 1797 drawing).

(Pl. 30c). Above the arcaded dado rises a narrow window with two lancets and an oculus. The tracery is in a single plane and there are no capitals or bases to interrupt the smooth flow of the rolls. In the upper parts, fine trefoils and a quatrefoil articulate the curves. This is a *svelte* and elegant elevation, and it shows that Etienne Tondu was working with the methods of current Rayonnant design, even if he was not a profound innovator.

By 1250 the Rayonnant style had matured in the Ile de France. The High Gothic speculation on colossal proportions and experiment with structure were well over and a series of new problems had been posed and solved. These involved, among other things, the use of a new scale and a new method of handling plastic effects, and both features had immediate repercussions in Burgundy, as is shown in the first design of the nave of Auxonne, about 1260 (Pl. 28a). In the easternmost bays, the triforium has four arches, each enclosed within a tall, rectangular frame. The frame is formed by colonnettes rising past the arcades to the string-course, which also group the arcades in pairs on either side of the central respond; each pair is further separated by a slimmer respond. In the original design, these responds were intended to rise into the clerestory, where they would have formed the mullions of the tracery. Before the top story was executed, however, the plan was revised. The Burgundian *chemin de ronde* was introduced, and in the remainder of the nave only three triforium arcades, without vertical dividers, were executed in each bay.

The similarity of the original design to an elevation such as St Denis or the cathedral of Troyes is striking.[6] One must also note that at Auxonne the tracery was planned in two distinct planes, a forward one dividing the bay into two major parts, and a recessed one subdividing each part into individual lancets. This is the principle of fractionization, of the subordination of parts to the whole and the repetition of the general design in increasingly smaller but otherwise identical units, one of the characteristics of the developed Rayonnant style.[7] The use of two planes of tracery instead of one facilitates and clarifies the design, but this detail did not make its appearance even at St Denis until about 1250 or 1255. The rapidity with which it reached the Saône Valley indicates that architects were still travelling widely and that even this rather provincial Burgundian town was in contact with the great foyers of the north.

Rayonnant shops continued to supply architects to Burgundian sites in the 1270's. The priory of St Thibault en Auxois, which acquired some relics of this saint about 1240 and shortly became an attraction for

6. For Troyes, see V. de Courcel in *Cong. arch.* (Troyes), 113, 1955, pp. 9–28, with bibliography.
7. As stated by E. Panofsky, *Gothic architecture and scholasticism*, Latrobe (Pa.), 1951, pp. 44–51.

pilgrims, had begun a modest church a decade or so later. The campaign here seems to have lagged and about 1270, another architect, instead of completing the edifice, reconstructed the north transept chapel dedicated to Saint Gilles (Pl. 30b). Such emphasis on the ritual parts of the church points up the desire to house the relics as splendidly as possible, and despite its small size, the chapel of St Gilles is rich and elaborate, a piece worthy of one of the great *chantiers*. But it is the apse of St Thibault, begun shortly before the end of the century, that must hold our attention (Pl. 31). The plain triforium and clerestory here were probably not erected until later in the fourteenth century, but the ground-story is certainly the work of an architect intimately familiar with Rayonnant design. There is a glazed Rémois passage here, a form which seems to have undergone a wide if sporadic revival at this time.[8] And as at St Urbain at Troyes, in the 1260's, the tracery is very delicate and the forms of the screen do not correspond with those of the windows, so that the complexity of these dark patterns against the light is increased. One should also note that the minor shafts in each bay pass through the central quatrefoils, an early example of the deliberate contradictions that were to preoccupy later Rayonnant architects.

Another Rayonnant master worked at St Germain in Auxerre, which had for centuries been one of the richest and most influential abbeys in France and whose patron was venerated in hundreds of towns and villages. Reconstruction here began in 1277 and continued intermittently into the late fourteenth century. As had been the case at Mâcon and at the cathedral of St Etienne across the city, the old crypt beneath the chevet was preserved as a foundation for the Gothic work, although it was also of course hallowed as the repository of the relics of Saint Germain. Certain alterations were made, however, such as the widening of the ambulatory, and the eastern rotunda, on a steep slope overlooking the Yonne, was wholly rebuilt.

8. It appears, for instance, at Sélestat (St Georges) in Alsace (G. Durand in *Cong. arch.* (Metz, etc.), 83, 1920, pp. 462–470) and at St Sulpice de Favières (Y. Sjöberg in *Cong. arch.* (Ile de France), 103, 1944, pp. 246–264), as well as in England (e.g., Durham).

The presence of the three-aisled Carolingian passage connecting the rotunda to the ambulatory obviously inspired the Gothic architect to use a similar arrangement in the new work (Pl. 33). The present passage is treated as a single, large bay covered by an eight-part vault, and aisles are suggested by two rows of thin columns on the eastern and western sides. The parti is similar to the entrance to the axial chapel of the cathedral and the architect seems to have had St Etienne in mind when he designed it, for one row of columns forms a screen across the entrance, and the ambulatory vault here has six ribs. Of greater interest in this respect is the resemblance of the two rows to the same parti in the south transept of Soissons cathedral, one of the predecessors of St Etienne of Auxerre in the late twelfth century. These two explanations, the adjustment of the Gothic work to the Carolingian, and the revival of a form some sixty years old, are not mutually exclusive, for the twelfth and thirteenth centuries offer many examples of an architect working out a design to fit a particular set of circumstances, that turns out to have been employed earlier in a totally different context.

Two other features of this first Gothic campaign at St Germain deserve our attention. Although the respond capitals are reduced in size, in good late thirteenth-century fashion, they disappear completely in the rotunda and the ribs of the vault descend uninterruptedly to the pavement. A sign of the increasing Rayonnant preoccupation with visual ellipses, this design was to be revived and widely used in the Flamboyant period of the fifteenth century. The second feature was born of the same spirit but it reveals closer historical affiliations. This is the prolongation of the window mullion down through the dado arcade. It had been used a decade or so earlier in the "vestibule" of the Virgin chapel at St Germer, built by Abbot Pierre de Wissencourt,[9] and was to reappear at Mantes and in the upper chapel of St Stephen's in London (founded in 1292).[10]

9. A. Besnard, *L'Eglise de Saint-Germer de Fly (Oise) et sa sainte chapelle*, Paris, 1913, plate following p. 88, and pp. 92–107.

10. At Mantes, in the axial chapel, about 1286; see J. Bony in *Cong. arch.* 104, 1946, p. 211 and view in *Cong. arch.* 82, 1919, following p. 218. See also M. Hastings, *St Stephen's Chapel*, Cambridge, 1955, pp. 84–86. A similar pattern appears at St Nazaire at Carcassonne about the same time, and in the early fourteenth century in the tribunes of the chevet of Paris Cathedral and in the baptismal chapel of St Denis.

As it very probably represents an imitation of the linkage between triforium and clerestory, of the sort used by Pierre de Montreuil at St Denis, simply transferred to another part of the building, this detail may be one of the indices of a "court" style, first elaborated by the architects surrounding Saint Louis and later expanded by those of King Edward.

St Germain is not a statement of the Burgundian style. There is no passage in the ambulatory or chapel walls and none in the clerestory of the hemicycle, or, for that matter, in the triforium itself (Pl. 32). Only the barest nod seems to be made to Burgundy: the triforium is rather tall and the clerestory quite a bit shorter than one would expect. But the triforium is very shallow and the screen reproduces a form well-known earlier in the century in the Ile de France, for instance at St Martin aux Bois, and in wide use around the year 1300. The sanctuary of St Germain is not particularly pure or inventive, but it is straight out of the Rayonnant book.

The same must be said for the nave of St Pierre at Varzy, which was begun about 1280 (Pl. 36b). The squat *piliers cantonnés* seem misplaced in this elevation, for the heavy triforium is quite tall and the clerestory is confined to the lunette of the vault, in the manner of the twelfth century and of early Burgundian style. The triforium passage has again been sacrificed for the solidity of the masonry, and as in the hemicycle of St Germain, the screen continues into the clerestory tracery. And finally, with the continuation of the transepts and nave of the cathedral of Auxerre, probably begun in 1309, we seem to have come full circle. Although the proportions of the elevation were not profoundly modified, the clerestory passage was abandoned and a fine Rayonnant triforium replaced the light one of the early thirteenth century.

None of the Rayonnant designs mentioned, whether of the earlier or later periods, were unusual in themselves, nor did they have a profound effect on the development of Gothic style at large. They mark the arrival of new architects in Burgundy and once again, as in the twelfth century, the importation of traditions developed elsewhere. It is clear that architecture in Burgundy could never again be what it had once been. The preference for Rayonnant forms during and after the mid-century was symptomatic of a general change of taste that took place over large portions of western Europe, and that altered the course of development of the Burgundian style. If a normal evolution was denied it, however, its firm entrenchment before 1250 unquestionably provided the force for its revival in the last decades of the century.

The Revival of the Burgundian Parti

The lapse of the Burgundian parti during the thirty years after 1250 was virtually complete, since the only clerestory passage with recessed wall begun at this time was in the nave of Auxonne. The revival of the parti in the 1280's was therefore somewhat abrupt. It was also limited, for it can be studied in only four buildings, although these are important ones and all but one are in cities that had earlier played roles in the Gothic architecture of the region. The first in time was the Benedictine monastery of St Bénigne at Dijon, where the crossing tower fell in 1272 and crushed a large part of the church (Pl. 34). The reconstruction was not begun immediately, and the first stone of the present edifice was laid only in 1281. By 1287 the new chevet and part of the transept had been completed, and the Burgundian revival was clearly marked out, although work continued on the nave until the early years of the fourteenth century. The apse of St Bénigne is an unremarkable design on a colossal scale, with a very tall clerestory and dark triforium passage. The austerity of the smooth surfaces is relieved only by the trefoiled arcades and complex supports of the triforium. When the eastern walls of the transept were erected, however, the design was altered to permit the introduction of a clerestory passage, and the triforium was gradually simplified until the final, plain version was arrived at in the nave, in the last decade of the century. The nave itself is, if anything, even more austere than the chevet. The triforium is spacious if not tall, and the arcade, even though it resembles a series of holes punched in a plate-like wall, is handled as a thin screen. The recessed window-wall above is also thin in appearance, and the large areas of masonry surrounding the openings recall the plain clerestory designs of the first half of the century. Clearly St Bénigne resisted all but the most minor elements of Rayonnant style.

The work projected as early as 1291 to complete the chevet of Nevers cathedral is also a Burgundian revival, but in a very different sense from St Bénigne. The unfinished work of the 1230's was taken into account, and the new work, like the old, contains a tall triforium and short clerestory (Pl. 37b). With these limitations, the architect made only one major alteration: he suppressed the partly executed transept, creating a long, continuous volume in the nave. For the rest, he seems to have concentrated his attention on the details of the edifice. The full elaboration of Rayonnant design is evident here, and if it is not profoundly creative, it is at least an excellent example of the optimism of 1300. The mouldings are uniformly fine, the triforium arcade and clerestory delicate. The resulting change of scale from the design of the 1230's is immediately apparent. The main arcades are sharply pointed, the triforium is placed a few centimetres higher in the elevation, and all the bays are equal in length (excepting, of course, the western one, where the transept had been begun). The glazing of the triforium makes each story light, and the openings are everywhere as large as possible. The recession of the clerestory windows has at last become unimportant, for the tracery patterns are prolonged into the triforium windows and the effect is completely logical: there is no contrast between glazed and open tracery, or between light and dark stories, and the window-wall is a continuous and visible external sheath.

The last three-storied Burgundian parti was executed in the Romanesque nave of the cathedral of Chalon in the course of the fourteenth century (Pl. 36a). The campaign undertaken by Bishop Robert de Decize in 1310 seems to have aimed at the completion of the old, unfinished nave, which still had a temporary wooden roof. The wall-responds were replaced, the main arcades and spandrels encased in new masonry and a new triforium and clerestory built above them. The triforium is not glazed, but it has the same form as the triforium at Nevers, a design we have already seen at St Thibault and Auxerre. The clerestory, however, is tall, even taller than the Gothic apse. Dedicated only in 1403, the nave of Chalon is a heavy, slow design that has neither the vivacity of Nevers nor the austerity of Dijon.

Fittingly enough, the final Burgundian design of the century has a two-storied elevation. The collegiate church of Mussy sur Seine, a summer residence of the bishops of Langres, had been founded in 1218, but the present edifice was not begun until about 1300 (Pl. 35). The plan is similar to those of Notre Dame at Dijon and St Urbain at Troyes, but the edifice is more ample in size and volume. This amplitude is enhanced by the two-storied elevation, and the consequent enlarged scale of the various parts. But the effect also depends upon the contrast of large, plain surfaces and the extremely economic use of thin rolls, as it were a thick structure with a gossamer pattern superimposed upon it. The arcades and the piers, which must here be understood as traversing both stories, are large and smooth, with their edges simply chamfered. Thin colonnettes are placed against these masses, as if to pick out a few major shapes, and it is of course the rectangle that is emphasized. The windows in the apse and the main arcades are framed like boxes and the edges of the crossing piers and arches subtly delineated. There is a certain family relationship in the smooth, simple tracery of Mussy to the upper stories of the apse of St Thibault.

The common element in these four monuments is the interior passage, clearly a revival of the spatial concept of the early thirteenth century. But a fundamental difference in approach to the effects of architecture divides them into two opposed groups. At Nevers and Chalon, the profound influence of Rayonnant design is apparent in the elaboration of detail and the proportions. At Mussy and Dijon, on the other hand, the keynote is sobriety and even grandeur, in the handling of tracery as well as masses and volumes. Although there is no evidence to link Mussy to the shop of St Bénigne, both mark a distinct rejection of Rayonnant aesthetics and the endeavour to regain an atmosphere of monumentality. These two approaches seem to have been the by-product of the revival.

Some fundamental features of the Burgundian style, for instance the technique of detached shafts, which had been replaced by Rayonnant monolithic mullions, were now, of course, inaccessible to these architects. Yet they do not reveal a full grasp of the principles of the early years of the century. And it is unfortunate that the success of the revival cannot be demonstrated, for other than the completion of Auxerre cathedral, no major new projects were begun in Burgundy in the first half of the fourteenth century. And when the abbey church of St Satur, the last two-storied Burgundian elevation, was begun in 1361, the design was drawn from other sources (Pl. 37a). Here, clarity and balance are foremost. The control of proportions is firm but not lacking in subtlety, and there is a certain refinement, even elegance, but one that does not depend on extreme elaboration. None of these features was inspired by Nevers or Dijon, but by the main stream of Gothic development that had taken place elsewhere in France.

*   *   *

In view of the wide and sometimes inexplicable movements of Gothic architects and shops, it is perhaps necessary to justify the term, "Burgundian style". Architecture in Burgundy followed no regular pattern of development from 1150 to 1350. The Romanesque traditions of the province were strong, and when the Gothic technique was first introduced, they tended to inhibit the formation of a local style. The second half of the twelfth century was in fact chiefly remarkable for the variety and frequence of importations from northern France. The last of these produced Auxerre and Clamecy, and it was here that a local Gothic tradition was first inaugurated, that a regional personality was formed. Of course even during this period of stability, from 1220 to 1250, there was no rigid uniformity of design, for the Chartrain element at Auxerre had, at the very start, provided an alternate elevation that became increasingly popular. Yet the parti of Clamecy and of Notre Dame at Dijon was also successful, and if an evolution took place in Burgundy, it reveals more the vitality of the area than a servile dependence on northern developments. The appearance of masters versed in Rayonnant design, in the late 1230's, and the weakness of the revival of the 1280's should not affect our conception of the original movement.

By most standards, however, thirty years is too short for the formation of a "style". Yet Burgundian architecture showed considerable breadth and flexibility. The forms and programmes varied from large to small and from cheap to costly and complex. Furthermore the Burgundian parti did not require a special ground-plan and did not impose a particular proportion. Considering the absence of artistic frontiers and the rapid expansion of Gothic architecture in the first half of the thirteenth century, the similarities of Burgundian edifices at this time are surely more out-standing than their differences. The same inner coherence and outward diversity characterized Plantagenet architecture in western France from 1160 to 1190. That both were short-lived was due more to external pressures than to their incapacity for expansion and development.

Fig. 28. Map of sites
in Catalogue.

61 Aignay le Duc
62 Minot
63 Montbard
64 Darcey
65 Cussey les Forges
66 Selongey
67 Grignon
68 Epoisses
69 Massigny lès Semur
70 Flavigny
71 Véronnes les Grandes
72 St Seine sur Vingeanne
73 Semur en Auxois
74 St Seine
75 Pichanges
76 Bèze
77 Marcigny sous Thil
78 St Thibault
79 Marsanny le Bois
80 Mirebeau sur Bèze
81 Orgeux
82 Talant
83 Fleurey sur Ouche
84 Dijon
85 Petit Ouges
86 Rouvres en Plaine
87 Vandenesse
88 St Philibert
89 Auxonne
90 Mimeure
91 La Bussière
92 Nuits St. George
93 Cîteaux
94 Corgoloin
95 Pernand
96 Gerland
97 Serrigny
98 Molinot
99 Beaune
100 Bourges
101 St Satur
102 St Verain
103 Entrains
104 Clamecy
105 L'Epau
106 Bellary
107 Varzy
108 Tannay
109 Prémery
110 Nevers
111 St Eloi
112 Chagny
113 St Loup de la Salle
114 Touches
115 Chalon sur Saône
116 St Marcel lès Chalon
117 Cluny
118 Mâcon
119 La Bénissons Dieu
120 Lyon

1 Villenauxe
2 Troyes
3 Bar sur Aube
4 Clairvaux
5 Mussy sur Seine
6 Boiscommun
7 Pont sur Yonne
8 Nailly
9 Ste Colombe lès Sens
10 Villeneuve l'Archévêque
11 Sens
12 Villeneuve sur Yonne
13 Dilo
14 St Julien du Sault
15 Chemilly
16 Pontigny
17 Appoigny
18 Monéteau
19 Montigny la Resle
20 Ligny le Châtel
21 Auxerre
22 Quenne
23 Chablis
24 Tonnerre
25 Quincy
26 Bléneau
27 Vaux
28 Chitry
29 St Bris le Vineux
30 St Cyr les Colons

31 Irancy
32 Vermenton
33 Sacy
34 St Sauveur
35 Sementron
36 Prégilbert
37 Montréal
38 Guillon
39 Vézelay
40 Avallon
41 Savigny en Terre Plaine
42 St Père sous Vézelay
43 Joinville
44 Blécourt
45 Chaumont
46 Bourbonne les Bains
47 Langres
48 Molesmes
49 Cerilly
50 Lachaume
51 Laignes
52 Châtillon sur Seine
53 Faverolles lès Lucey
54 Val des Choux
55 Recey sur Ource
56 Asnières en Montagne
57 Essarois
58 Bure les Templiers
59 Rougemont
60 Fontenay

Catalogue of Monuments

Nᴏᴛ all the twelfth and thirteenth-century monuments of Burgundy could be listed in the accompanying Catalogue, nor are all the edifices that are listed properly speaking Burgundian. An effort has been made to record the data pertinent to the thesis of the text, on a wide but representative basis, with especial attention to destroyed monuments. Brackets indicate buildings or studies not seen by the author. The plans and drawings are diagrammatic and are not in scale with each other. Monographs are cited in the Catalogue; the full titles of articles listed briefly can be found in R. de Lasteyrie du Saillant, *Bibliographie générale des travaux historiques et archéologiques publiés par les sociétés savantes de la France*, Paris, 1888– (continued to 1940 by R. Gandilhon). The numbers following the place-names in the Catalogue refer to Fig. 28; the bibliographies are divided into the following categories for convenient reference:

(a) historical material
(b) archaeological studies
(c) additional bibliographical notices.

AIGNAY LE DUC (Côte d'Or) (61)
St Pierre & St Paul, parish in the diocese of Autun patronized by the bishop.
See Plates 41b and 44a.

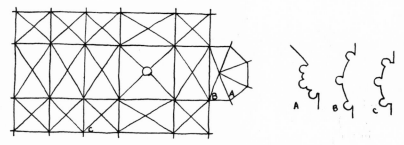

Fig. 29. Aignay le Duc, plan and responds.

Begun at the east in the late 1230's, the building was completed without major interruptions in about twenty years. It was restored in 1780 and again in the XIX c.

There are a transept and a crossing tower, but no flying buttresses. The apse has two stories with a sharp string-course between, and the upper descends slightly below the vault departures. Each bay of each story has one plain lancet. The responds have the rounded pilaster, the ogive is similar to the wall-rib of Clamecy. The choir, transept and nave have two stories without the separative string-course, with small, plain lancets in the vault-zone and a large expanse of plain wall below. The transept terminals have three equal lancets and a small rose well above them (view in Flipo), the west façade a small rose over twin lancets, as on the façade of Minot. The crossing piers are circular with four large and four small engaged colonnettes; the chevet and aisle responds form segments of the same (with three colonnettes), in the aisle the whole being set forward slightly from the wall. The nave has *piliers cantonnés* with one shaft continuing uncut by the capital, into the wall-respond.

An example of the monastic style. The format and style of the nave capitals are close to St Pierre at Flavigny. The crossing piers are the common coin of the period, as at Nevers, Semur, Appoigny, and so on, all resembling the piers at Bourges Cathedral, to which the chevet and aisle responds also bear a certain resemblance.

(a) Courtépée 4, 202; Longnon, *Lyon*, 87 (XVI c.); Roserot 4. (b) V. Flipo, *Mémento pratique* ... [Paris, 1930], with view, p. 161; Guillaume 310.

APPOIGNY (Yonne) (17)

St Pierre, collegiate church in the diocese of Auxerre, said to have been founded by Bishop Guillaume de Seignelay (1207–1220).

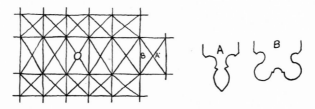

Fig. 30. Appoigny, plan and rib profiles.

The apse and transept were constructed about 1230–1235, the nave (by a different master and shop) about 1240–1255.

The rectilinear plan of the chevet is complemented by a clear massing of large, cubical volumes with no horizontals. There is a crocket cornice here. The interior has a single story with a tall, arcaded dado supporting a narrow, open passage running around the chevet from the west side of the transept terminals. It is cut behind the crossing piers but corbelled in front of the responds in the corners of apse and transept. The vaults extend to the window wall, which is plain and has twin lancets in the lateral bays of the apse, east walls of the transept and north terminal wall (where the presence of a staircase reduces the available space), and triplets in the east wall of the apse, the south transept terminal and the west walls of the transept (now blocked in); the latter are placed high in the vault zone to surmount the aisle roofs. The eastern crossing piers reveal a change of plan above the bases, which resulted in the suppression of one of the shafts on each pier. The corner responds consist of three detached shafts surrounding a larger core, as at Auxerre; in the north corner of the apse, this respond is coursed, perhaps in restoration. The vaults have horizontal crowns and tall, vertical departures for the transverse arches and the wall-ribs; the lateral wall-ribs are stilted on detached shafts with high capitals. There are no wall ribs on the west walls of the transept. The key-stones are sculpted and boss-like, having, in the transepts, crockets to mask the rib joints.

In the nave, a tower was apparently planned but never executed for the second bay. The main bays are wide and long, the aisle bays almost square. The elevation has three stories, with squat Chartrain piers, of which the shaft on the nave side rises to the vault departure. The triforium is of the Sens type and originally opened onto the roofs; the arcades are trefled, the relieving arches round-headed, and corbels appear beneath some of the bases. The clerestory is very short, with a single lancet in each bay. The western crossing piers are circular, with alternating large (coursed) and small (detached) shafts on the major and minor axes. The wall-respond has the rounded-pilaster behind the major colonnette, and two large engaged shafts set forward of the wall. The median triforium support has a coursed circular core flanked by three detached shafts. The vaults, with tall vertical departures for the transverse arches, are like those of the chevet, and it is likely that they were all mounted at the same time. The façade wall has an open interior passage, covered by an arch, connecting the aisle roofs, and a plain triplet window. There are long, low flying buttresses above the aisles, the projection of which is diminished by the height and angle of the roofs. The lateral portal is round-headed, with a trefled tympanum; the west portal is similar to the one at Prégilbert. The whole building is thoroughly restored.

The chevet may have been constructed by masons from Auxerre, but it is in fact merely a poor copy of the cathedral, since the minor spaces are undeveloped; certainly the Auxerre Master himself did no work here. A further reduced version is found at Sacy, suggesting a small, local stylistic eddy after 1230. The nave was designed by a man who knew Prémery and St Cyr at Nevers, but who was working in the tradition of Sens cathedral.

(a) Lebeuf 3, 383. (b) Quantin, *Dictionnaire topographique du département de l'Yonne*

(*Comité des travaux historiques* . . .), Paris, 1862, 3; *id.*, *Rép.*, 17; Hautecœur 89–91 and Pls. 91–94; J. Vallery-Radot in *Cong. arch.* (Auxerre), 116, 1958, 97–106. (c) Besse 6 (1913) 76.

ASNIERES EN MONTAGNE (Côte d'Or) (56)

St Pierre, parish in the diocese of Langres, at the presentation of the abbot of Moûtiers St Jean.

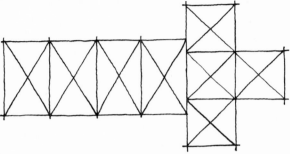

Fig. 31. Asnières en Montagne, plan.

The apse and transept, and then the nave, were constructed in two consecutive campaigns, about 1240–1250.

The small church has one story and a crossing tower. The apse and transept walls have single lancets, the responds are single colonnettes. The crossing piers have alternately large and small engaged shafts around a roughly circular core. The nave responds have three contiguous engaged colonnettes. The profile of the ogives is similar to the one in the chevet of Appoigny.

The country style, showing the persistence of early Gothic forms in the hinterland.

(a) Longnon, *Lyon*, 148 (1436); Roserot 14. (b) Guillaume 281.

AUXERRE (Yonne), in the Archdiocese of Sens (21)

A. Cathedral St Etienne

See pp. 38–47, Plates 1, 13a, 14 and 15, and Figs. 8–11.

The old cathedral possessed a nave and two aisles with an ambulatory and a single radiating chapel on axis. The chevet was flanked by two towers, the exact location of which is not known. Guillaume de Seignelay's immediate predecessors had embellished the edifice with a new, raised pavement, new roofing and possibly vaults over the aisles, and they had reworked the west façade, adding lateral portals and larger windows with stained glass. The old chevet foundations determined the width of the new chevet, as at Chartres and many other sites, although the overall length, as well as the length of the individual bays, may have been altered. The thirteenth-century axial chapel is supported by extra walls and arches thrown around the older chapel at the level of the crypt.

On the XIIc. sacristy (now totally rebuilt), see Porée (1907), 80. It was probably constructed under Bishop Guillaume (1167-1182).

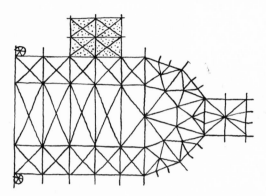

Fig. 32. Auxerre Cathedral, plan of the chevet with XII c. sacristy.

The Gothic chevet was begun about 1215 – perhaps in this very year, when three guardians were appointed to the cathedral (Lebeuf 4, 77 [no. 124]) – and it is known to have been in progress in 1217, when the Romanesque towers collapsed (see p. 39); the latter date is given in the *Gesta Pontificum*, 475, and by the second continuer of the chronicle of Robert de Saint Marien, in *Monumenta Germaniae Historica, Scriptores*, 26, 277, 282 and n. 6. The work was terminated shortly before 1234 (see p. 39); in 1233, the duties of the guardians were redefined, as if the new edifice had just come into use (Lebeuf 4, 97 [no. 165]).

The south tower at the western end of the nave seems to have been begun about 1235, but not even the ground story was completed in this campaign. The fabric was extensively reworked at the end of the century.

The weak piers of the choir directly to the east of the crossing were rebuilt at the end of the XIII c. (Porée, 1906) and the arcade departures above the weak piers farther to the east also seem to have been altered, contrary to the opinion of Porée. It is likely that the square masonry piers now obtruding into the triforium passage in the hemicycle were also added at this time, since they do not match the trapezoidal plan of the lintels they support. This work was probably terminated before the dedication of the main altar in 1334.

The transepts and nave were under construction from about 1309, when the relics of Saint Amâtre were translated by Bishop Pierre de Corbeil. By about 1400, the south transept and the lower stories of the nave had been completed.

(b) *On the earlier edifices:* M. Quantin, "Restitution par les textes des cathédrales élevées successivement à Auxerre avant le XIIIe siècle", *Bull. Soc. Yonne*, 4, 1850, 369–379 (uncritical; largely drawn from the *Gesta Pontificum*); R. Louis, *Les églises d'Auxerre*, Paris, 1952, 111–124; J. Hubert (1952), no. 28. *On the present edifice:* C. Porée, "Le chœur de la cathédrale d'Auxerre", *Bull. mon.*, 70, 1906, 168–181; id., *La cathédrale d'Auxerre (PM)*, Paris, 1925; M.-L. Springer, in *Notre Dame in Dijon*, Stettin, 1934, 50–52; R. Fourrey, *Dans la cathédrale Saint Etienne d'Auxerre*, Auxerre, 1935; Jantzen, 11–17; J. Vallery-Radot in *Cong. arch.* (Auxerre), 116, 1958, 40–50. (c) Besse 6 (1913), 73, n. 1.

B. St Eusèbe, priory of canons with titular abbot in the XII c., at the presentation of the abbot of St Laurent. The church and cloister served as a cemetery for the cathedral chapter.

See pp. 30–31 and Plate 9a.

The chevet (destroyed) may have been begun in the early XII c. By mid-century, the nave, including the tower over the north aisle, was under construction, although probably not even the ground story had been completed before the fire of 1188, which burned the market in the adjacent square and presumably attacked the church itself. The triforium in the eastern bays and the main piers in the western were undertaken soon after, although progress was still slow, since the western end of the nave had not been completed when fire seems to have struck again in 1216 (discounted by Porée). The façade wall and the adjacent bays of the triforium were built about 1225–1235, in a style close to that of the cathedral, with clusters of detached shafts and heads serving as corbels in the triforium. The main vaults over the whole nave were the last work to be executed.

(a) Lebeuf 1, 284; 2, 539; 3, 122 (fire of 1188) and 150 (fire of 1216, confirmed in *Monumenta Germaniae Historica, Scriptores*, 26, 277); cf. 2, 538–545; Longnon, *Sens*, 257 (late XV c.). (b) F. Vachey, "Eglise Saint Eusèbe d'Auxerre", *Bull. Soc. Yonne*, 2, 1848, 131–192, with many illustrations; C. Porée in *Cong. arch.* (Avallon), 74, 1907, 188–193; J. Vallery-Radot in *Cong. arch.* (Auxerre), 116, 1958, 87–96. (c) Cottineau (1) 216.

C. St Germain, Benedictine abbey.

See pp. 94–96 and Plates 32 and 33.

The Gothic edifice was begun in 1277 under Abbot Jean de Joceval, who seems to have constructed most of the ambulatory. The triforium and clerestory were probably erected under Abbot Gauthier Dignon (1309–1334) and the transept and nave in the second half of the XIV c. (1362 ff.). That the latter was never completed (work was still going on in the XV c.), is indicated by the existence, up to 1811, of three bays of the Carolingian nave immediately to the west of the present one. The extant tower (XII c.) seems originally to have formed part of the church.

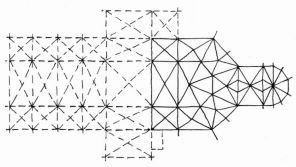

Fig. 33. Auxerre, St Germain, plan with 1277 and 1362 campaigns.

(b) *For the earlier buildings*, see J. Hubert, "L'avant-nef carolingienne de Saint Germain d'Auxerre", *Cahiers archéoloqiques*, 5, 1951, 151–162, and R. Louis, *Les églises d'Auxerre*, Paris, 1952, 35–110. *On the present edifice*, C. Porée in *Cong. arch.* (Avallon), 74, 1907, 182–188; J. Tillet, *ibid.*, 627–653; L. Schürenberg, *Die kirchliche Baukunst in Frankreich*, Berlin, 1934, 164–167; J. Vallery-Radot in *Cong. arch.* (Auxerre), 116, 1958, 26–39. (c) Cottineau (1) 216–218.

[D. St Pèlerin, Augustinian priory of St Père en Vallée from 1145. Destroyed.] In the late XII c. the edifice was reconstructed on much earlier foundations. It had an apse flanked by rectangular chapels. The elevation is unknown.

(b) R. Louis, "Les fouilles de l'ancienne église St Pèlerin d'Auxerre", *Bull. Soc. Yonne*, 1927, 123–147, and *op.cit.* (1952), 25–30. (c) Cottineau (1) 219.

AUXONNE (Côte d'Or) (89)

Notre Dame, parish of the Cluniac priory of St Vivant, Vergy, in the diocese of Besançon.

See pp.65–66 and Plates 23a and 28a.

An edifice seems to have been built soon after 1189 (traditional date). Remains are to be seen in the low transepts, which were to support towers somewhat in the fashion of the Saône Valley. About 1235 (possibly 1237, when Auxonne became a possession of the duke), the apse was reconstructed, together with the unequal oriented chapels. The shop seems to have worked earlier on the chevet of Notre Dame at Dijon and at St Vincent at Chalon, although the different elevation of Auxonne suggests that this master had no hand in their design. The continuous mouldings, without capitals, surrounding the apse lancets, are reminiscent of

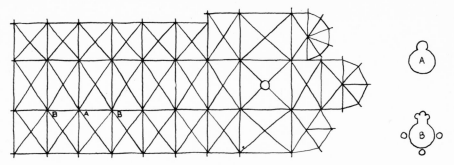

Fig. 34. Auxonne, plan and piers.

Montréal and the Yonne Valley in the decades before 1200. The responds here are composed of detached shafts set against masonry cores; in the main responds, the cores are undulated, although this feature seems at once to have developed into the rounded pilaster and then into the normal pilaster as work progressed.

The construction of the nave followed immediately upon the completion of the chevet, about 1250, but it lasted well into the second half of the XIII c. and was perhaps never terminated according to the original project. The piers were originally circular, with three clustered, engaged shafts on the nave-side, to support the ribs of the four-part vaults. In the western bays of the south file, there appear *piliers cantonnés* with detached shafts set well away from the core, although the suggestion of a plan for two six-part vaults here (and at least one more bay than at present) may be incorrect. The piers bear a certain resemblance to those at Dol in Brittany (see A. Rhein in *Bull. mon.* 74, 1910, esp. 372–377). The elevation has three stories, with a triforium passage and an interior clerestory passage. The present triplet windows in the eastern bays recall certain XIII c. Burgundian edifices, and the passage represents a change of plan. In the remaining bays to the west, the clerestory window is a single opening filled with twin lancets and an oculus, all executed in tracery. There is a certain relationship here to the apse of St Bénigne at Dijon (1281 ff.), as noted by Oursel, but the earlier work on the nave is certainly based on Ile de France and central Champenois design of the 1240's. The XIII c. edifice is disfigured by a considerable amount of restoration and rebuilding in the XIV c. and XV c. (see Oursel).

(a) Roserot 19; Calmette-Clouzot, *Pouillés des provinces de Besançon* . . ., Paris, 1940, 18 (1275). (b) [C. Pichard, *Souvenirs sur l'église Notre-Dame d'Auxonne*, Auxonne, 1847 (36 pp.)]; J. Tillet in *Conq. arch.* (Dijon), 91, 1928, 450–456 (to be corrected by Oursel); C. Enlart, *Manuel d'archéologie française*, 3d ed., Paris, 1929, 693 (dated 1309–1360, to be corrected by Schürenberg); L. Schürenberg, *Die kirchliche Baukunst in Frankreich*, Berlin, 1934, 174, n. 59; C. Oursel, *Notre-Dame d'Auxonne (Côte-d'Or)* (*La Bourgogne Touristique*, ed. Syndicat d'Initiative d'Auxonne), n.p., 1957, 10 pp. (important).

AVALLON (Yonne) (40)

[St Martin du Bourg, Benedictine priory of St Martin at Autun, in the diocese of Autun.]

See p. 17 and Fig. 2f.

The rectangular apse, with a ribbed vault, constructed about 1155, is among the earliest in the Yonne Valley. The remainder of the edifice is groin-vaulted (several bays of the nave have been destroyed).

(a) Courtépée 3, 607; E. Petit, *Avallon et l'Avallonnais. Etude historique,* 2d ed., Auxerre, 1890, 144. (b) C. Porée in *Cong. arch.* (Avallon), 74, 1907, 10–12; J. Richard in *Annales de Bourgogne,* 31, 1959, 146–147. (c) Cottineau (1) 221.

BAR SUR AUBE (Aube), in the diocese of Langres (3)

A. St Maclou, collegiate church in the former château of the counts of Champagne, replacing their private chapel, founded in 1159 by Henri le Libéral; the dean was named by the canons of St Quiriace at Provins. A relic of Saint Maclou was obtained only in 1220.

See pp. 23–26, Figs. 4 and 6c, and Plates 5b and 7b.

Fig. 35. Bar sur Aube, St Maclou, ogive profiles.

The present church was begun shortly after 1159 (but probably before 1165, when a first parish at Bar was granted), and it was largely terminated by the end of the century. Some capitals suggest the re-use of older materials, possibly from the earlier chapel. The apse and chapels were rebuilt in the late XIV c.

(a) H. d'Arbois de Jubainville, *Histoire . . . des comtes de Champagne,* 3, Paris-Troyes, 1861, 172, n. 1; E. Chapin, *Les villes des foires de Champagne* (*Bibliothèque de l'Ecole des Hautes Etudes, sciences historiques et philologiques,* 268), Paris, 1937, Pl. 3 and *passim.* (b) A.-F. Arnaud, *Voyage archéologique et pittoresque dans le département de l'Aube,* Troyes, 1837, 201–203; d'Arbois, *Rép.,* 34. (c) A. Prévost in Baudrillart 6 (1932) 550; Laurent-Claudon (1941), 171–174.

B. St Pierre, Benedictine priory of St Claude, adjacent to the *halles* of Bar.

See p. 28 and Plate 5a.

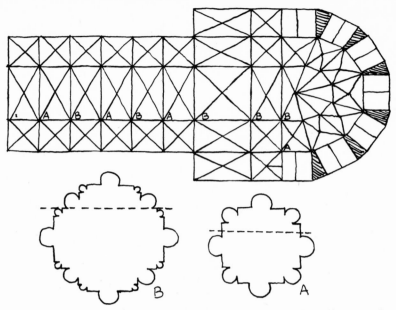

Fig. 36. Bar sur Aube, St Pierre, plan and piers, with wall-responds.

The church was constructed slowly from west to east, without major interruptions. The nave was begun about 1195, the hemicycle was in progress about 1235.

The nave has alternating piers and three stories separated by string-courses. There is a short clerestory with simple lancets and a triforium with passage (now walled up in some bays) but surmounted by an expanse of plain wall. The triforium had six arcades per bay, formed into groups of three by twin colonnettes in the centre, with round-headed arches (with a small chamfered moulding) and no imposts; in the transept terminals there are two groups of four arcades flanking an arch with twin colonnettes on either side (in the north transept, the passage is covered by a series of small arches corresponding to the arcades). The vaults have alternately heavy and light transverse arches; all the departures are set back from the supporting capitals as if the vaults were added after a change of plan. The ogive and the minor transverse arches have two tori separated by a pointed moulding. There is a Cistercian rose in the nave terminal. The hemicycle is horseshoe-shaped, with columns and a single colonnette wall-respond; the triforium (probably always blind) has moulded, pointed arches and imposts, as in the eastern wall of the transept. Each clerestory bay has one round-headed lancet. The hemicycle vault was rebuilt in the XIX c. The radiating chapels have pointed barrel vaults (probably not original) on trapezoidal buttress-walls.

The nave is closely related to St Maclou at Bar by the details, including the capital sculpture, and it was perhaps built by members of this shop. The alternation recalls St Etienne at Troyes but even more Notre Dame en Vaux at Châlons sur Marne, since six-part vaults were probably not intended. The triforium passage marks an advanced technique for the area. The chevet is clearly Cistercian in plan, although probably not derived from nearby Clairvaux.

(a) E. Chapin, *op. cit.*, *passim*. (b) A.-F. Arnaud, *op. cit.*, 200–201; Abbé Tridon in *Cong. arch.* (Troyes), 20, 1853, 125. (c) Laurent-Claudon (1941), 458–459 and n. 4.

BEAUNE (Côte d'Or), in the diocese of Autun (99)

A. Notre Dame, collegiate church and parish (1789)

About 1220–1240 three bays were added to the Romanesque nave. A porch was constructed in a second campaign, the termination of which is perhaps marked by a transfer of relics on 9 Nov. 1265 (mention of the *opus* in 1249 might therefore indicate construction was still in progress).

The nave bays are a careful copy of the Romanesque work, with minor modifications such as a single clerestory window and no fluting on the pilasters. They are barrel-vaulted. The three portals formerly bore an elaborate programme of sculpture. The porch is two bays deep and three wide, with a six-part vault on ringed, columnar shafts. The outer corner supports have undulated hollows between the colonnettes. Sculpted heads are used as corbels.

Both campaigns are very sophisticated: the nave bays by their adherence to a design long out of style, and the porch by its lightness and elegance, in keeping with Burgundian developments of the XIII c.

(a) Courtépée 2, 291 (where the "portal" is dated 1332); Petit 6, 192 and no. 2659; Roserot 28. (b) Foisset 149–154; Abbé Vinceneux, "Notes sur l'histoire de la construction de l'église Notre-Dame", *Mémoires, Société d'archéologie de Beaune (Côte-d'Or)*, 41, 1920–1925, 60–71; Hautecœur, 54, 127–129, 180; pls. 224–225.

B. St Nicolas, parish church at the presentation of the chapter of Notre Dame.

The plan comprises an apse, a choir bay, a crossing and transept arms of the same size (with diagonal buttresses), two shorter nave bays and an axial, square tower to the west, over a bay flanked by two equally small groin-vaulted bays. The whole edifice has been totally rebuilt. It is said to date from the early XIII c., although the church proper is obviously later than the mid-century.

(b) Foisset 155; A. Perrault-Dabot, "L'église Saint-Nicolas à Beaune et les clochers de la région beaunoise au moyen âge", *Mémoires de l'académie des sciences, arts et belles-lettres de Dijon*, 1925–1926, 203–212; R. Oursel, "Une église-porche en Bourgogne au XIII siècle: Saint-Nicolas de Beaune", *Mém. com. C.-d'Or* 23, 1947–1953, 205–207.

BELLARY (Nièvre, commune of Châteauneuf-Val de Bargis) (106)

[Notre Dame, Carthusian priory, founded in 1209 by Hervé, Count of Nevers.]

The church was probably erected in the mid-XIII c. It is destroyed. The chevet was flat. The nave had five bays without aisles, with ribbed vaults resting on colonnettes corbelled from the wall at the level of the base of the windows.

(a) Lebeuf 1, 385. (b) Soultrait, *Rép.*, 94–95; Barat – Bussières – Morellet, *Le Nivernais*, Nevers, 1840, 2, 93 and view, pl. xcvi; L. Charrault, "La chartreuse de Bellary (1209–1793)", *Bull. Soc. nivernaise*, 22, 1908, 541–632. (c) Cottineau (1) 328.

LA BENISSONS DIEU (Loire) (119)

Cistercian abbey of Clairvaux, founded in 1138 by Louis VII, in the diocese of Lyon.

Fig. 37. La Bénissons Dieu, profile of nave rib.

The nave was built about 1170.

There are seven bays of the nave extant, with groin-vaulted aisles and four-part ribbed vaults over the main vessel. There are three stories, with small openings in a plain wall between the main arcades and the clerestory.

(b) Aubert, *Arch. cist.*, 1, 163, 269 (view) and *passim*; Dimier, 83–84 and pl. 34.

BEZE (Côte d'Or) (76)

St Remi, parish church of the Benedictine abbey of St Pierre & St Paul at Bèze, in the diocese of Langres; at the presentation of the Langres chapter.

See p. 65.

The church was rebuilt about 1230–1240, perhaps as a result of the fire that destroyed the village in 1215. The core of the crossing and transept remain.

The church is small and the apse, replaced in the XVIII c., apparently was heptagonal. The transept masses are tall and dominated by a still taller crossing tower, resembling somewhat the XII c. project at Auxonne. The interior volumes of the transept are quite low, however, and there are vaulted chambers above them that open onto the crossing. The latter has three interior stories on the north and

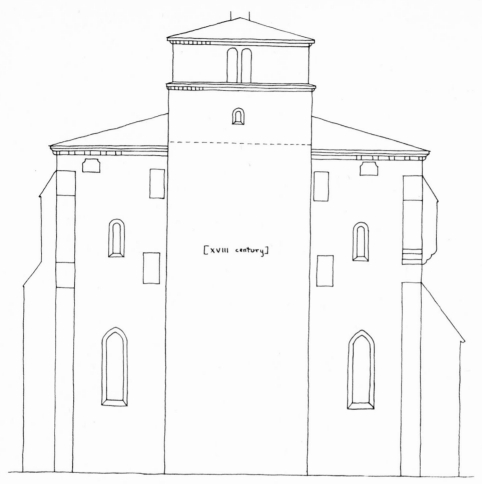

[XVIII century]

Fig. 38a. Bèze, eastern elevation of the chevet.

south faces, and simple arches to the apse and nave, both the latter taller than the openings onto the transept arms. The crossing piers have three small and two large colonnettes on the major faces, and three detached shafts (one of which is for the dado arcade) on the transept faces. The eastern wall of the transept has single lancets recessed well behind the wall-rib, giving the impression of layering as in the Catherine chapel at Chalon. The corner colonnettes in the transept are ringed by the moulding prolonged from the bases of the wall-rib responds. The transept chamber vaults have ogives with large chamfers resting on heavy but plain corbels. The doorways at two levels in the eastern wall of the transept suggest that the apse may have had an exterior passage at the clerestory level. The purpose of the second set of openings is obscure.

The shop was familiar with the chevet of Notre Dame at Dijon and the Cathedral of Chalon.

(a) Dumay in Courtépée 4, 697–699; Roserot 37. (b) Foisset 116; H. Chabeuf, "Excursion à Bèze", *Revue de l'art chrétien*, s.4, v.6 (44), 1894, 179–384; A. Colombet, "Quelques particularités de l'église de Bèze", *Mem. Com. C.-d'Or*, 24, 1957–1958, 165–170. (c) Cottineau (1) 373–374; on the abbey, see Heurtebize in Baudrillart 8 (1935) 1344; Laurent-Claudon (1941) 587, n.2.

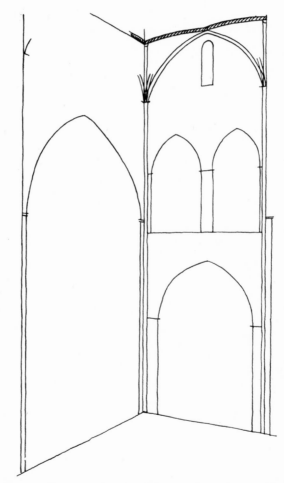

Fig. 38b. Bèze, schematic sketch of the crossing, from the north-east.

BLECOURT (Haute Marne) (44)

Notre Dame, parish in the diocese of Châlons sur Marne, at the presentation of the abbot of St Urbain.

See p. 30 and Plate 40b.

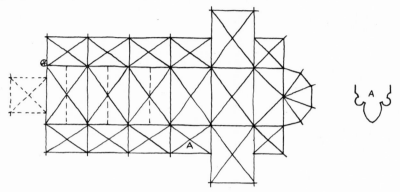

Fig. 39. Blécourt, plan and rib profile.

The church was built from west to east. The first campaign was executed about 1235–1250 and comprised the lower stories of the three western bays of the nave. The remainder of the church, including all the vaults, was built in a second campaign in the third quarter of the century, by a different shop. A dedication is said to have been performed in 1272.

First campaign: the elevation has three stories with a false triforium. The original parti called for compressed six-part vaults and single lancets in each lunette, where there are now four-part vaults and small windows with oculus and twin lancets in tracery. The two western piers are polygonal with eight alternating large and small colonnettes (engaged); the four others are the same, but around a circular core. The capitals form a continuous band. The wall-responds have five colonnettes engaged into pilasters. The triforium supports are detached shafts set against masonry cores, with circular bases; there are round-headed relieving arches above twin "arcades" consisting of lintels with trefoils cut on the surface; the imposts are circular, the bases without cavetti here. The aisle vaults have level crowns and narrow, round-headed lancets in each bay. The west façade was originally preceded by a one-bay porch with a lean-to roof. The clerestory here has an interior passage with three isolated openings, the central one wider and taller and framing a rosette (the passage is covered by an arch here).

Second campaign: the eastern bay of the nave has the same elevation as the western, but it was planned for a four-part vault. The main arcade is slightly taller and the triforium fills the bay (the supports here are coursed). The crossing piers are large and cylindrical with single shafts on the major axes. The transept wings are long and tall, with quasi-Cistercian roses above a clear expanse of plain wall. The apse has one story and is of nave-height, with tall oculus-and-twin-lancet windows arched from impost level and not filling the lunettes (as in the outer bays of the western walls of the transept); there is a trefoiled dado arcade below. All the ribs have concave chamfers. The rectangular chapels have diagonal buttresses. There is a crossing tower. The flying buttresses have independent *culées* and thinner flights resting on colonnettes corbelled above the aisle roof.

See Bony (1958) for the compressed six-part vaults. The eastern nave bay belongs to the extension of the Sens revival in the XIII c., if only by coincidence. The shop may also have worked at Joinville.

(a) Roserot, *Dictionnaire topographique du département de la Haute-Marne*, Paris, 1903, 18. (b) T. Pinard, "Notre-Dame de Blécourt", *Revue archéologique*, 3 (1), 1846, 47–52; J. Royer, *Blécourt, son églises et ses environs*, Joinville, 1898.

BLENEAU (Yonne) (26)

St Loup de Troyes, parish in the diocese of Auxerre, under the patronage of the bishop of Auxerre.

See p. 18 and Fig. 2c.

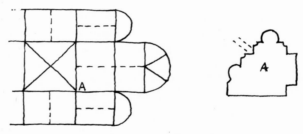

Fig. 40. Bléneau, plan and pier.

The crossing vault was erected about 1160, the apse about 1160–1170.

The transept bears pointed barrel vaults, as do the choir and the bays preceding the half-domed apses (that in the south transept is now ribbed). The main apse has a three-part ribbed vault, with a rectangular ogive and tiny tori lightly indicated at the angles; the respond capitals and the imposts are not turned to follow the angles of the ribs.

This is among the earliest Yonne Valley ribbed vaults.

(a) Dey, "Etudes historiques sur la ville de Bléneau", *Bull. Soc. Yonne*, 1, 1847, 167–200, with lithograph of the interior of the crossing and the apse following p. 170 (V. Petit); Longnon, *Sens*, 252 (late XV c.). (b) Quantin, *Rép.*, 130–131; Philippe 62–63.

BOISCOMMUN (Loiret) (6)

Notre Dame, Augustinian priory of St Jean at Sens, in the diocese of Sens, founded in 1172 by Archbishop Guillaume de Champagne.

See p. 30 and Plate 40a.

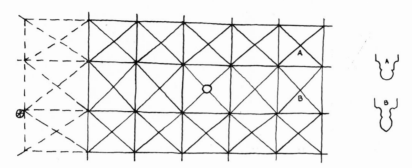

Fig. 41. Boiscommun, plan with XV c. western end, and rib profiles.

The church was built in three campaigns, from east to west: the three eastern bays, about 1220; the next two bays, about 1240; and the western bay in the XIV c. or XV c.

A tower was planned over the third bay from the east. There are no flying buttresses. The first campaign has, in the terminal wall, two stories of triplet windows, the upper one somewhat wider and taller than the others. The main vessel here has three stories, with a Sens-like false triforium and single, plain clerestory lancets descending below the vault departure and the peak of the triforium arcades. The triforium supports consist of colonnettes engaged into wide, long pilasters. The piers are cruciform with extra pilasters on the transverse axes. The second campaign represents the modernization of the same design: there is a triforium passage and an exterior clerestory passage passing through the buttresses. The clerestory window has an oculus above two lancets, with pierced spandrels and chamfered mullions, and the triforium has a quatrefoil pierced above trefled arcades and a support consisting of a coursed colonette cluster. The imposts here are *à bec*.

The plan of Boiscommun is typical of the Ile de France in the early XIII c., and only the squarish nave bays indicate a provincial or older design. The elevation seems inspired by the Sens revival of the Yonne Valley. The shop probably came from here and was perhaps engaged through the abbey of St Jean at Sens.

(b) F. Deshoulières in *Cong. arch.* (Orléans), 93, 1930, 370–376. (c) Cottineau (1) 406.

BOURBONNE LES BAINS (Haute Marne) (46)

Notre Dame, Benedictine priory of St Vincent at Besançon, in the diocese of Besançon, under the patronage of the abbot of St Vincent or of Faverney.

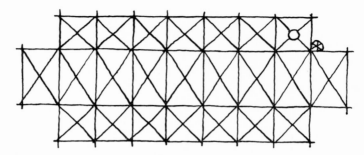

Fig. 42. Bourbonne les Bains, plan.

The medium-sized church was built in two consecutive campaigns, from east to west, from about 1220 on.

There is a tower over the north chapel. The eastern terminal wall has three lancets with heavy arches and ringed columns, and a rose in the lunette underlined by a string-course. The responds and piers are rectilinear; in the eastern bays of the nave, they are slightly taller and have a square core with a pilaster added to each face, while in the western bays there are engaged colonnettes. The nave has two stories with a single lancet above plain wall in each bay. All the ogives are various forms of the single heavy-torus type, except in the apse, where there appears a standard XIII c. type as at Appoigny. There are no flying buttresses.

This is one of the widespread rectilinear plans of eastern France. The elevation and especially the form of the eastern piers, are similar to Montréal and Epoisses, but the overall decoration is more sober.

(a) Roserot, *Dictionnaire topographique du département de la Haute-Marne*, Paris, 1903, 22; Calmette-Clouzot, *Pouillés des provinces de Besançon . . .*, Paris, 1940, 86–87.
(b) H. Ronot, *Les églises de Bourbonne-les-Bains et de ses environs (Nefs et Clochers)* [Paris, 1950], 24 pp., with plates and summary bibliography. (c) Cottineau (1) 457.

BOURGES (Cher) (100)

St Pierre le Guillard, parish in the archdiocese of Bourges, under the patronage of the archbishop.

See pp. 74–75 and Plates 24a and b.

Begun about 1220–1225 at the western end, the edifice was completed quickly although probably not by 1230, the traditional date of consecration. The ambulatory was under construction about 1235.

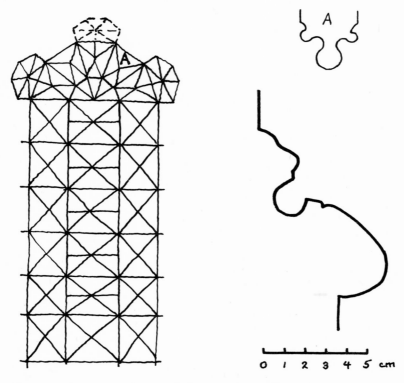

Fig. 43. Bourges, St Pierre, plan, ambulatory rib profile and base profile of pier at entrance to south chapel.

(a) H. Boyer – R. Latouche, *Dictionnaire topographique du département du Cher*, Paris, 1926, 61. (b) A. Buhot de Kersers, *Histoire et statistique monumental du Cher*, II, Bourges, 1883, 194–200; J. Vallery-Radot in *Cong. arch.* (Bourges), 94, 1931, 17–38; F. Deshoulières in *Cher* (*Les églises de France*), Paris, 1932, 39–41; I am indebted to M. Robert Gauchery, of Bourges, for the communication of his article, to be published in the *Union des Sociétés savantes du Centre*, which gives account of the evidence brought to light during recent restorations of the church. M. Gauchery has verified the later addition of the north and south-eastern radiating chapels. Only the axial chapel has not been examined.

BURE LES TEMPLIERS (Côte d'Or) (58)

St Georges, parish in the diocese of Langres, under the patronage of the Templar commandery of Bure.

A two-bay rectangular apse was added, about 1210–1220, to the south of the XII c. edifice, which has an eastern tower over a groined vault.

The apse has one story with a rosette above three isolated lancets in the eastern terminal wall. The eastern corners have detached responds, the supports between the bays have colonnettes engaged into pilasters. There are heavy imposts and ribs, and ogives with the Pontigny (chevet) profile; the transverse arch has two tori and a pointed fillet, both terminating in four inverted cusps. The capitals have *feuilles d'eau* and incipient crockets.

The apse marks the persistence of early Gothic forms. It is a rather elaborate example, perhaps due to Templar patronage.

(a) Longnon, *Lyon*, 160 (1436); Roserot 65. (b) Guillaume 253. (c) on the commandery, Laurent-Claudon (1941), 598, n. 5.

LA BUSSIERE (Côte d'Or) (91)

Notre Dame, Cistercian abbey of Cîteaux, founded in 1131, in the diocese of Autun.

The rectangular apse, with a five-part ribbed vault, was rebuilt about 1230. The ogives have concave chamfers and rest on corbels.

The vault is common coin for the period; the plan, alone, is somewhat exceptional.

(b) Foisset 242–243; Aubert, *Arch. cist.*, 1, 67, 231 (where the vault is called XIV c.) and 255; Dimier, 92 and pl. 58.

CERILLY (Côte d'Or) (49)

St Martin, parish in the diocese of Langres, at the presentation of the abbot or Pothières.

A small, rectangular apse with a six-part vault was built about 1260. The ogives have chamfers and rest on corbelled columns. The capitals are covered by foliage, animals and birds.

In the country style.

(a) Longnon, *Lyon*, 148 (1436); Roserot 72. (b) Guillaume 305.

CHABLIS (Yonne), in the diocese of Langres. (23)

A. St Martin, collegiate church and priory of St Martin at Tours.

See pp. 31–32 and Plate 8b.

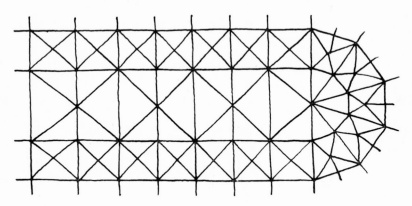

Fig. 44. Chablis, St Martin, plan.

The church was begun at the eastern end, perhaps in 1212, when St Martin at Tours purchased a quarry at Chablis, apparently as part of a programme of local expansion for which there are several suggestive texts of 1216. Some of the masons may have come from Vézelay and Pontigny. The western bays were continued in 1279, when a two-towered façade was projected; the present façade was built in the XVII c.

(a) Quantin III, nos. 173 and 181. (b) Quantin in *Ann. Yonne*, 1839, 313–316 and *Rép.* 23; von Veltheim, 52–53, where St Martin and St Pierre are evidently confused in name; G. Bonneau, "La collégiale de Saint-Martin de Chablis", *Bull. Soc. Sens*, 30, 1916, 32–84; Hautecœur, 86–88 and pls. 89–90; F. Salet in *Cong. arch.* (Auxerre), 116, 1958, pp. 197–212. (c) Cottineau (1) 664; Laurent-Claudon (1941), 166–168 (where the edifice is said to have been begun about 1160, possibly on the basis of Bonneau) and n. 1.

B. St Pierre, parish in the diocese of Langres, under the patronage of the provost of Chablis.

See pp. 19, Fig. 6a and Plate 6a.

The church was probably begun about 1155 at the eastern end, which was later replaced by a XVI c. structure, the latter since destroyed; the transept was under construction about 1160–1165, and the nave continued until the end of the century.

(a) Longnon, *Lyon*, 147 (1436). (b) Quantin, *Rép.*, 23; a view from the east appears in *Ann. Yonne*, s.2, v. 21 (46), 1882, following p. 224; Bonneau, *loc. cit.*, 66–68; F. Salet in *Cong. arch.* (Auxerre), 116, 1958, 212–213.

CHAGNY (Saône et Loire) (112)

St Martin, parish in the diocese of Chalon; after 1220 under the patronage of the abbot of St Ruf.

About 1170: the crossing vault, with an ogive profile similar to Pontigny (nave) and short fluted pilasters beneath the transverse arch. About 1200: a three-bay nave of two stories, with single lancets above plain wall. There are rectangular transverse arches, but advanced ogive profiles in the four-part vaults. The piers are cruciform with, on the nave-side, pilasters and engaged colonnettes turned to the angles of the ribs.

(a) Courtépée 3, 326–327; Longnon, *Lyon*, 184 (XVI c.). (b) mentioned in Y. Fernillot, "Les églises gothiques de l'ancien diocèse de Chalon", *Positions de thèses de l'Ecole des Chartes*, 1946, 55–61.

CHALON SUR SAONE (Saône et Loire), in the archdiocese of Lyon (115)

A. Cathedral of St Vincent.

See pp. 64–65 and Plates 20, 36a and 42a.

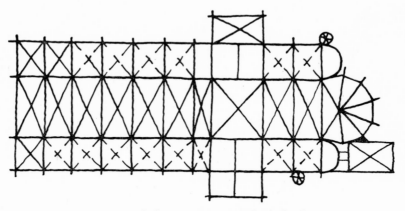

Fig. 45. Chalon sur Saône Cathedral, plan.

The apse of the Romanesque edifice was rebuilt and enlarged under Dean Artaud (1230–1233), and a small chapel originally dedicated to Saint Catherine was added east of the old southern apse. At this time, the transept was vaulted and a taller vault, beneath a projected tower, was established over the crossing. The entire campaign may have been terminated by 1241, when money was left to the *opus*, but not for the construction. An unexplained passage runs through the apse buttresses at ground level.

The Romanesque nave seems to have been left incomplete in the XII c., for Bishop Robert de Decize inaugurated a long series of renovations in 1310. At this time, the walls above the main arcades were reworked and the wall-responds altered, the present triforium and clerestory were constructed and the nave was vaulted (1374 ff.); alterations were also effected in the chevet, particularly in the vaults, and the balustrade was added to the clerestory passage.

(a) the 1241 text is in Dom Plancher, *Histoire . . . de Bourgogne*, vol. 2, 13. (b) J. Virey in *Cong. arch.* (Dijon), 91, 1928, 426–534; R. Violot, "La cathédrale Saint-Vincent de Chalon et l'école bourguignonne", *Mémoires, Société d'histoire et d'archéologie de Chalon-sur-Saône*, s.2, v. 16 (24), 1930–1931, 83–96; *id.*, "A propos des restaurations . . .", *ibid.*, 29, 1940, 185–186; P. Gras, "Les anciennes chapelles de la cathédrale Saint-Vincent", *ibid.*, 31, 1945, 5–51; *id.*, "La date du chœur de la cathédrale", *ibid.*, 32, 1947, 15–16 (fundamental). (c) P. Gras in Baudrillart 12 (1958), 286–302, especially for the diocese.

[B. Temple]

Built about 1230–1250.

The rectangular edifice had three bays and one story, with windows over a dado. There was a triplet in the west wall. The present groined vaults date from the XVIII c., and the original form is unknown.

(b) P. Gras, "L'ancienne église du Temple de Chalon", *Mémoires, Société d'histoire et d'archéologie de Chalon-sur-Saône*, 32, 1947, 32–40, with figures and plans.

CHATILLON SUR SEINE (Côte d'Or), in the diocese of Langres (52)

Both Notre Dame (St Pierre) and St Nicolas, begun respectively in the mid and late XII c., are distinctly copies of the Cistercian style, with pointed barrel vaults over the nave and transverse barrels over the aisles.

(b) F. Deshoulières in *Cong. arch.* (Dijon), 91, 1928, 205–214 and 214–220. (c) Laurent-Claudon (1941), 381, n.

CHAUMONT (Haute Marne) (45)

St Jean Baptiste, collegiate church in the diocese of Langres.

The edifice was built from east to west. The extant portions of the XIII c. are in the nave, about 1235–1260.

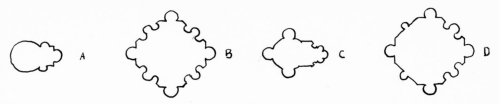

Fig. 46. Chaumont, nave piers from the south file: a. eastern weak; b. eastern strong; c. western weak; d. western strong.

The eight-bay nave has extremely wide aisles, but two squarish towers at the west. There are alternation and six-part vaults. The elevation has two stories with single lancets in the lunettes and a large expanse of plain wall below, with a string-course at the summit of the main arcades.

An example of the monastic style, with details found elsewhere in the extreme east.

(b) H. Ronot, *Les églises de Chaumont* (*Nefs et clochers*) [Paris, 1949] 24 pp., with plates and bibliography. (c) Laurent-Claudon (1941), 185, n. (1) f.

CHEMILLY (Yonne) (15)

St Georges, parish in the diocese of Auxerre, at the presentation of the cathedral chapter.

See p. 18.

The apse was built about 1155–1160.

The rectangular apse was added to the east of the tower surmounting a groined vault. There are two lancets in the eastern wall, and one in the north and south. A four-part vault covered the bay; the ogives have two tori and a fillet. There are no wall-ribs. The capitals have *feuilles d'eau* and are quite flat; one has concentric lines similar to those at St Loup de Naud. The imposts are sculpted.

One of the earliest rib-vaulted edifices of the Yonne Valley.

(a) Lebeuf 4, 79. (b) Quantin, *Rép.*, 64; Philippe 69.

CHITRY (Yonne) (28)

St Valérien (St Jean Baptiste), parish in the diocese of Auxerre, under the patronage of the bishop.

Constructed at the very end of the XII c., the small nave (originally a single aisle) has both four and six-part vaults, with weak and strong responds. These have engaged colonnettes set into the angles, and their form, as well as the style of the capitals, indicates a relationship with the shop at Pontigny (1186 ff.) The elevation has only one story, with windows, and the vaults have horizontal ridge-lines. The wall-ribs are stilted on independent orders with detached shafts. The chevet was rebuilt in the late XIV c., when the south aisle was added and the church was fortified.

(a) Lebeuf 1, 17; Courtépée 4, 384. (b) Quantin, in *Ann. Yonne* 1841, 2, 47–62, esp. 61–62; *id.*, *Rép.*, 24–25; J. Vallery-Radot in *Cong. Arch.* (Auxerre), 116, 1958, 189–196.

CITEAUX (Côte d'Or, commune of St Nicolas lès Cîteaux) (93)

[Notre Dame, chief abbey of the Cistercian Order, founded in 1098.]

See p. 28.

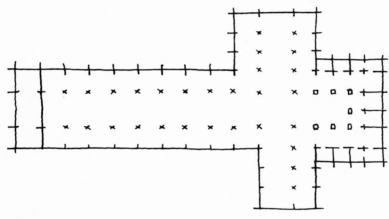

Fig. 47. Cîteaux, plan (after Dimier).

The new chevet was begun at an unknown date in the second half of the XII c. and dedicated in 1193. It is destroyed.

(b) Aubert, *Arch. cist.*, 1, 191–193 and *passim*; Dimier, 99 and pls. 78–80; H. Hahn, *Die frühe Kirchenbaukunst der Zisterzienser (Frankfurter Forschungen zur Architek-turgeschichte, 1)*, Berlin, 1957, 122–124 and *passim*. (c) J. M. Canivez in Baudrillart 12 (1953), 852–874.

CLAIRVAUX (Aube, commune of La Ville sous la Ferté) (4)

[Notre Dame, Cistercian abbey of Cîteaux, founded in 1115 by Hugh de Champagne.]

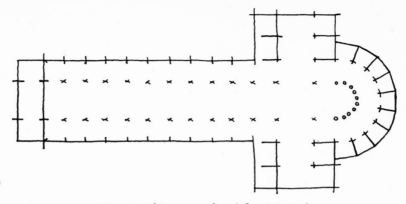

Fig. 48. Clairvaux, plan (after Dimier).

See p. 28.

A dedication took place in 1145 in the Romanesque church. The new and larger chevet was begun in 1154 and dedicated in 1174, with partial dedications in 1157 (the first radiating chapel) and 1166 (the Lady chapel). Destroyed. Known largely from the plans made in 1708 by Dom Milley and from various bird's-eye views.

(b) Aubert, *Arch. cist.*, 1, 249–250 and *passim;* Dimier, 100 and pls. 82–84; H. Hahn, *Die frühe Kirchenbaukunst der Zisterzienser (Frankfurter Forschungen zur Architekturgeschichte,* 1), Berlin, 1957, 119–122 and *passim.* (c) J. M. Canivez in Baudrillart, 12 (1953), 1050–1061.

CLAMECY (Nièvre) (104)

A. St Martin (St Potentien), collegiate church in the diocese of Auxerre, founded in 1075 by Guy de Clamecy.

See pp. 47–50, Figs. 12–14 and Plate 13b.

Fig. 49. Clamecy, profiles of ribs from the first campaign: a. ogive; b. transverse arch;
c. wall-rib.

There are no texts pertaining directly to the XIII c. construction; the enfranchisement of the town in 1213 cannot be directly related to the work, although the campaign probably opened about 1215. By about 1220, the ambulatory and the two eastern bays of the aisle wall were terminated, and by about 1225, the triforium and clerestory had been erected over this section and two more aisle bays put up to the west. The superstructure over these parts was finished by about 1230, when the first major interruption occurred. About 1240, work was resumed on the next three bays to the west. The church was dedicated on 10 January 1438 and the present façade and tower were built from 1497 on. François I provided the funds for the brace in the choir, which was rebuilt in stone in mock-Gothic style in the late XIX c.

(a) Lebeuf 3, 54; 4, 26–27. (b) J. J. Bourassé, *Esquisse archéologique . . . de Nevers*, Nevers, 1844, 107–114; Crosnier, "Notice archéologique et iconographique sur l'église de Clamecy", *Bull. Soc. nivernaise*, s. 2, v. 1 (1), 1863, 381–388; Soultrait, *Rép.*, 41; [(Courot), "Notice historique sur l'église de Saint-Martin de Clamecy", *Bulletin, Société des sciences de Clamecy*, 1–2, 1879, 79 ff., 99 ff.]; J. Charrier, *Notice historique sur la collégiale de Saint-Martin de Clamecy*, Nevers, 1887 and *Bull. Soc. nivernaise*, s. 3, v. 3 (13), 1890, 37–73; A. Philippe in *Cong. arch.* (Avallon), 74, 1907, 155–161; M. Epron, *L'église Saint-Martin et l'évêché de Bethléem*, Clamecy, 1934; Jantzen, 24–25. (c) Besse 6 (1913), 16, n. 4.

B. Chapel of the see of Bethlehem, in the hospital established in 1147 by Guillaume II, Count of Nevers, and given to the bishops of Bethlehem by Count Guillaume IV in 1168 (now the dining-hall of the Hôtel de la Boule d'Or).

The present chapel was begun about 1200 and built in several campaigns, east to west. These were originally three squarish but tall, one-storied bays with four-part vaults. Three isolated, tall lancets in triplet formation fill the eastern terminal wall, and each bay of the lateral walls has a single lancet. The eastern responds comprise single shafts set in the angles of half-pilasters, with small colonnettes engaged into chamfered corners; the shafts have capitals, the colonnettes have cusped terminations. The central responds comprise three colonnettes (two small, one large), with two detached shafts for the ogives. The western responds comprise five engaged colonnettes. The eastern ogive has a large, slightly pointed torus; the central rib a long, almond-shaped torus flanked by concave chamfers. The building was recently restored.

With certain reminiscences of XII c. Avallonnais style, it is otherwise a typical example of a XIII c. chapel.

(a) Lebeuf 3, 101. (b) Barat-Bussières-Morellet, *Le Nivernais*, v. 2, Nevers, 1840, fig. p. 162 (exterior); J. J. Bourassé, *Esquisse archéologique . . . de Nevers*, Nevers, 1844, 93–94; Soultrait, *Rép.*, 40–41; A. Philippe in *Cong. arch.* (Avallon), 74, 1907, 161–163; M. Epron, *L'église Saint-Martin et l'évêché de Bethléem*, Clamecy, 1934, 65–78.

CLUNY (Saône et Loire), in the diocese of Mâcon (117)

[A. St Pierre & St Paul, Benedictine abbey. Destroyed.]

See pp. 11–13 and 24–27.

Fig. 50. Cluny, St Pierre & St Paul, profiles of ribs from the narthex (after Conant):
a. eastern bay; b. western bays.

The narthex, projected in the early XII c., was designed about 1125 but not constructed at once. The first plan, partly executed in the eastern bays, comprised
a three-story elevation similar to, but smaller than, that of the nave. About 1170
or shortly before, these bays were covered by ribbed vaults, the lunettes of which
formed a fourth story in the elevation. The lower portions of the western bays
were erected to about 1180–1185, and a new, three-story elevation with a Sens-
like triforium put above them (the triforium was later apparently converted into
a passage by the addition of a rear wall). The western terminal, with an interior
passage before the rose, probably was made under Abbot Roland (1220–1228),
when the flying buttresses were added.

(b) K. J. Conant, "The third church at Cluny", *Mediaeval Studies in Honor of
A. K. Porter*, Cambridge (U.S.A.), 1939, (2), 327–357; *id*., "Some observations
on the vaulting problems of the period 1088–1211", *Gazette des Beaux-Arts*, s. 6,
26 (86), 1944, 127–134, revised *in litteris* to the author. (c) G. de Valous in Baudrillart 13 (1956), 149–157, with bibliography, 169–174. I am profoundly indebted
to Professor Conant for advising me on this structure prior to the publication of
his monograph on Cluny.

B. Notre Dame, parish church.

See pp. 78–79 and Plate 25b.

The Gothic church was in all probability built after the fire of 1233. Considerable
use was made of the old foundations and walls, and construction moved from east
to west. The sculpted heads serving as corbels in the transept are not unlike those
of the cathedral of Auxerre, the western bays of St Eusèbe in this city, and Notre
Dame at Semur. The crossing tower forms a lantern and has an interior passage.
The western terminal of the nave has a rather deep, slab-covered interior passage,
and the portal was once preceded by an open porch of two stories, the upper
possibly with an external passage through the buttresses.

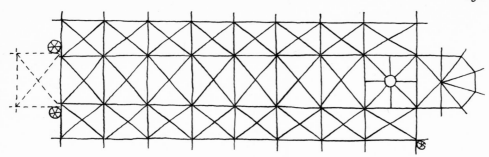

Fig. 51. Cluny, Notre Dame, plan.

(b) J. Virey in *Cong. arch* (Moulins-Nevers), 80, 1913, 68–72; *id.*, *L'Abbaye de Cluny* (*PM*), Paris, n.d., 32–40; Hautecœur 157 and pls. 156–157.

CORGOLOIN (Côte d'Or) (94)

St Pierre, parish in the diocese of Autun, under the patronage of the chapter of Beaune.

About 1250 or later, the rectilinear apse, crossing and transept, projecting one bay, were erected. The vaults are four-part, with simple chamfered ogives on corbels. There is one story with plain lancet windows. *Passages berrichons* connect the transept and the wider, aisleless nave of five very short bays. There are no vaults extant here. The edifice burned in 1636.

(a) Courtépée 2, 391–392; Longnon, *Lyon*, 79 (XIV c.). (b) Foisset 222–223; Guillaume 80.

CUSSEY LES FORGES (Côte d'Or) (65)

St Remi, parish in the diocese of Langres (after 1171), at the presentation of the abbot of St Etienne at Dijon.

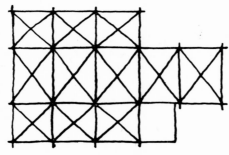

Fig. 52. Cussey les Forges, plan.

The apse and choir, next to the older tower, were built about 1200–1210; the nave not before about 1250.

The chevet is low and has four-part vaults with wall-ribs and large ogives with big pointed tori and cyma recta mouldings, as at Nailly and Massigny. The nave has two stories, the upper short and windowless. There are columnar piers, with eight large and small colonnettes, of which a segment serves as wall-respond. The aisle ribs have chamfers and rest on corbels.

The chevet is provincial Gothic and the nave a reduced version of the monastic style, related to Chitry, Pont sur Yonne and to Aignay le Duc.

(a) Dumay in Courtépée 4, 743; Roserot 136. (b) Foisset 98–99; Guillaume 349.

DARCEY (Côte d'Or) (64)

St Bénigne, parish in the diocese of Autun, under the patronage of the abbot of Flavigny or the bishop of Autun.

From the mid-XIII c. comes the small, rectangular apse of one story, with a six-part vault resting on plain corbels. The ogive has simple chamfers. The wider nave may originally have had aisles (fragments of the vault remain in the western corners).

Country style.

(a) Courtépée 4, 263; Roserot 138. (b) Guillaume 257–258.

DIJON (Côte d'Or), in the diocese of Langres (84)

A. Notre Dame, parish under the patronage of St Etienne at Dijon.

See pp. 54–62, Figs 15–17 and Plates 17a, 18 and 19.

Of the mid-XII c. portal unearthed in the porch, the bases are now in the *Musée archéologique* (cf. Fyot, 5–10) and the fragments of bas-reliefs were incorporated in the terminal walls of the Gothic transept by the XIX c. restorers (see Pl. 17a).

The Gothic chevet was begun about 1220 and the transept and eastern bays of the nave were underway about 1230. In March 1230, £20 was left to the *opus* (Oursel, 1927, 147). About 1240, according to an account by Etienne de Bourbon, the gargoyles on the west façade are assumed to have been in position (Oursel, 1938, 30). In January 1251, Barthélemy de Saumaize obtained permission to erect an altar of the Magdalene and for the burial of himself and his family, especially his wife, "postquam ecclesia predicta consecrata fuerit . . ." (Oursel 1927, 147–148). In 1269, 100 s. were given to the *opus* (*id.*, 148), and the dedication was performed on 8 May 1334 (Fyot 23). The church does not seem to have served as the communal hall before the XV c.; in 1260, communal meetings were held in the Maison du Singe (Boudot).

The edifice was constructed quickly in two campaigns, apparently without interruption, although the western end was never finished. The first campaign comprised the chevet and eastern walls of the transept, the second the rest of the transept and the nave. Certain details differentiate these from one another, such as the change from the trilobed dado arcade to the simple, semicircular arches in the chapels, the absence of the "Braine buttress" on the transept walls, and the absence of the Rémois passage in the nave. The original form of the crossing tower and the chevet triforium is discussed by Oursel (1938). With respect to Viollet-le-Duc's analysis of the nave, it must be said that the pilasters behind the triforium do not seem to rest on corbels but on normal slab footings that are supported by the haunches of the aisle vaults. I have not had an opportunity to verify this on the south side, however.

(a) *On the origins*, see M. Chaume, "Ste-Marie-de-Charancey et les origines possibles de Notre-Dame de Dijon", *Mém. com. C.-d'Or*, 20, 1933–1935, 366–367; *id.*, "Les anciennes paroisses de Dijon", *ibid.*, 29–34; see also Boudot in *ibid.*, s. 1, v. 1, 1834, 85–102. (b) *On the present edifice*: J.-B. Patte in J.-F. Blondel, *Cours d'architecture*, v. 6, Paris, 1777, 218–222 and illustrations, pls. cx-cxi; H. Chabeuf, "Notre-Dame de Dijon et la cathédrale de Cantorbéry", *Mém. com. C.-d'Or*, 16, 1909–1913, 163–171 (very weak); E.-E. Viollet-le-Duc, *Dictionnaire . . .*, *passim*, esp. v. 4; E. Fyot, *L'église Notre-Dame de Dijon. Monographie descriptive*, Dijon, 1910; J. Vallery-Radot, in *Cong. arch.* (Dijon), 91, 1928, 39–70; E. Lambert, *L'art gothique en Espagne*, Paris, 1931, 154–158; C. Oursel, "Un petit problème de chronologie à propos de l'église Notre-Dame de Dijon", *Mém. com. C.-d'Or*, 19, 1927–1932, 146–148; *id.*, "Les origines monumentales de l'église Notre-Dame de Dijon", *ibid.*, 20, 1933–1935, 171–172; *id.*, "La question des origines architecturales de Notre-Dame de Dijon", *Annales de Bourgogne*, 6, 1934, 299–300; *id.*, *Notre-Dame de Dijon (PM)*, (Paris, 1938); M.-L. Springer, *Notre Dame in Dijon. Ein Beitrag zur Stilgeschichte der burgundischen Gotik*, Frankfurt-Stettin, 1934; H. Jantzen (1949), 18–24; *on restorations*, H. Chabeuf, "Notre-Dame et Saint-Michel au commencement du XVIIIe siècle", *Mém. com. C.-d'Or*, 13, 1895–1900, 215–224; (A. de Baudot), "Rapport sur les restaurations faites à l'église Notre-Dame de Dijon", *ibid.*, 7, 1865–1869, 5–8 and 27–38; *id.*, "Restauration de la cathédrale [sic] de Dijon", *Encyclopédie d'architecture*, s. 4, v. 4, 1891–1892, 36–38 and pls. 151–152; *for the sculpture*, see H. David in *Mém. com. C.-d'Or*, 17, 1913–1921, cclxxxvi-cclxxxvii; E. Fyot, *Dijon. Son passé évoqué par ses rues*, Dijon, 1928, 135 ff.; H. David, "Les sculptures du grand portail de Notre-Dame de Dijon", *Mém. com. C.-d'Or*, 19, 1927–1932, 31–33; L. Schürenberg, "Spätromanische und frühgotische Plastik in Dijon . . .", *Jahrbuch der Preussischen Kunstsammlungen*, 58, 1937, 13–25. (c) P. Gras in Baudrillart, 14 (1958), 466–480.

B. St Bénigne, Benedictine abbey.

See pp. 25–27, 97–98, Figs 5a, 6f and Plate 34.

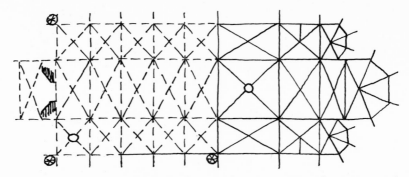

Fig. 53. Dijon, St Bénigne, XIII c. plan, with campaigns, and XII c. portal.

Only the most recent bibliography, with a few fundamental earlier studies, is listed here.

(a) *On the cult*, see H. Grégoire, "Saint Bénigne de Dijon et son prototype by-zantin, le mégalomartyr Benignos (Menignos) de Parion (Hellespont)", *Comptes-rendus, Académie des inscriptions et belles-lettres*, 52, 1953, 204–213. (b) *On the rotunda* and the older Romanesque buildings, see L. Chomton, *Histoire de l'église de Saint-Bénigne de Dijon*, Dijon, 1900; Hubert (1952), no. 91; and A. S. Wethey, "The legend of the alternate system at St Bénigne of Dijon", *Journal, Society of Archi-tectural Historians*, 17, 1958, 3, 2–9; *on the XII c. nave*, see Chomton, "Note sur la reconstruction partielle de l'église Saint-Bénigne au XIIe siècle", *Mém. com. C.-d'Or*, 16, 1909–1913, 21–27; *on the present church*, see V. Flipo, *La cathédrale de Dijon (PM)*, Paris, 1928; M. Aubert, in *Cong. arch.* (Dijon), 91, 1928, 16–38; L. Schürenberg, *Die kirchliche Baukunst in Frankreich*, Berlin, 1934, 169–170; and P. Quarré, "Saint-Bénigne de Dijon d'après la tombe de l'abbé Hugues d'Arc", *Bull. mon.*, 103, 1945, 231–242; a plan and details by F. Sagot are published in the *Moniteur des architectes*, s. 2, v. 3, 1889, Pls. 3–4; the restorations are discussed by H. Chabeuf, "France et Italie. Causerie à propos de la cathédrale de Dijon", *Revue de l'art chrétien*, s. 4, v. 14 (53), 1903, 308–312; *on the monastic buildings*, see C. Poinssot "Note sur le réfectoire de l'abbaye de St-Bénigne de Dijon", *Bulletin des relations artistiques France-Allemagne*, 1951; *on the sculpture*, see P. Quarré, "La sculpture des anciens portails de Saint-Bénigne de Dijon", *Gazette des Beaux-Arts*, s. 6, v. 50, 1957, 177–194. (c) Cottineau (1) 966–968 and Laurent-Claudon (1941), 584–585, nn.

C. St Philibert, parish of the abbey of St Bénigne.

See p. 27, n. 29 and Fig. 6g.

A groin-vaulted basilica probably begun after the 1137 fire and completed in the 1160's.

(b) P. Foisset, "Saint-Philibert de Dijon et l'architecture romane en Bourgogne", *Mém. com. C.-d'Or*, 6, 1861–1864, 1–32 (placing St Philibert in the Cluniac group!); F. Deshoulières, in *Cong. arch.* (Dijon), 91, 1928, 98–109.

[D. Ste Chapelle, private chapel of the duke, founded in 1172 by Hugh III. Destroyed in 1802.]

See p. 57.

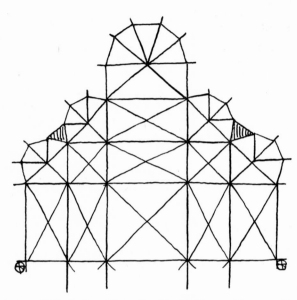

Fig. 54. Dijon, Ste Chapelle, plan (after Vallery-Radot).

An undated obit mentions a Master Hugh the stonecutter, who was master of the work of the church (Petit 2, 185, n.2), but no particular part of the edifice can be attributed to him. According to Pérard and Fyot, the land was freed and the first stone laid in 1173 (d'Arbaumont, 68). The church is mentioned in 1196 (Vallery-Radot, 305). In 1244, Innocent IV granted an indulgence for the continuation of the work (Petit 6, 193–194), in 1248 vacant prebends were ordered turned over to the work for a year (Petit 4, 367) and legacies are recorded for the years 1253–1256 and 1283; another indulgence was granted in 1290 and the bishop of Langres asked for assistance for the construction in 1302 (Petit, 6, 193–194). £300 a year were granted in 1349 (Courtépée 2, 102). It is therefore clear that major campaigns were underway around 1240, again in 1300 and as late as 1350. This does not mean, however, that the edifice was begun only in the 1240's (despite the phrase, "capellam ampliare coeperint opere sumptuoso" in the 1244 bull, which technically indicates only that the enlargement had been begun before this year), since the fragments discovered and published a century ago by d'Arbaumont, from the western end of the nave, date clearly from the 1240's and suggest that the chevet was begun earlier. There was no Rémois passage in either the chevet or the nave; the latter had three stories, with a triforium passage and a tall clerestory with an interior passage. The piers here would seem to date from the XIV c. if, in fact, they were elliptical and not round (d'Arbaumont, 90), but this is questionable. There were spiral staircases in all four corners of the transept and at the western end. The plan of the clerestory reveals that each bay had a single lancet, as did the transept terminals, but these were probably filled with tracery.

(a) Courtépée 2, 102; Petit 2, 185; 4, 367; 6, 193–194. (b) J. d'Arbaumont, "Essai historique sur la Sainte-Chapelle de Dijon", *Mém. com. C.-d'Or*, 6, 1861–1864, 63–187; J. Vallery-Radot, "Une réplique peu connue de Saint-Yved de Braine. La Sainte-Chapelle de Dijon", *Bull. mon.*, 85, 1926, 299–306; a plan of the apse is in Paris, *Archives Nationales*, N. III 3 (Côte-d'Or); and a view of the west façade, *ibid.*, N. II 1 (Côte-d'Or). (c) Laurent-Claudon (1941), 576 and n. 2.

[E. Clairvaux cellar.]

See p. 19.

About 1190.

A two-storied edifice, two bays wide and eight bays long. The vaults of each story are at the same level. The transverse and longitudinal arches are slightly pointed, the ogives round-headed.

(b) H. Chabeuf, "Les celliers de l'ancien hôtel de Clairvaux", *Mém. com. C.-d'Or*, 14, 1901–1905, 9–14; J. Tillet, in *Cong. arch.* (Dijon), 91, 1928, 121–126; Aubert, *Arch. cist.*, 2, 169–171.

DILO (Yonne) (13)

[Premonstratensian abbey of Valsecret, founded in 1132 by Louis VI. The church was dedicated on 10 May 1164 and destroyed in 1843.]

The plan and elevation are unknown; a view of the interior of the apse was made by V. Petit, probably before the destruction (Paris, *Bibl. Nat., Est.*, Va 417).

(a) V. Petit in *Ann. Yonne* 1844, 2, 84–85. (b) Quantin, *Rép.*, 141–124. (c) Cottineau (1) 970–971.

ENTRAINS (Nièvre) (103)

St Sulpice, parish in the diocese of Auxerre, under the patronage of the bishop. The church was probably built in the 1220's.

The edifice is essentially a chapel. There remain the choir (the apse was rebuilt much later), lateral chapels (the northern one is narrower than the southern), a transept and a three-bay, aisleless nave with a western porch. The transverse arches and wall-ribs are rectangular; the nave ogive is almond-shaped. The whole is very restored.

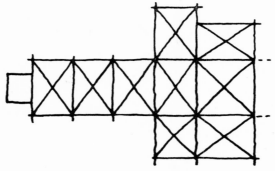

Fig. 55. Entrains, plan.

(a) Longnon, *Sens*, 252 (late XV c.). (b) Soultrait, *Rép.*, 69; [J. F. Baudiau, *Histoire d'Entrains depuis les temps les plus reculés jusqu'à nos jours*, Nevers, 1879].

L'EPAU (Nièvre, near the commune of Donzy) (105)

Notre Dame, priory of Val des Choux, founded in 1214 by Hervé de Donzy, Count of Nevers.

See p. 72 and Plates 40c and 43b.

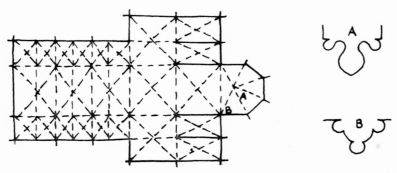

Fig. 56. L'Epau, plan (after Barat) with rib-profile and respond from the apse.

The church was built in two campaigns (chevet, nave) about 1230–1240. It is now in ruins.

The apse has a single, tall story and the chapels are somewhat shorter. The former has single, long lancet windows. The respond here is a simple coursed colonnette; those between the sanctuary and the choir consist of three shafts on a rounded core. The eastern crossing pier is cruciform with one colonnette in the angle and three clustered on the face; the western is circular with alternating colonnettes, and on the aisle side, the ogive departs from a small capital slightly below the main capital. The nave piers are lost, but the western responds are semicircular with a single colonnette on axis, suggesting they may have been *piliers cantonnés* as shown by Morellet, who also indicates an alternation with plain columns. The elevation has two stories with panels of wall above the arcades. The west wall of the transept has windows with twin lancets surmounted by an oculus.

The chevet plan is Cistercian, but the nave alternation suggests a local formula. The nave was undoubtedly in the monastic style and by a shop related to Flavigny.

(b) Barat-Bussières-Morellet, *Le Nivernais*, v. 2, Nevers, 1840, p. 97 and pl. 6, and v. 1, pl. 74 (plan); Soultrait, *Rép.*, 99–100. (c) Cottineau (1) 1055.

EPOISSES (Côte d'Or) (68)

St Symphorien, collegiate church in the diocese of Langres.

See p. 23.

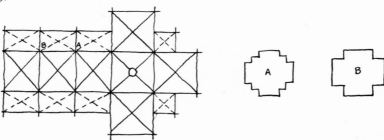

Fig. 57. Epoisses, plan and piers.

The chapter was founded by Bernard, lord of Epoisses, in his castle chapel, according to Laurent-Claudon about 1200, but probably as much as a decade earlier, if the present church were erected for this purpose.

The edifice is small, and there is a crossing tower. The terminal wall of the apse has a rose above three equal lancets. The nave has two stories with single windows in plain wall in the clerestory. The aisles and the chapels are groin-vaulted. The piers are rectangular with added pilasters, the wall-responds similar. The ogive in the chevet is of the Pontigny type; that in the nave has a heavy, pointed torus flanked by two smaller tori.

The church is a reduced and simplified version of the collegiate of Montréal.

(a) Courtépée 3, 540–541; Roserot 152. (b) Guillaume 234. (c) Laurent-Claudon (1941), 174–175 and n. 1.

ESSAROIS (Côte d'Or) (57)

St Médard, parish in the diocese of Langres, under the patronage of the bishop.

The church was built about 1260 or later. It has a small, rectangular apse with corner buttresses at 45° and a four-part vault with chamfered ogives. The three-bay nave is slightly wider, and there is a small porch to the west.

The country style, with very archaic forms.

(a) Roserot 154. (b) [Mignard, "Note archéologique sur Essarois", *Bulletin historique et archéologique de Dijon*, 1, 1883, 116–117.]

FAVEROLLES LES LUCEY (Côte d'Or) (53)

St Pierre, branch of the parish of Lucey in the diocese of Langres, under the patronage of the bishop.

Built after 1250, the edifice comprises a vessel of three bays with an apse and a half-bay at the west. Here, there are two columns on axis and a tower over the southern half. The vaults are four-part, with chamfered ribs resting on corbels. The responds are rectilinear, in two planes. The corner buttresses are at 45°.

Country style, with a very complex western end.

(a) Longnon, *Lyon*, 151 (1436); Roserot 159 and 219. (b) Guillaume 354, who says it is a Templar construction.

FLAVIGNY (Côte d'Or), in the diocese of Autun (70)

A. St Pierre & St Prix (Préject), Benedictine abbey, now largely destroyed. XII c. and XIII c. remains can be seen in the Anis de Flavigny factory and in the home of M. Jean Troubat.

See pp. 25, n. 27, and 72, Fig. 6h and Plates 38a and 39a, b and d.

Mid-XII c. work, probably in the conventual buildings, is indicated by the column now in the Louvre. About 1170–1175, a narthex of three bays (with two towers?) was built in front of the old nave. The Gothic nave was put up about 1245–1250.

The narthex is closely related to the Langres-Bar-Dijon shops. The fluted trumeau (now serving as a support in the porch of the church at Seigny) suggests an affiliation with the Cluniac tradition. The portal formerly had a Virgin and two other figures sculpted on it.

The nave had two stories with a blank area between the main arcades and the clerestory. The latter extended slightly below the main capitals and terminated in a sharp string-course. There was a single lancet in each bay. The *piliers cantonnés*

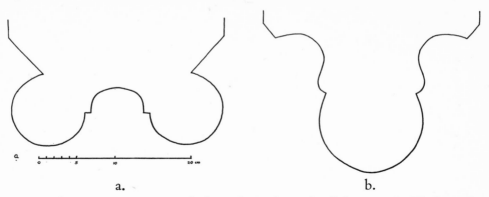

a.   b.

Fig. 58. Flavigny, St Pierre: a. rib from the main vault of the nave; b. rib from the
aisle vault of the nave (now in Museum).

had a single colonnette forming a wall-respond, except at the eastern end, where
the respond was segmental with three shafts, or was formed by a cluster of three
colonnettes, and at the western end, where a similar cluster was found. The
opening above the main arcade in the western bay suggests there was a passage
across the inner wall of the narthex. Probably all the vaults were four-part (cf.
the two keystones now preserved, from the main and the aisle vaults), although
the western bays may have been covered by a six-part vault. The capitals form
bands, with extra, smaller unsupported cores for the wall-respond colonnettes.

An example of the monastic style, on a rather large scale. The shop is related to
Semur, but also to Aignay le Duc, and even l'Epau.

For the pre-Gothic buildings, see Hubert (1952), nos. 85–97 (excavations at the
eastern end were in progress in 1958–1959). (a) Courtépée 3, 492–495. (b) P. de
Truchis, in *Cong. arch.* (Avallon), 74, 1907, 53–63. The plan (from the *Archives
nationales*) is reproduced by J. Hubert, *L'art préroman* (*Les monuments datés de la
France*), Paris, 1938, pl. IIc and E. Lambert, "Monuments disparus et documents
d'archives", *Phoebus*, 1, 1946, fig. 1; a bird's-eye view is in *Monasticon Gallicanum*,
no. 34; an 1840 view of the nave reproduced by Petit, 6, fig. 12; *for the sculptural
remains*, see M. Aubert–M. Beaulieu, *Catalogue raisonné des sculptures du moyen
âge . . .* (*Musée du Louvre*), I, Paris, 1950, nos. 7–11 and 27. (c) Cottineau (1)
1149–1150.

B. St Genès, parish church of the abbey.

The church was begun about 1250–1260. It has a flat chevet, a crossing tower and
a three-storied nave with tribunes. The proportions of the interior volumes are
very tall. The transept arms are isolated by heavy walls. The six-part vault in the
apse is at the same level as the crossing (and the present XV c. nave vaults), with
stilted wall-ribs. Each lateral wall of the apse has two very tall lancets separated

by a mullion but with a solid lunette above. The nave has thin, short *piliers cantonnés*, repeated in the tribunes. The clerestory here originally was short, with one lancet in each bay.

The tribunes are unique in XIII c. Burgundy and were perhaps designed to accommodate the large population of the town that had grown up around the abbey. The nave capitals are similar to those in the abbey church, suggesting that members of the same shop worked at St Genès.

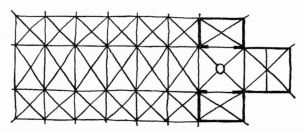

Fig. 59. Flavigny, St Genès, plan.

(a) Courtépée 3, 490–492; Roserot 164. (b) P. de Truchis in *Cong. arch.* (Avallon), 74, 1907, 49–52, with section showing original elevation of nave; Hautecœur (1) 33–34 and pls. 36–37; Guillaume 192–194, with view of nave, p. 192.

FLEUREY SUR OUCHE (Côte d'Or) (83)

St Jean Baptiste (St Georges), parish in the diocese of Langres, under the patronage of St Marcel lès Chalon.

The church dates from the late XIII c. and is said to have been built by Agnès, Duchess of Burgundy (1279–1317).

There is a rectangular apse with two four-part vaults. The crossing is surmounted by a tower, and the transept arms project, although each is covered by a single four-part vault. The nave has three bays with aisles, all with four-part vaults. The ogives are chamfered and rest on corbels. The crossing piers are cruciform. The edifice was totally rebuilt in the XIX c.

(a) Courtépée 2, 192–194; Roserot 164. (b) Foisset 67–68; Guillaume 116–117, who places it among the earliest Gothic edifices of the region!

FONTENAY (Côte d'Or, commune of Marmagne) (60)

Notre Dame, Cistercian abbey of Clairvaux, founded in 1119 by Rainard de Montbard.

See pp. 18–19 and Plates 3a and 4a.

The chapter house was built about 1155. It originally had nine bays (3 × 3) and was vaulted as a hall. The arches are all round-headed, with differing chords, as in the chapter house of Vézelay.

(b) L. Bégule, *L'abbaye de Fontenay* (PM), Paris, (1912), pp. 41–44; Aubert, *Arch. cist.*, 2, 62–63.

GERLAND (Côte d'Or) (96)

St Pierre, parish in the diocese of Autun, at the presentation of the abbot of Ste Marguerite or the chapter of Beaune.

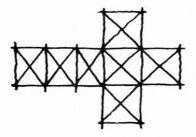

Fig. 60. Gerland, plan.

The apse and transept were built about 1230, the nave about 1245. The edifice is small and has a crossing tower. The ogives of the apse rest on pilasters, the wall-ribs on corbels. The rib has one pointed torus flanked by two concave chamfers. In the transept, there are no wall-ribs and the ogives are corbelled, as in the nave, where the profiles consist of simple chamfers. The apse has a small rose framed, on the exterior, by two columns in the Cistercian fashion.

A provincial rendering of forms found in the major regional shops.

(a) Courtépée 2, 393–394. (b) Foisset 224; E. Mairet in *Encyclopédie d'architecture*, v. 11 (51), 1861, cc.116–117, and pls 77–87; Guillaume 422.

GRIGNON (Côte d'Or) (67)

St Jean l'Evangéliste, priory of Flavigny in the diocese of Autun.

The nave, about 1260, has four bays and is aisleless. It has one story with four-part vaults. The responds are complex, with seven shafts, and the rib-profiles are very sophisticated. The eastern end was rebuilt at a later time.

(a) Courtépée 3, 566. (b) P. de Truchis in *Mém. com. C.-d'Or*, 18, 1922–1926, 61–75; Guillaume 272. (c) Cottineau (1) 1345.

GUILLON (Yonne) (38)

St Remi, Benedictine priory of Notre Dame at Semur, established in 1211 by Guy de Montréal, in the diocese of Auxerre.

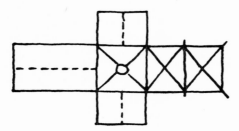

Fig. 61. Guillon, plan.

The church was built about 1250. The crossing is surmounted by a tower; both this and the two-bay chevet were added to a late Romanesque edifice with pointed barrel vaults. The apse has one story, the terminal wall a rosette over two lancets. There are no wall-ribs; the ogives rest on corbels in the apse, and on single colonnettes in the choir.

The Romanesque edifice is late and provincial, and the Gothic additions are also provincial, in an Avallonnais idiom.

(a) E. Petit in *Bull. Soc. Yonne*, 19, 1865, 209–210. (b) Quantin, *Rép.*, 92; V. Petit, *Description des villes et campagnes du département de l'Yonne (arrondissement d'Avallon)*, Auxerre, 1870, 99–100; Parat, "Nouveau répertoire archéologique", *Bull. Soc. Yonne*, s. 5, v. 4 (74), 1920, 111–131. (c) Cottineau (1) 1361.

IRANCY (Yonne) (31)

St Germain, parish in the diocese of Auxerre, at the presentation of the abbot of St Germain at Auxerre.

See p. 26 and Fig. 5b.

The nave was begun about 1190 and shows a certain relationship to Pontigny in the capitals and pier forms. The colonnettes on the latter are, however, in less sharp relief than at Pontigny. The nave has two stories, without windows, and the present vaults, although plastered over, seem to date from the XVIII c. It is therefore doubtful whether Irancy belongs to the northern group of groin-vaulted basilicas listed by Oursel (see above, p. 11, n. 2.)

(a) Longnon, *Sens*, 256 (late XV c.). (b) Quantin, *Rép.*, 31.

JOINVILLE (Haute Marne) (43)

Notre Dame, parish in the diocese of Châlons sur Marne, at the presentation of the abbot of St Urbain.

See p. 30.

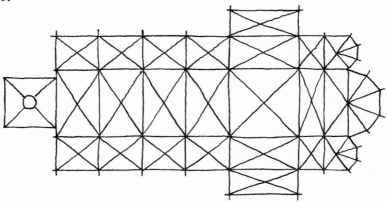

Fig. 62. Joinville, plan.

The edifice was built from west to east from about 1210. The nave is preceded by a porch with a tower, the latter now all XIX c. masonry. There is another tower over the crossing, and flying buttresses. There are four wide bays in the nave, and three stories, including a Sens-like triforium on heavy, coursed piers, and a clerestory descending below vault-departure. The piers have square cores with a pilaster and three colonnettes added to each face, of which one such group forms the wall-respond. The present main vaults and clerestory windows date from the late XIII c.–early XIV c., although the wall-ribs (on corbels) may be original. The façade verso has a rosette above four arcades fronting a wall-passage. The inner bays of the transept have twin lancets with ringed orders, and simpler triforium supports than the nave. The terminal walls here have full-sized roses above triplets. The chevet, now totally XIX c., has two stories with a single lancet in each bay.

(a) A. Roserot, *Dictionnaire topographique du département de la Haute-Marne*, Paris, 1903, 90. (b) A. de Caumont, in *Bull. mon.*, 17, 1851, 314, 316; J. Fériel, "Joinville. Eglise Notre-Dame", *Mémoires, Société historique et archéologique de Langres*, 1, 1847, 286–292.

LACHAUME (Côte d'Or) (50)

Notre Dame, parish in the diocese of Langres, under the patronage of the bishop.

The edifice was erected about 1260 or later. It has a cross-shaped plan with a rectangular apse, a transept projecting one bay and a three-bay, aisleless nave.

There is a crossing tower, and the corner buttresses are placed at 45°. There is only one story, with fenestration in the eastern wall consisting of a rosette above three isolated lancets. The vaults are four-part, mostly on corbels.

In the country style.

(a) Longnon, *Lyon*, 135 (XIV c.); Roserot 96. (b) Guillaume 355 (who says the church is a Templar foundation).

LAIGNES (Côte d'Or) (51)

St Didier, parish in the diocese of Langres, at the presentation of the abbot of St Germain at Auxerre, or the prior of Griselles.

See p. 23.

The nave was built from about 1160 to about 1190. It has six bays with a pointed barrel vault, and groins over the aisles. The piers are square, with one column on the aisle and nave sides, only; the latter forms the wall-respond. There is only one story.

An example of Romanesque forms in XII c. north-central Burgundy.

(a) Longnon, *Lyon*, 152 (1436); Roserot 207. (b) Guillaume 302.

LANGRES (Haute Marne), in the archdiocese of Lyon (47)

A. Cathedral St Mammès.

See pp. 23–26, Figs. 6d, e and Plate 7a.

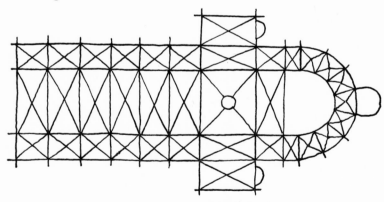

Fig. 63. Langres Cathedral, plan.

The present edifice was probably begun about 1160, although Ache and Ronot advance a date of 1141–1153 for the first campaign. The terminal date of 1196, indicated by the consecration of an altar, is rejected by Laurent-Claudon (142).

The cathedral was erected in two major campaigns and three phases, with remarkable uniformity. The first campaign comprised the chevet and the eastern walls of the transept, to and including part of the transept chapels; this was followed at once by the completion of the transept and the construction of the first bay of the nave at ground level, while the triforium was erected over the earlier portions. The second campaign completed the parts brought to readiness as well as the next five bays of the nave. At this time, the flying buttresses were added to the chevet, as is indicated by the style of their capitals.

The ground plan is probably related to St Pierre at Senones (dedicated in 1124: see G. Durand, *Eglises romanes des Vosges*, Paris, 1913, 352–360), as well as to the XI c. cathedral of Auxerre, and so on.

(b) [J. Ache, *Histoire monumentale de la ville de Langres* (dissertation, Faculté des Lettres, Paris)]; H. Ronot, *La cathédrale Saint-Mammès et l'église Saint-Martin de Langres* (*Nefs et Clochers*), Paris, n.d., with bibliography; H.-P. Eydoux, "L'abbatiale de Morimond et la cathédrale de Langres", *Mémoires, Société historique et archéologique de Langres*, 5, 1957, 1–16. (c) Laurent-Claudon (1941), 136–144, with bibliography.

B. St Didier, priory of Molesmes (now the Musée lapidaire)

About 1210, a rectangular apse was added to the Romanesque edifice (now vastly altered). The ogives have a large, pointed torus and two smaller tori, and rest on single, coursed colonnettes. The springers are sculpted, one with a figure. The wall-respond is rectangular. The whole apse forms a single, tall story.

(b) J. Tillet in *Cong. arch.* (Dijon), 91, 1928, 515–518, where the apse is dated in the late XIII c. (c) Cottineau (1) 1554–1555; Laurent-Claudon (1941), 435–437 and n.

C. St Martin, Benedictine priory of St Seine.

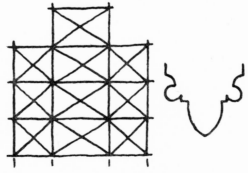

Fig. 64. Langres, St Martin, plan, and profile of apse ogive.

The Gothic church was begun about 1220, perhaps on older foundations that seem to be visible on the exterior of the chevet. The plan originally had a square apse and a three-bay choir with collaterals, a low transept (suggested by the wider bay here) and a three-aisled nave, the latter built in the late XIII c. The main vessel has one story with blind vault-lunettes and small, square openings above the string-course, that give onto the aisle roofs. The chevet piers were perhaps originally *piliers cantonnés* with octagonal cores. The whole is considerably altered and restored.

The first work is related to St Didier and is another example of the widespread rectilinear plans of eastern France. The piers belong to the group of Chaumont, Blécourt, Pouan (Aube), and even Troyes (cathedral) and Voulton.

(b) H. Ronot, *op. cit.*, 27–32. (c) Cottineau (1) 1555; Laurent-Claudon (1941), 450 and n. 1.

LIGNY LE CHATEL (Yonne) (20)

St Pierre & St Paul, parish in the diocese of Langres, under the patronage of the chapter.

See p. 18 and Fig. 2d.

The crossing vault was built about 1155. The nave has six bays with aisles, square piers and pointed arches. It is one story tall and has a wooden roof. The crossing vault, beneath the tower, has a ribbed vault; the ogives rest on single, coursed colonnettes.

The ribbed vault is among the earliest in the Yonne Valley.

(a) Longnon, *Lyon*, 147 (1436). (b) Cornat, "Notice religieuse, historique, archéologique et statistique sur la ville de Ligny-le-Châtel", *Bull. soc. Sens*, 8, 1863, 33–257; 9, 1867, 106, 302; Quentin, *Rép.*, 44–45; Philippe 62–63, 69; J. Vallery-Radot in *Cong. arch.* (Auxerre), 116, 1958, 154–162.

LYON (Rhône) (120)

Cathedral St Jean, in the metropolitan see.

See pp. 84–86, Fig. 23 and Plate 29.

The first campaign of the present edifice was begun under Archbishop Guichard (1165–1180), the second probably was inaugurated when the chapter reserved stone in the quarries at Fourvière (1192). The main altar was dedicated before 25 May 1246, at which time the vaults were in place over the chevet, transept and probably the crossing and possibly two bays of the nave (the presence of a fillet on the face of the ribs does not necessarily indicate an advanced date in the XIII c., as Aubert says; cf. the profiles in Reims Cathedral [1210 ff.]). For the many donations, often for specific parts of the edifice, see Bégule.

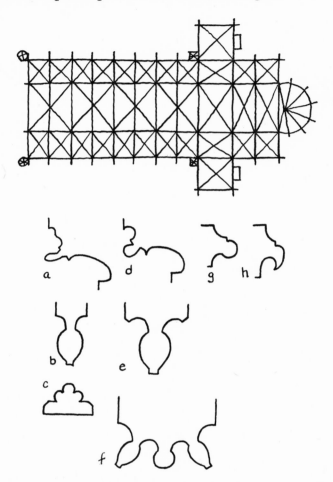

Fig. 65. Lyon Cathedral, plan and details: a. base; b. triforium rib profile; c. respond plan, all from north transept, west wall, south bay; d. base from the second pier from the west, south file, nave; e. rib profile from the crossing and nave; f. rib profile from the south transept and the transverse arch of the nave; g. impost from the transept; h. impost from the triforium, south bay of the south transept.

(b) L. Bégule–M.-C. Guigue, *Monographie de la cathédrale de Lyon*, Lyon, 1880; M. Aubert in *Cong. arch.* (Lyon-Mâcon), 98, 54–90; Bony (1958), 44–45 and *passim*.

MACON (Saône et Loire) (118)

Former cathedral St Vincent, in the archdiocese of Lyon.

See pp. 90–92, Fig. 27 and Plates 30a and c.

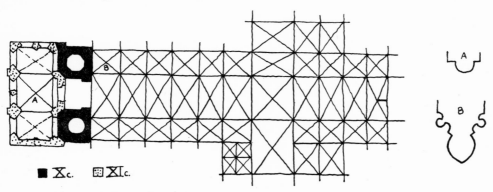

Fig. 66. Mâcon, former Cathedral, plan (after Virey) and rib profiles.

Ribs were added to the narthex vault about 1160–1170. About 1239 ff., the body of the church was reconstructed, probably from west to east, and possibly by Master Etienne Tondu, mason and master of the works for 21 years (known in 1239 and 1244). The arch "supra introitum chori" was made before 1253, and chaplaincies were founded in 1277. The older narthex and fragments of the western aisle bays are extant.

The elevation had three stories with a triforium passage and an exterior clerestory passage. In some bays of the choir, the rear wall of the triforium was pierced and the exterior drip-wall raised, to form a sort of gallery like a tribune. This appears in the 1797 section, but that it was an addition can clearly be seen in the inharmonious joining of the drip-wall to that of the aisle.

(a) Petit 6, 190–191 and n. 1. (b) J. Virey, *L'architecture romane dans l'ancien diocèse de Mâcon*, Paris, 1892, 222–232, with approximate profile of the narthex rib, p. 231; *id.*, in *Cong. arch.* (Lyon and Mâcon), 98, 1935, 464–472; *id.*, *Les églises romanes de l'ancien diocèse de Mâcon*, Mâcon, 1935, 320–338; A. Morgand, "Les dernières années de l'ancienne cathédrale Saint-Vincent de Mâcon (1790–1799)", *Annales de l'académie de Mâcon*, 30, 1933, 245–272; L. Decloître, "Les véritables dimensions de la cathédrale Saint-Vincent de Mâcon", *ibid.*, 35, 1940–1941, 62–65; see also Decloître, *loc. cit.*, xcvi–xcvii, for the remains of the X c. crypt.

MARCIGNY SOUS THIL (Côte d'Or) (77)

Notre Dame, priory of Semur in the diocese of Autun, under the patronage of the bishop.

The small, two-bay chevet, above a small, groin-vaulted crypt, is from the mid-XIII c. The corner buttresses are at 45°. The elevation has one story, with single, plain lancets in the lateral walls and twin, round-headed lancets in the eastern one. The wall-responds are pilasters, the ribs have long chamfers and rest on either corbels or shafts.

The country style.

(a) Longnon, *Lyon*, 100 (XIV c.). (b) Guillaume 209. (c) Cottineau (2) 1740.

MARSANNY LE BOIS (Côte d'Or) (79)

Notre Dame, parish in the diocese of Langres (under the patronage of the abbot of St Bénigne at Dijon?)

The small, two-bay chevet was built about 1260. The corner buttresses are at 45° and there are four-part vaults. There is only one story, and the ribs, with chamfers, rest on responds of three merged colonnettes. There is also a ribbed vault beneath the older crossing, but the short transept retains its Romanesque barrel vaults.

A rather elaborate example of the country style.

(a) Roserot 240. (b) Foisset 106; Guillaume 360–361.

MASSIGNY LES SEMUR (Côte d'Or) (69)

St Pierre ès Liens (St Martin), parish in the diocese of Autun, at the presentation of the abbot of Flavigny.

The small, two-bay chevet was erected about 1270–1280. There are four-part vaults and the corner buttresses are at 45°. There is only one story, with two plain lancets in the eastern wall. The ribs have a single pointed torus and lateral cavetti; the transverse arch profile is similar to that at St Bénigne at Dijon. The respond is formed of three juxtaposed colonnettes.

(a) Roserot 241. (b) Guillaume 228, who sees a Cistercian influence and says the chevet was built by a monk from Flavigny.

MIMEURE (Côte d'Or) (90)

St Pierre & St Paul, parish in the diocese of Autun, under the patronage of the abbot of St Bénigne at Dijon.

After the mid-XIII c., a small, square apse with a very low six-part vault. There is only one story, and the ribs have simple chamfers.

In the simplest country style.

(a) Roserot 251. (b) Foisset 188; Guillaume 148.

MINOT (Côte d'Or) (62)

St Pierre & St Paul, parish in the diocese of Langres, under the patronage of the bishop.

See Plate 41a.

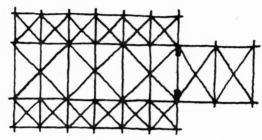

Fig. 67. Minot, plan.

The church was built in two campaigns: the apse and choir in the early XIII c., and nave about 1240–1250. A dedication is recorded on 9 October 1454.

The apse and choir vaults are domed laterally and have no wall-ribs; the ogives have a simple chamfered profile, close to that in the chapels of St Seine. The nave was perhaps planned for two towers at the west (only the northern one was executed, and rests on an octagonal pier), and for four-part vaults. These were altered at the top of the main arcades. There are two stories, with a long section of plain wall below the small lancets set high in the lunettes. The piers are columnar, and the responds and wall-responds consist of three contiguous colonnettes. The ribs here also have simple chamfers.

The earlier campaign represents the first extension of Gothic technique into the region. The second is an example of the monastic style, with relations to Flavigny.

(a) Courtépée 4, 279; Longnon, *Lyon*, 159 (1436). (b) G. Potey, "L'église Saint-Pierre de Minot", *Bulletin d'histoire, de littérature et d'art religieux de Dijon*, 25, 1907, 5–18; 85–115, with plans and view; Guillaume 337.

MIREBEAU SUR BEZE (Côte d'Or) (80)

St Pierre (Notre Dame), priory in the diocese of Langres, under the patronage of the abbot of St Etienne at Dijon.

The edifice was built from east to west, from about 1190–1200 to about 1230 (it may have been in use in 1232); the apse was then modified about 1240.

The nave has a tower in the second bay, and a low vault (at the height of the apse vaults) in the eastern bay. There is no transept. The edifice was perhaps begun with groined vaults (the vault beneath the tower is now XIV c.), but the ogives over the three western nave bays are original. There are no wall-ribs, but fairly level crowns. The piers are cruciform, with a colonnette on each major face. There are two stories, with no windows or decoration. The rib profile is a developed oval torus with a fillet, flanked by undulated cavetti and chamfers. The lateral walls of the apse have two short stories of plain lancets, not on the same axis, and a rosette over two lancets in the eastern wall.

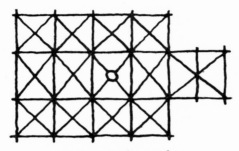

Fig. 68. Mirebeau, plan.

The first campaign may have been in the groined group, with ribbed vaults introduced only after 1200, in the nave. The nave itself is in the simpler monastic style, and the later work in the apse fairly cosmopolitan.

(a) Courtépée 2, 221–222; Longnon, *Lyon*, 157 (1436). (b) Foisset 113–114; Guillaume, 384. (c) Laurent-Claudon (1941), 595 and n. 2.

MOLESMES (Côte d'Or) (48)

Ste Croix, church of the novices and then parish (XIII c.) of the Benedictine abbey of Notre Dame (diocese of Langres).

The choir was built about 1250, the transept and nave in the late XIV c.

The choir has one story with plain lancet windows. The vault departures are *en tas-de-charge*. The ogives consist of an almond-shaped torus flanked by undulated cavetti and small chamfers, the transverse rib has two tori and a wide fillet. The median respond consists of three colonnettes around a pilaster. The capitals are spiky with crockets. There is a crossing tower, and the nave has five double bays, of which only the eastern pair were covered by a six-part vault (there are, however, two flying buttresses on the exterior here). There are two stories with clerestory windows here, and the piers are alternately octagonal and Chartrain.

The choir is in a simple but not unsophisticated style, such as at Mirebeau, and is perhaps related to Flavigny.

(b) An exterior view is in the *Monasticon Gallicanum*, no. 39 Cc; Guillaume 308. (c) Laurent-Claudon (1941), 305.

MOLINOT (Côte d'Or) (98)

Notre Dame, parish in the diocese of Autun, under the patronage of the bishop.

The west bay was erected about 1240. It has a six-part vault, beneath a tower, and a single story with plain lancets. The ribs have concave chamfers, and some rest on corbelled capitals with finished terminals. The wall-ribs are on stilts.
   In the country style.

(a) Courtépée 2, 331–332; Roserot 254. (b) Foisset 212; Guillaume 136.

MONETEAU (Yonne) (18)

St Cyr, Benedictine priory of St Germain at Auxerre, from 1215.

The apse and choir were rebuilt about 1235. There are two rectangular bays with four-part vaults, and one story with lancets; the eastern terminal has a triplet with asymmetrical arches. The median respond consists of three colonnettes and a rounded pilaster, all set forward of the wall. The capitals for the transverse arch are well above those of the ogives; the capitals of the latter are prolonged across the intervening pilaster. The vault departures are *en tas-de-charge;* the transverse rib has two tori and a cavetto, the ogive an almond-shaped torus and undulated cavetti.
   The XIII c. work is indirectly related to Auxerre cathedral and was perhaps by a mason from this shop. The local spread of the rounded pilaster and the differing heights of the capitals are interesting.

(a) Lebeuf 1, 382. (b) Cotteau-Petit in *Ann. Yonne*, 1853, 247–249; Quantin, *Rép.*, 20; H. Bouvier in *Bull. Soc. Yonne*, s. 4, v. 1 (51), 1897, 21–23. (c) Cottineau (1) 1884.

MONTBARD (Côte d'Or) (63)

St Urse (St Jean Baptiste), parish in the diocese of Langres, under the patronage of the abbot of Moûtiers St Jean.

There are some remains of the construction of about 1240, chiefly at the eastern end. The apse is rectangular and is flanked by smaller square chapels, adjacent to the crossing tower. There is one story, with a string-course below the windows, and four-part vaults on single colonnettes. The departures are *en tas-de-charge*, with inverted cusps at the terminations.
   Country style.

(a) Longnon, *Lyon*, 149 (1436); Roserot 257. (b) Guillaume 280–281.

MONTIGNY LA RESLE (Yonne) (19)

Notre Dame, parish in the diocese of Auxerre, under the patronage of the cathedral chapter from 1130.

Begun at the eastern end about 1220–1225, there are five rectangular bays covered by four-part vaults. There is a single story, with a dado below the lancets. The eastern wall has a small oculus above three lancets, all unornamented but with deep splays. The eastern responds are single colonnettes with circular imposts; the western, groups of three around a pilaster. The vault-departures are *en tas-de-charge*, the wall ribs are pointed but the transverse arches nearly semi-circular. In the eastern bay, the north wall has a dado of four arches united by two relieving arches, all with a dog-tooth moulding (including the edges of the pilasters behind the detached colonnettes); on the south here, there is a door with a four-petalled, pyramidal ornament on the jamb.

The edifice is quite elaborate, although the ornament is rather naïve.

(a) Courtépée 4, 398–399; Longnon, *Sens*, 256 (late XV c.). (b) Quantin, *Rép.*, 46–47; von Veltheim, 64–65 and pl. 25, where a date in the second half of the XII c. is advanced.

MONTRÉAL (Yonne), in the diocese of Langres (37)

A. St Bernard, Augustinian priory and hospital of Mont Joux.

See p. 18, n. 4.

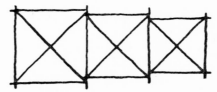

Fig. 69. Montréal, priory of St Bernard, plan.

Begun at the eastern end about 1170, the small edifice was probably completed before 1200 in three distinct campaigns. The western bay is now inaccessible. There is one story, with a round-headed lancet in each bay. The eastern responds are colonnettes on bases with "feet" similar to those in the chevet of Vézelay (about 1185). The transverse arch has chamfered edges (the roll on the western side belongs to the second campaign), the wall-rib has a single torus, and the ogive a heavy torus flanked by cyma recta mouldings and terminating in inverted cusps.

This edifice must be numbered among the early ribbed monuments of the Yonne Valley and shows certain relationships to Avallonnais design.

(b) Quantin, *Rép.*, 95; Breuillart in *Mém. com. C.-d'Or*, 9, 1874–1877, vi–xiii;

F. Brunet, *Montréal en Basse Bourgogne*, Auxerre, 1936, 67–68. (c) Cottineau (2) 1972.

B. Notre-Dame, collegiate church, founded by Anséric de Montréal in fulfilment of a vow made upon his departure for the crusade of 1147.

See pp. 19–20, Fig. 6b and Plate 6b.

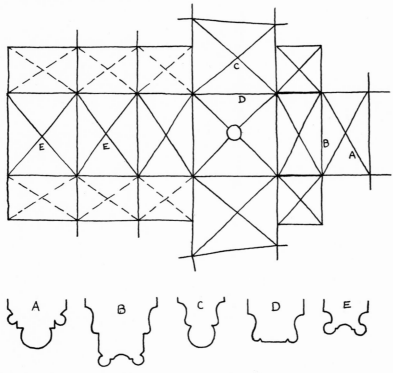

Fig. 70. Montréal, collegiate church, plan and rib profiles.

The edifice was begun about 1160 and built rather slowly until the early years of the XIII c. A narrow tribune, for the lords of Montréal, juts in above the western portal and adjoins a passage in the thickness of the façade wall covered by an arch (see Viollet-le-Duc, *Dictionnaire*, 9, 264 and figs. 265–266, and Hautecœur (2), pl. 96. 1). The details of the western piers of the nave (about 1195) reveal an influence, and possibly masons, from the shop working at Vézelay at this time.

(a) E. Petit in *Ann. Yonne*, 1861, 121–127 and *Bull. Soc. Yonne* 19, 1865, 68–261.
(b) Quantin, *Rép.*, 93–94; C. Porée in *Cong. arch.* (Avallon), 74, 1907, 97–101; F. Brunet, *op. cit.*; F. Salet in *Cong. arch.* (Auxerre), 116, 1958, 329–344, and *Encyclopédie d'architecture*, 3, 1875, for details.

MUSSY SUR SEINE (Aube) (5)

St Pierre ès Liens, collegiate church in the diocese of Langres, founded in 1218 by Bishop Guillaume de Joinville.

See p. 99 and Plate 35.

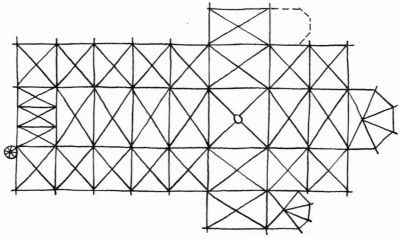

Fig. 71. Mussy sur Seine, plan.

The edifice was begun about 1300 and seems to have been terminated without interruptions in one campaign. A low, covered corridor runs around the exterior of the apse, traversing the buttresses as at Chalon, but it is accessible from the interior. There are flying buttresses. The piers of chevet and nave consist of flattened octagons with thin colonnettes on nave and aisle sides; the crossing piers are rectangular on the far sides, a detail found earlier at Chartres and Meaux.

(a) Longnon, *Lyon*, 151 (1436). (b) Tridon in *Cong. arch.* (Troyes), (20), 1853, 126–127; E. Lefèvre-Pontalis in *Cong. arch.* (Troyes), 69, 1902, 295–297; d'Arbois, *Rép.*, 77; L. Schürenberg, *Die kirchliche Baukunst in Frankreich*, Berlin, 1934, 212–213. (c) Laurent-Claudon (1941), 176–177 and n. 1.

NAILLY (Yonne) (8)

St Pierre, parish in the diocese of Sens, under the patronage of the archbishop.

The nave was built in the second half of the XII c. (the aisles are now destroyed); the transept and apse about 1230. The nave was to have had four-part vaults. The chevet has one story, with single lancets in the lateral walls of the apse and a plain triplet in the terminal. The responds here consist of one engaged colonnette, of a polygonal pilaster in the corners of the transept. There are niches in the eastern wall of the transept. The ogives have a pointed torus and cavetti, as at Cussey and Massigny.

The plan of the chevet is related to Appoigny and Sacy.

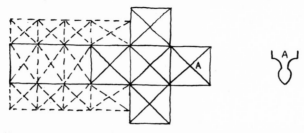

Fig. 72. Nailly, plan with destroyed nave bays and rib profile from apse.

(a) Longnon, *Sens*, 5 (about 1350). (b) Quantin, *Rép.*, 201; J. Perrin in *Bull. Soc. Sens*, 35, 1926–1927, 89–110.

NEVERS (Nièvre), in the archdiocese of Sens (110)

A. Cathedral St Cyr.

See pp. 68–71, 98, Fig. 19 and Plates 22a, 37b, 42b and d.

The construction of the XIII c. edifice is generally attributed to Bishop Guillaume de St Lazare (1201–1221), after the fire of 1211 ("Obiit Guillelmus a Sancto Lazaro . . . sedes in choro construxit. Ecclesiam opere lapideo primus incepit et pro magne parte peregit propriis sumptibus . . .", Parmentier), and it is suggested that he began the work at the eastern end, which was later rebuilt. The close examination of the edifice reveals, however, that the early XIII c. campaign was located in the western transept, both arms of which were covered with ribbed vaults. The crossing vault here was not constructed until later, and this may be the meaning of the phrase, *pro magna parte peregit*. On the other hand, *ecclesiam . . . incepit* obviously does not refer to a total reconstruction, since the Romanesque western transept is still standing (see Serbat for the interpretations of *opere lapideo*).

The work on the nave and chevet was inaugurated at the west, possibly as a result of the fire of 1228, although the text makes no mention of the cathedral. The campaign may have been deferred by the death of Bishop Regnault (28 July 1230) and the ensuing two years of vacancy of the see. It does not seem to have been undertaken much before 1235. The nave was completed, the transept begun and the foundations and lower courses of the chevet were implanted, when work seems to have been suspended, probably in the 1250's. If in fact the north transept portal (St Christophe or Doyenné) was built in 1280 (Crosnier), this would have been a *reprise* of work. A projected quest for funds in 1291 indicates that work was once again contemplated, undoubtedly to terminate the transept and chevet.

It may have been interrupted by the fire of 1308, but the completion of the eastern end is indicated by the dedication of 26 March 1331. It is therefore possible that Guillaume's choir-stalls and his tomb, if, in fact, they should be associated in space, were placed in the eastern choir of the old edifice, and that his tomb was again placed in the choir after the present edifice had been completed. The transept begun in the 1235 campaign was suppressed at the end of the century.

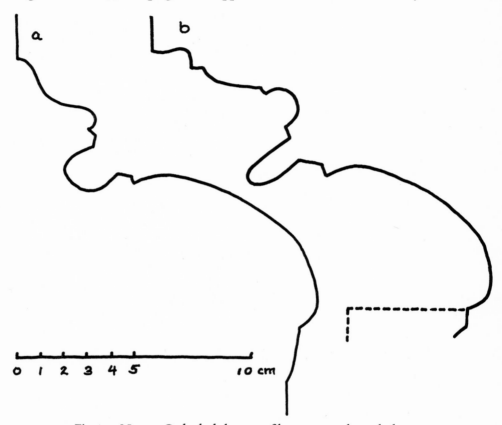

Fig. 73. Nevers Cathedral, base profiles: a. nave; b. ambulatory.

   The archaeological evidence for this chronology speaks for itself. For the work of 1211–1221, see pl. 43a. Serbat's observation of the composite nature of the ambulatory responds is correct – the inner respond bases are earlier, those framing the chapel entrances are later (see pl. 43b) – but the profile of the former could not be from the time of Guillaume. Since the capitals over both elements are from whole cloth, and obviously from the late XIII c., I assume that it was not completed in the 1235 campaign. Serbat's deduction as to the existence of the Rémois passage in the nave aisle, of the transept and of the presence of straight chapels in this programme can easily be confirmed.

(a) The obituary of Guillaume de Saint Lazare is in Parmentier, *Histoire sommaire des monseigneurs les évêques de Nevers* (manuscript of the *Société d'archéologie nivernaise* on deposit in the *Archives départementales de la Nièvre*), p. 314; the 1228 fire indicated in a XVI c. chronicle is in *anon.*, "Chronique ou histoire abrégée des évêques et des comtes de Nevers", *Bull. Soc. nivernaise*, s. 2, v. 5, 1872, 10–106, esp. 77; the 1291 quest is in a communication of Morellet on the texts copied by F. Gautron (1827–1853), *ibid.*, (s. 1), v. 2, 1855, 146. (b) Bourassé, *Esquisse archéologique . . . de Nevers*, Nevers, 1844, 1–28; Crosnier, *Monographie de la cathédrale de Nevers*, Nevers, 1854, 71 ff.; G. de Soultrait, *Guide archéologique dans Nevers*, Nevers, 1856, 8; L. Serbat in *Cong. arch.* (Moulins-Nevers), 80, 1913, 301–339; J. Palet, "La cathédrale de Nevers à travers le passé", *Bull. Soc. nivernaise*, v. 28 (29), 1930, 83–96; 1931, 249–291; 1932, 369–391, is fundamental for the tomb of Guillaume de Saint Lazare and the church furnishings; L. Schürenberg, *Die kirchliche Baukunst in Frankreich*, Berlin, 1934, 56–58; Jantzen, 17–18. (c) Besse 6 (1913), 107 and n. 2. For the older buildings and recent excavations, Hubert (1952), no. 34.

B. St Gildard, priory of St Laurent.

See pp. 76–77 and Fig. 22.

Fig. 74. Nevers, St Gildard, rib profile.

The edifice was erected about 1245–1250. It was restored and considerably altered in the XIX c., when the pavement was lowered about 30 cm. and the eastern end enlarged. It originally contained four rectangular bays with four-part vaults, and with portals in the north and south walls of the sanctuary (Crosnier, f. p. 264). There are two stories with an area of plain wall supporting an arched, interior passage in the lunette. The responds consist of three clustered colonnettes set forward of the wall. The passage is recessed behind the piers. The vault departures are *en tas-de-charge*, the ogives and transverse arches have an oval torus and fillet, two cavetti and chamfered edges; the terminals have undulated, inverted cusps. The capitals are similar to contemporary work in the nave of Bourges cathedral, although this may be due to the restorations.

An example of the Burgundian two-storied elevation on a traditional chapel plan.

(a) Crosnier, in *Bull. soc. nivernaise*, 1, 1854, 263–266; L. Roubet, "Saint-Gildard, Saint-Gildas", *ibid.*, s. 3, v. 3 (13), 1890, 134–143. (b) Soultrait, *Rép.*, 163–164; L. Serbat in *Cong. arch.* (Moulins-Nevers), 80, 1913, 360–361. (c) Cottineau (2) 2065–2066.

NUITS ST GEORGES (Côte d'Or) (92)

St Symphorien, parish in the diocese of Autun, from 1144 under the patronage of the chapter of Vergy.

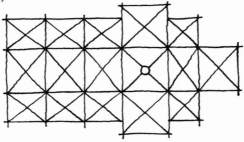

Fig. 75. Nuits St Georges, plan.

The present church was built about 1235 ff., possibly on older foundations. The massing is rectilinear and there is a crossing tower. The elevation has two stories, with a single, round-headed lancet in the clerestory. The eastern terminal has a large, open rose placed well above three lancets. The apse responds are simple colonnettes to the east, but the median one has three shafts around a pilaster. The crossing piers are cruciform, with colonnettes engaged to the faces and detached shafts in the angles. The nave elevation is similar to the chevet, but the aisles are groin-vaulted here. The vaults are slightly domed and without wall-responds, the ogives (with simple chamfers) now resting on corbelled capitals.

An example of the monastic style having considerable clarity of line. Situated between Chalon and Dijon, it is remarkable for the retention of archaic forms, especially since some of the details (such as the exterior of the apse) reveal direct contact with the large, nearby shops.

(a) Courtépée 2, 365 ("grossièrement construite en 1280!"); Longnon, *Lyon*, 81 (XIV c.). (b) Foisset 217–218; V. Flipo, *Mémento pratique . . .*, Paris, 1930, interior view, p. 216; Guillaume, 72, with exterior view, p. 73.

ORGEUX (Côte d'Or) (81)

Notre Dame, parish in the diocese of Langres, at the presentation of the abbot of St Bénigne at Dijon.

See p. 23.

A small rectangular apse was built about 1190 to the east of a Romanesque tower, probably replacing an older apse. It has a four-part vault. The ogive profile has an almond-shaped torus flanked by a cyma recta moulding; the ribs rest on corbelled capitals and the departures are ornamented by a series of inverted cusps.

In the country style, the apse represents the persistence of the earliest ribbed types in the Dijonnais.

(a) Longnon, *Lyon*, 156 (1436); Roserot 289. (b) Foisset 58–59; Guillaume 369.

PERNAND (Côte d'Or) (95)

St Germain, parish in the diocese of Autun, under the patronage of the cathedral chapter of Chalon sur Saône.

A small rectangular apse, about 1220, replaced a Romanesque one on the cruciform, barrel-vaulted edifice. It has a four-part vault with simple, chamfered ogives resting on polygonal corbels. The western tower also has a ribbed vault in the lowest story, the ogives here having concave chamfers. The whole is very restored.

A provincial edifice.

(a) Longnon, *Lyon*, 79 (XIV c.); Roserot 296. (b) Foisset 170; Guillaume 95.

PETIT OUGES (Côte d'Or) (85)

St Pierre, parish in the diocese of Autun, under the patronage of the cathedral chapter.

See Plate 41c.

Built about 1240, the edifice has two small rectangular bays for a choir (beneath a tower) and an apse, both with six-part vaults. There is only one story with three plain, trilobed lancets in the terminal wall and one round-headed lancet beneath a deep wall-rib in each lateral bay. The median responds are trapezoidal with five detached shafts, and the bases have an overhang of about 2 cm., with corbels beneath them. The ribs, with chamfers, rest on corbelled capitals. The departure of the eastern wall-rib is higher than that of the ogives, that of the lateral wall-ribs even higher and on stilts with individual capitals. There has been severe restoration.

An engaging example of mid-thirteenth-century provincial style.

(a) Longnon, *Lyon*, 186 (XIV c.); Roserot 291. (b) Foisset 69; Guillaume 402.

PICHANGES (Côte d'Or) (75)

St Laurent, branch of the parish of Gémeaux in the diocese of Langres, under the patronage of the abbot of St Etienne at Dijon from 1120.

See p. 23.

Built about 1190, the edifice has three bays and a tower, with four-part vaults. There are two stories with lancets above a string-course. The responds have detached shafts beneath the ogives. The transverse arches are rectangular, the ogives have a large, slightly pointed torus flanked by cyma recta mouldings and the departures are ornamented by inverted cusps.

The church represents the persistence of the earliest ribbed types in eastern Burgundy, and was probably built by a shop from the Yonne Valley.

(a) Courtépée 2, 231; Longnon, *Lyon*, 160 (1436); Roserot 299. (b) Foisset 107–108 (where the nave is dated mid-thirteenth century and the portal about 1200); Guillaume 362, who notes the church was once fortified.

PONT SUR YONNE (Yonne) (7)

Notre Dame, parish in the diocese of Sens, from 1162 under the patronage of the metropolitan chapter.

See pp. 29–30.

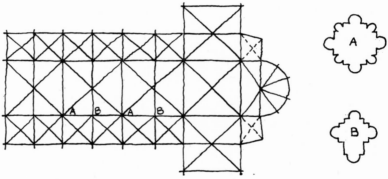

Fig. 76. Pont sur Yonne, plan and nave piers.

The church was built from east to west from about 1200 to about 1225.

The seven-part, one-storied apse is flanked by mis-shapen, groined chapels. The transept and nave are covered by six-part vaults and the nave has alternating piers, the weak ones with higher plinths. There are no windows here, and basically only one story, for the pointed main arcades rise above the vault departure into the lunette, although they are crowned by a string-course. There are no wall-ribs in the nave or transept, but the lunettes are semicircular. The transverse ribs of the crossing are simply chamfered, as are the main arcades; the ogives are of the Pontigny type and not unlike those of the Quincy hostelry and the chevet of Montréal. There is a tower over the south aisle; the corresponding bay on the north was restored in the XV c.

The weak piers are reduced versions of Pontigny. The nave elevation is not unlike St Pierre at Chablis. The church represents the spread of the six-part vault and the persistence and slow transformation of the groined parti.

(a) Longnon, *Sens*, 8 (about 1350). (b) V. Petit in *Ann. Yonne*, 1845, 2, 116–118; Quantin in *Annales archéologiques*, 13, 1853, 97 and plate (longitudinal section) and 25, 1865, 374–376 (plan and transverse section of chevet), both criticized by M. Prou in *Bull. Soc. Sens*, 14, 1888, 22–43; Quantin, *Rép.*, 191; interior view in *Bull. mon.*, 81, 1922, 282.

PONTIGNY (Yonne) (16)

Notre Dame, Cistercian abbey of Cîteaux, founded in 1114.

Begun at the eastern end about 1145, the nave was terminated not long after 1155. The chevet was rebuilt from about 1186, when a quarry is mentioned, to about 1208–1210.

See pp. 16–17, 29, Figs 2a, b and Plates 3b and 10.

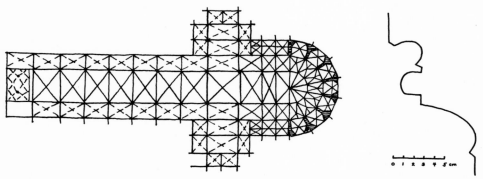

Fig. 77. Pontigny, plan (after Dimier) and base of a respond in the chevet.

For the cellar, see Fontaine, 101–117 and Aubert, *Arch. cist.* 127.

(b) Aubert, *Arch. cist., passim*; Dimier, 148–149, with bibliography, and pls. 235–237; G. Fontaine, *Pontigny* (*Etudes d'art et d'archéologie publiées sous la direction d'Henri Focillon*, 1), Paris, 1928; M. Aubert, "Les fouilles de l'église de Pontigny", *Bulletin, Société nationale des Antiquaires de France*, 1942, 243–246; *id.*, in *Cong. arch.* (Auxerre), 116, 1958, 163–168. (c) Cottineau (2) 2331–2332.

PREGILBERT (Yonne) (36)

Notre Dame, parish in the diocese of Auxerre, under the patronage of the abbess of Crisenon.

Only the two western bays of the nave, and a part of a third, with a tower on the north side, all about 1222–1230, are extant. The plan of the chevet is unknown. The edifice was seriously restored in the XVI c. and XIX c.

The elevation has three stories with string-courses separating the clerestory, with its unadorned lancet, and the central story, with its false-tribune opening, from the main arcades. The tribune opening has two arches framed by a round-headed relieving arch and opened onto the roof, without any preparation for a gallery or walk behind it. The proportions of the nave are narrow and tall. The aisle window has a tall lancet, the dado is plain. The responds consist of three colonnettes separated from each other and from the wall. The ribs have two contiguous tori. There is an arched passage across the façade verso and another interior passage here at clerestory level, also arched. There are flying buttresses.

Prégilbert must be numbered among the extremely late examples of a XII c. elevation and structure, such as Gamaches (Somme), Fauquembergues (Pas de Calais) and Trouan le Grand (Aube). The portal is close in style to the one at Appoigny.

(a) Longnon, *Sens*, 259 (late XV c.). (b) Quantin, *Rép.*, 78; von Veltheim, 75–76; and especially Hautecœur (2), 100–101 (with plan) and pl. 101.

PREMERY (Nièvre) (109)

St Marcel, collegiate chapter founded slightly before 15 April **1196** by Jean de Fontenay, Bishop of Nevers, and under episcopal patronage.

See p. 76 and Fig. 21.

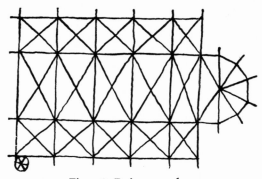

Fig. 78. Prémery, plan.

Begun about 1220, the first campaign comprised the apse and two bays of the aisle walls. In the second campaign, about 1235–1240, the two eastern nave bays were completed, and the remaining three bays were erected in the last third of the century. There are many restorations from the XV c.

The low, broad apse has a seven-part vault and two stories of windows above a decorated dado. The clerestory is limited to the short vault-zone, and the axial lancet has cusped edges. The arcade summers of the dado bear crockets, as at Clamecy and Dijon.

The two-storied nave has an interior clerestory passage (arched) in the vault-zone. The piers are Chartrain, with the shaft on the nave-side running up to the vault departure but cut by the string-course. The spandrels of the main arcades are surmounted by several feet of solid wall. The west façade was to have been surmounted by two towers, but only the south one was executed.

The apse is in a provincial idiom. The eastern nave bays derive from St Cyr at Nevers and show relationships to the naves of Clamecy and Appoigny, but they are executed in a much heavier manner.

(b) Bourassé, *Esquisse archéologique . . . de Nevers*, Nevers, 1844, 115–118; Soultrait, *Rép.*, 118–120; L. Serbat, in *Cong. arch.* (Moulins-Nevers), 80, 1913, 417–423. (c) Besse 6 (1913), 109, n. 2.

QUENNE (Yonne) (22)

Notre Dame, priory and parish in the diocese of Auxerre, under the patronage of the abbot of St Pierre at Auxerre.

See p. 18, n. 14.

The small edifice was built about 1155. The plan comprises four bays and a polygonal, three-sided apse. There is only one story, with lancets above a plain dado. The responds consist of a pilaster with three engaged colonnettes. The ogive is similar to those in St Pierre at Bar sur Aube. The three western bays now have XVI c. vaults.

The apse is among the first ribbed vaults in the Yonne Valley.

(a) Longnon, *Sens*, 257 (late XV c.). (b) Quantin, *Rép.*, 14–15; Philippe 69. (c) Cottineau (2) 2388.

QUINCY (Yonne, commune of Commissey) (25)

Cistercian abbey of Pontigny, founded in 1133. Destroyed.

See pp. 19, 28.

The dedication of 1139 undoubtedly referred to the first church, since the fragments of the one recorded in the XVII c. by Israel (Silvestre) and seen by Quantin in 1863 dated from the late XII c. The latter edifice had rounded transepts, each of which, according to Martène and Durand, had seven altars, suggesting seven chapels. These must have been embedded in a continuous wall, as at Clairvaux, but without an ambulatory, since the engraving shows only one low, normal mass here. The general plan seems a direct forerunner of Chaalis (1203–1219). Dimensions: length 85 m.; width at transept: 45 m. The chevet was reworked during the Renaissance. Quantin records a pier 2 m. tall with eight colonnettes and capitals *en bourrelet*. One arch, probably separating two bays of the nave aisle, can still be seen, although it is half buried. Quantin also records "bâtiments des moines" with a massive XII c. vault, and "bâtiments de l'abbé" with semicircular vaulted rooms from the late XII c. Either may have been the extant "hostelry", a typically Cistercian structure of six bays (2 × 3) of the hall-type, of about 1170.

(a) Martène-Durand, *Voyage littéraire . . .*, 1717, 1, 107; Quantin, *Rép.*, 243–244; E. Lambert, "Histoire de l'abbaye de Quincy", (part 2), *Ann. Yonne*, s. 2, v. 4 (28), 1864, p. 4; Héliot in *Bull. mon.* 108, 1950, 113; Aubert, *Arch. cist.*, 1, 211; 2, 79 and 81 (salle des moines); 155–157 (hostelry). (b) The exterior view is in Paris, *Bibl. Nat., Est.*, Va 418 (reproduced in Petit, 9, following p. 176, and Aubert, *Arch. cist.*, 1, p. 212). (c) Laurent-Claudon (1941), 355–359.

RECEY SUR OURCE (Côte d'Or) (55)

St Remi, parish in the diocese of Langres, under the patronage of the bishop.

Fig. 79. Recey, ogive profile.

A small edifice, with a Romanesque nave. To it was added, about 1230, a rectangular apse with a four-part vault and a similar vault over the crossing. After about 1250, the aisles and transept were reworked and the nave vaulted. The ogives have simple chamfered angles and rest on corbels. The western vault is six-part.

(a) Longnon, *Lyon*, 151 (1436); Roserot 321. (b) Guillaume 352–353.

ROUGEMONT (Côte d'Or) (59)

Notre Dame (St Julien), Benedictine convent depending from Moûtiers St Jean.
See pp. 75–76 and Plate 25a.

Built from east to west, the extant portions date from about 1245 to about 1265; the *opus* received small legacies in 1257, 1261 and 1263, possibly for the construction. The porch and tower were later fortified, perhaps during the Hundred Years' War.

Four bays of the nave are now extant, the entire eastern portion having been destroyed. An axial tower over a low vault surmounts the western bay, and the façade is preceded by a porch one bay deep and three wide. The elevation of the nave has two stories with an interior clerestory passage. The piers closely resemble those in the nave of Semur, both in plan and proportions; those beneath the tower are square with a colonnette and pilaster added to each face. The clerestory passage

Fig. 80. Rougemont, pier and ogive profile.

is slab-covered, but a supplementary wall-rib frames the window wall. The south window has a quadrilobe above two lancets separated by a mullion; the north has simply two lancets. The present main vaults have rectangular ribs. The bases toward the west have an overhanging lower torus supported by a corbel. The main portal has a sculpted tympanum and a series of statues.

This nave is one of the later examples of the two-storied Burgundian elevation and is close to Semur.

(a) Petit, 6, 197; Roserot 332. (b) *id.*, communication in *Mém. com. C.-d'Or*, 13, 1895–1900, cvi–cvii (where the church is related to Aignay le Duc!); Schanosky, "Notice", *Mém. com. C.-d'Or*, 14, 1901–1905, xi–xiv; Guillaume 285, with view of portal, 284. (c) Cottineau (2) 2551; Laurent-Claudon (1941), 398–400.

ROUVRES EN PLAINE (Côte d'Or) (86)

St Jean Baptiste, parish in the diocese of Chalon, under the patronage of the chapter of Beaune.

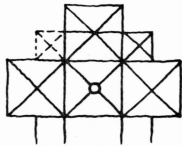

Fig. 81. Rouvres, plan of eastern end.

A small edifice, said to have been begun in 1233 outside the ducal château. The apse may be about this time or slightly later; the transept and nave were built in the late XIII c. and XIV c.

The apse is square, with a six-part vault, the minor transverse arch resting on corbels. It is flanked by two rectangular chapels (XVI c. on the north). The terminal wall has a rosette above three plain, pointed lancets; the lateral walls have two lancets each, on two levels but not on the same axis. There is a tower over the crossing and the five-bay nave, with aisles, has octagonal piers and corbelled vaults similar to those in the transept. The whole edifice is now completely restored.

The church is the work of a very provincial shop, even though ostensibly working for the dukes of Burgundy.

(a) Courtépée 2, 236–237; Roserot 333. (b) Foisset 85–87; J. Tillet-J. Verrier in *Cong. arch.* (Dijon), 91, 1928, 435–441; Guillaume 404.

SACY (Yonne) (33)

St Jean Baptiste, parish in the diocese of Auxerre, under the patronage of the abbot of Vézelay.

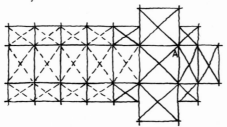

Fig. 82. Sacy, plan and pier.

The eastern portion of the Romanesque edifice was rebuilt about 1240–1250 perhaps as a result of the agreement of 1235 (Lebeuf).

The chevet and transept were enlarged and the two eastern aisle-bays of the Romanesque church rebuilt. The former are in one tall story. The eastern terminal has a triplet, the lateral walls a single lancet each. The median transverse rib of the choir rests on corbels. The responds have engaged colonnettes and rounded pilasters.

The Gothic work is related in general effect to Appoigny and may represent the ultimate impact of Auxerre cathedral on the hinterland. Certainly the same master was not responsible for all three, as has been suggested.

(a) Lebeuf, 4, no. 169; Longnon, *Sens*, 258 (late XV c.). (b) Quantin, *Rép.* 79; Philippe, 69, with section; von Veltheim, 77; Rose, 130; view in Hautecœur (2) pl. 107, 2; J. Vallery-Radot in *Cong. Arch.* (Auxerre), 116, 1958, 265–270.

ST BRIS LE VINEUX (Yonne) (29)

St Bris & St Cot, parish in the diocese of Auxerre, under the patronage of the chapter from 1181, and necropolis of the lords of Mello.

The nave was constructed from east to west about 1210 ff. The chevet is Renaissance.

    The nave may originally have had nine bays, of which five of the north, six of the central and nine of the south aisles remain (in part from the XIV c.). There is a tower above the eastern Gothic bay of the north aisle. The elevation has two stories with a string-course between and a plain lancet in each clerestory bay. The piers have no less than sixteen colonnettes of three different sizes engaged into pilasters or angles, of which five rise uninterrupted to the vaults. The latter are all four-part, with horizontal crowns and all the ribs slightly stilted. The ogive profile resembles those at Gerland and Massigny.

    The shop is related to those of Pontigny and St Martin at Chablis. The edifice is essentially a Gothic rendering of the groined basilica.

(a) Lebeuf, 1, 342; Longnon, *Sens*, 256 (late XV c.). (b) Quantin in *Ann. Yonne*, 1838, 2, 290–293; *id.*, *Rép.*, 15–16; von Veltheim 50; L. Prieur in *Cong. arch.* (Auxerre), 116, 1958, 169–183. (c) Besse 6 (1913), 100 and n. 9.

STE COLOMBE LES SENS (Yonne) (9)

[Ste Colombe (St Loup), Benedictine abbey in the diocese of Sens]

See p. 69 and Plate 45b.

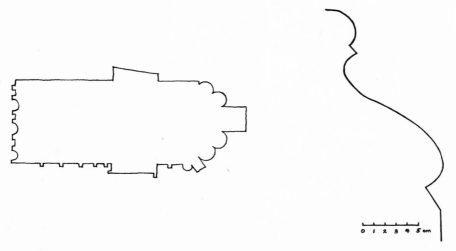

Fig. 83. Ste Colombe lès Sens, outline plan and profile of base unearthed by Brullée.

An edifice was begun on 25 March 1142 and dedicated on 26 April 1164; another campaign is recorded from 1218 to before 1235. The church is destroyed.

There exists an outline plan of the church and abbey buildings by Gondet, dated 1756 (*Archives de l'Yonne*, H 141) and engraved in 1779 (Paris, *Bibl.Nat.*, *Est.*, Va 416), from which the accompanying plan is freely taken. No interior plans or views are known. The total interior length, including the axial chapel, was about 74 m.; the width of the nave, about 28 m. 25; of the transept, about 36 m. 65. It is uncertain whether the XII c. or XIII c. building, or both, is represented; both were unquestionably vaulted, even though Abbot Robert de la Ménardière "fit paver et voûter l'église" at the end of the XVI c. (Paris, *Bibl. Nat.*, *Collection de Champagne*, 42, f. 28 Ro). The north flank was adjacent to the monastic buildings, with the cloister touching the transept; the south flank undoubtedly had a row of later, additional chapels. The description by Dom Morin, as cited by Petit, is useless; Petit himself added that the interior was about 29 m. high. Fragments of various periods were discovered by Brullée during excavations in 1852, but the site is now inaccessible beneath the church erected in 1874. The remains, still visible in the modern convent, include two bases (one from the XII c. and one from the XIII c. campaigns) and a capital from the XII c. work that must originally have surmounted a columnar pier.

(a) L.-M. Duru, *Bibliothèque historique de l'Yonne*, 1, Auxerre-Paris, 1850, 209–210, 213; Quantin, II, 176. (b) V. Petit in *Ann. Yonne* 1854, 2, 110–112; Brullée, "Rapport sur les fouilles executées à la fin de 1852 . . .", *Bull. Soc. Sens* (v. 4), 1853, 68–81. (c) Cottineau (2) 2638–2639.

ST CYR LES COLONS (Yonne) (30)

St Cyr & Ste Julitte, parish in the diocese of Auxerre, under the patronage of the abbot of St Laurent.

See p. 18, n. 14.

The small, rectangular apse, of about 1170, was built east of the older tower. Both have ribbed vaults, slightly domed, with rectangular ogives and no wall-ribs. The terminal wall contains two round-headed lancets with a tiny oculus above, the lateral walls merely single lancets. The window jambs have detached shafts, but not the responds. Some capitals bear Romanesque animals. The nave is totally new, but may have been in the groin-vaulted group.

This is one of the early rib-vaulted structures in the Yonne Valley.

(a) Lebeuf, 1, 284; Longnon, *Sens*, 257 (late XV c.). (b) Quantin, *Rép.* 27; Philippe 69; Rose 22.

ST ELOI (Nièvre) (111)

St Eloi, parish in the diocese of Nevers, under the patronage of the prior of
St Etienne at Nevers.

The parish was founded in 1235, the church built about 1250.
   The plan consists of three rectangular bays with four-part vaults and buttresses
at 45° angles. There is one story, with single lancet windows. The rib in the eastern
bay has simple chamfered angles and rests on corbels; the vault in the western bay
is much later. The whole edifice is totally restored.

(a) Longnon, *Sens*, 524 (1478). (b) Soultrait, *Rép.* 172.

ST JULIEN DU SAULT (Yonne) (14)

A. St Julien, chapel of the château of Vauguilain, atop the hill, owned by the
archbishop of Sens, temporal lord of St Julien.

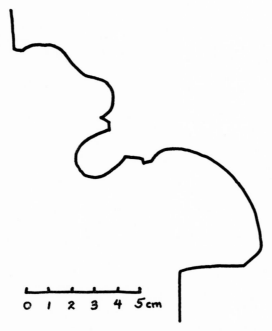

Fig. 84. St Julien du Sault, base of ambulatory respond.

The chapel, built about 1190, has two (originally three) rectangular bays covered
by four-part vaults. It is of one story, with a single lancet in either lateral wall of
the eastern bay and a triplet in the terminal; a small door opens in the north side of

the western bay. The eastern responds are single engaged colonnettes, the central ones three colonnettes of differing size separated by sunken but flat panels. The imposts, following the angles of the ribs, are merged. The ogives bear two tori separated by a sunken, flat panel, the transverse arch is rectangular with chamfered angles. Both the latter and the wall-rib are stilted. In the western bay, the formeret is supported by a corbel in the form of a grotesque head.

An ornate but not too rich château chapel of essentially simple form.

(b) Exterior view by V. Petit in *Ann. Yonne* 1853, following p. 270; Quantin, *Rép.*, 167; J. Vallery-Radot in *Cong. arch.* (Auxerre), 116, 1958, 355–357.

B. St Pierre, collegiate chapter in the diocese of Sens, founded before 1193 by Guy de Noyers.

See pp. 87–88, Fig. 24 and Plates 27a and 28b.

The edifice was begun about 1235 at the eastern end; the traditional foundation date of 1205 is therefore too early for the present building (Hautecœur). The transept was under construction about 1245. The Renaissance work probably dates from the mid-XVI c.

(a) Vignon in *Bull. soc. Sens*, 1, 1846, 73. (b) J. Tonnellier, "Notice . . .", *Ann. Yonne*, 1842, 2, 99–118; Vignon in *Cong. arch.* (14), 1847, 118–122; Quantin, *Rép.*, 167–168; Hautecœur (1) 63–65 and pls. 70–71; J. Vallery-Radot in *Cong. arch.* (Auxerre), 116, 1958, 357–365. (c) Besse 6 (1913), 13 and n. 3.

ST LOUP DE LA SALLE (Saône et Loire) (113)

St Loup, parish in the diocese of Chalon sur Saône, patronized by the bishop.

See p. 27, n. 29.

The nave, from the very end of the XII c., has three bays of two stories, with plain lancets in the clerestory above an unornamented wall. The aisles are groin-vaulted and the main vessel, vaulted with ribs resting on corbels, may originally have been planned for groins. The whole design seems a simplification of St Marcel lès Chalon.

(a) Courtépée 3, 401; Longnon, *Lyon*, 184 (XIV c.). (b) mentioned in Fernillot, "Les églises gothiques de l'ancien diocèse de Chalon", *Positions de thèses de l'école des chartes*, 1946, 55–61.

ST MARCEL LES CHALON (Saône et Loire) (116)

St Marcel, Cluniac priory (1060) in the diocese of Chalon sur Saône.

See p. 27, n. 29.

The church was begun in the later XII c. and was perhaps planned for barrel vaults (the barrel-vaulted south chapel is probably a XIX c. invention). The nave was underway about 1190 and was perhaps to have been groined. The present apse dates from about 1245 and the nave vaults from about 1250.

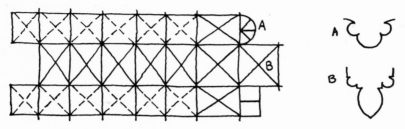

Fig. 85. St Marcel lès Chalon, plan and ogive profiles.

A crossing tower and two towers to the west were originally projected. The nave has two stories with small lancets in the clerestory, above plain wall. The piers are square, with four colonnettes, two of which serve as wall-responds (one pier, west of the crossing and on the south side, has an added pilaster and colonnette). The aisles are groin-vaulted. The ribs in the nave spring from the joint of the wall and the transverse arch and are unsupported. The apse windows comprise rosettes over twin lancets.

This is possibly an example of the late use of the barrel vault and the groined-vault in eastern Burgundy, as well as of the relatively late appearance of ribbed vaults in the immediate area.

(a) Cazet, "Notice historique et archéologique . . .", *Mémoires, Société d'histoire et d'archéologie de Chalon-sur-Saône* (v. 1), 1844–1846, 139–192 (to the XII c.). (b) A. de Baudot, *Eglises de bourgs et villages*, v. 2, Paris, 1867, two unnumbered plates; J. Evans, *Romanesque architecture of the order of Cluny*, Cambridge, 1938, *passim*, with interior view, fig. 57; mentioned in Y. Fernillot, "Les églises gothiques de l'ancien diocèse de Chalon", *Positions de thèses de l'école des chartes*, 1946, 55–61. (c) Cottineau (2) 2780.

ST PERE SOUS VEZELAY (Yonne) (42)

Notre Dame, chapel at the presentation of the abbot of Vézelay, and then in the diocese of Autun (late XVI c.) and deaconry of Avallon.

See pp. 79–80 and Plate 26a.

The present edifice may have been begun as early as 1235–1240 at the eastern end, which was rebuilt in the XIV c. The earliest extant parts of the nave were under construction about 1245 and the whole was terminated before 1258, at which time a tomb was placed against one of the façade buttresses (the inscription is in part cut into the portal jamb). The porch was added in the last third of the century.

The original chevet plan is virtually impossible to reconstruct, even with the peculiar, seven-ribbed keystone mentioned by Bruand. The nave, with alternating piers, is clearly related to the nave of St Martin at Clamecy, although Bruand

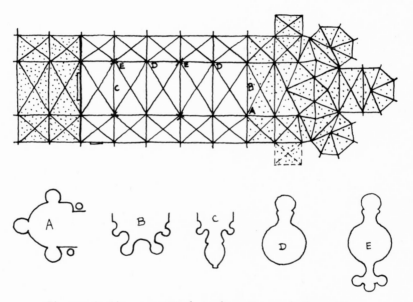

Fig. 86. St Père sous Vézelay, plan, piers and rib profiles.

thinks the central strong piers were reworked. The upper of the two stories contains a slab-covered interior passage. All the supports are coursed, except for some minor shafts on the easternmost XIII c. piers, which suggest a different shop for the now-replaced chevet, perhaps one in the *mouvance* of ideas centring in the cathedral of Auxerre. The western bays were to have been surmounted by towers, of which only the extraordinary north one was executed. The façade and gable have long been studied for their sculpture. The one-story porch, open on all sides, recalls Beaune and, ultimately, Dijon.

(a) Longnon, *Lyon*, 90 (XIV c.). (b) C. Porée in *Cong. arch.* (Avallon), 74, 1907, 17–23; Hautecœur (1) 23–24 and pls. 24–26; Jantzen, 34; Y. Bruand in *Cong. arch* (Auxerre), 116, 1958, 251–264.

ST PHILIBERT (Côte d'Or) (88)

St Philibert, parish in the diocese of Langres, at the presentation of the Grand Prior of Champagne, Order of the Knights Templar.

About 1220, a small rectangular apse was added to an older edifice. The vault is four-part, the responds detached shafts with rings.

In the country style, with some XII c. features.

(a) Roserot 358. (b) Foisset 94; Guillaume 68.

ST SATUR (Cher) (101)

St Satur, Augustinian abbey in the diocese of Bourges (1131).

See p. 100 and Plate 37a.

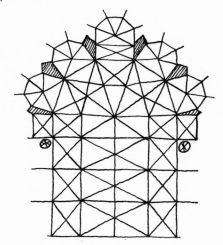

Fig. 87. St Satur, plan.

Begun in 1361, work on the church was interrupted in 1405, at which time the transept and nave were not yet complete.

(b) A. Buhot de Kersers, *Histoire et statistique monumentale du Cher*, vol. 7, Bourges, 1895, 50–53; F. Deshoulières, in *Cher (Eglises de France)*, Paris, 1932, 234–237; L. Schürenberg, *Die kirchliche Baukunst in Frankreich*, Berlin, 1934, 59–62 and *passim*. (c) Cottineau (2) 2876–2877.

ST SAUVEUR (Yonne) (34)

St Jean Baptiste, parish in the diocese of Auxerre, at the presentation of the abbot of St Germain at Auxerre.

See p. 18, n. 14 and Fig. 2.

The apse was built about 1160. It is rectangular, small and has only one story. The eastern wall has two lancets with orders and mouldings. The vault covering the bay to the west, on corbels and with departures *en tas-de-charge*, is from the XIII c.

The apse is among the early ribbed vaults in the Yonne Valley.

(a) Longnon, *Sens*, 256 (late XV c.). (b) Quantin, *Rép.*, 59–60; Philippe 69.

ST SEINE (Côte d'Or) (74)

Notre Dame (St Seine), Benedictine abbey in the diocese of Langres.

See p. 73 and Plate 24c.

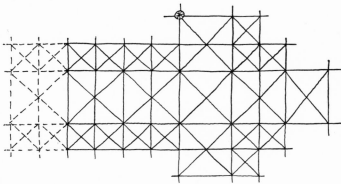

Fig. 88. St Seine, plan with uncompleted western bays.

Begun between 1205 and 1209, the first campaign comprised two phases: the lower walls of the chevet and transept, and those of the nave. Work was suspended by 1226 and resumed about 1235 or slightly later. This second campaign saw the curtailment of the nave by two bays and the construction, over most of the edifice, of the clerestory and vaults. These were damaged in the fire of 1255 (Vallery-Radot, 151) and funds for the restoration and completion of the edifice were sought at once and again in 1266. Extensive rebuilding was carried out in the XIV c. and XV c., and the entire monument was restored in the XIX c.

(a) Roserot 362. (b) C. Rossignol, in *Mém. com. C.-d'Or*, 2, 1842–1846, 193–286; Mignard, in *ibid.*, 6, 1861–1864, 220–264; Foisset 124–128; H. Chabeuf, in *Mém. com. C.-d'Or*, 11, 1885–1888, 31–223; J. Vallery-Radot in *Cong. arch.* (Dijon), 91, 1928, 148–183; Jantzen, 31–33. (c) Cottineau (2) 2885; Laurent-Claudon (1941), 586–587 and n.

ST SEINE SUR VINGEANNE (Côte d'Or) (72)

St Seine, parish in the diocese of Langres, under the patronage of the abbot of Bèze.

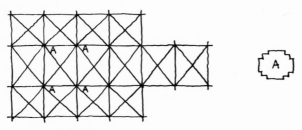

Fig. 89. St Seine sur Vingeanne, plan and pier.

The edifice is said to have been founded in 1300, according to the interpretation of an inscription on the respond at the south side of the entrance to the choir ("Odito lapis me fecit MCCC"), but its authenticity and transliteration are doubtful. The building was probably erected about 1260–1270 on older foundations.

The chevet has one story, with a tower over the eastern bay of the nave. The nave has two stories with a small lancet in a tall and very pointed lunette, above a stretch of plain wall. The piers at the western side of the tower are cruciform (the aisle respond here is a single pilaster); further west, they have a square core with pilasters on the faces (the aisle and wall-responds here consist of one pilaster engaged into another). There are no wall-ribs in the aisles, and the main arcades are rectangular. The design is rather austere, with a minimum of sculpture.

A late example of the monastic style, related to Bourbonne les Bains and perhaps ultimately to Epoisses.

(a) Courtépée 2, 244; Longnon, *Lyon*, 156 (1436); Roserot 362. (b) Foisset 79; Guillaume 378.

ST THIBAULT EN AUXOIS (Côte d'Or) (78)

St Blaise (St Thibault), Benedictine priory of St Rigaud en Mâconnais.

See pp. 93–94 and Plates 30b and 31.

There are remains of the transept built about 1240–1250, and the portal sculpture is well-preserved. According to Colombet, the St Gilles chapel was erected about 1270–1280 and the apse about 1290, although the upper stories of the latter seem later. The work does not seem to have been terminated, and there was considerable revision of the programme in the XVI c. and XVIII c.

(b) A. Colombet, *Saint-Thibault-en-Auxois*, Dijon (1957), with bibliography (add Petit 6, 198–199 and L. Schürenberg, *Die kirchliche Baukunst in Frankreich*, Berlin, 1934, 172–174); Hautecœur (2) 113–114 and pls. 110–111; on the sculpture, see L. Lefrançois-Pillion, "L'église de Saint-Thibault-en-Auxois et ses œuvres de sculpture", *Gazette des Beaux-Arts*, s. 5, v. 5 (25), 1922, I, 137–157. (c) Cottineau (2) 2900.

ST VERAIN (Nièvre) (102)

St Verain & St Blaise, Benedictine priory of St Germain at Auxerre, in the diocese of Auxerre.

The nave, with groin-vaulted aisles, probably originally had a pointed barrel vault; the present ribbed vaults, all four-part, and the clerestory were added about 1220.

(a) Longnon, *Sens*, 256 (late XV c.: parish). (b) Soultrait, *Rép.*, 125–126; von Veltheim, *passim*. (c) Cottineau (2) 2914.

SAVIGNY EN TERRE PLAINE (Yonne) (41)

St Bénigne, parish, given in 1148 to the canons of St Lazare at Avallon by the bishop of Autun; in the diocese of Autun.

About 1195–1200, a small, rectangular apse of one story was constructed. It has a four-part vault resting on corbels. The eastern wall bears a triplet crowned by continuous mouldings. The ogive is similar in profile to Epoisses and Langres, St Didier. There are no wall-ribs.
   A late example of the earliest type of ribbed apse.

(a) Longnon, *Lyon*, 88 (XIV c.). (b) Anon., in *Mém. com. C.-d'Or*, 4, 1853–1856, 317–325; Petit in *Bull. Soc. Yonne* 19, 1865, 229; Quantin, *Rép.*, 97; von Veltheim 92–94, with plan.

SELONGEY (Côte d'Or) (66)

St Remi, parish in the diocese of Langres, at the presentation of the abbot of St Bénigne at Dijon.

The nave was built about 1250, on foundations apparently of about 1210–1220; the upper parts were again rebuilt at the end of the XIII c. The crossing was altered about 1300.
   The nave has four bays with aisles. The piers are cruciform with colonnettes on the faces and in the angles. The wall-responds are thickened outward above the pier capitals, and the four-part vaults set immediately above the main arcades, producing a low, two-storied design without a clerestory.

(a) Courtépée 2, 249–252; Longnon, *Lyon*, 159 (1436); Roserot 375. (b) Foisset, 131–132; Guillaume 346, with interior view, 345.

SEMENTRON (Yonne) (35)

St Pierre, parish in the diocese of Auxerre, under the bishop.

See p. 18, n. 4 and Fig. 2c.

The apse was built about 1160–1170. It is small and rectangular, with a four-part vault. There is one plain lancet in the eastern wall, and two in each lateral wall. The crowns of the vault are slightly sloping.
  Among the earliest ribbed vaults in the Yonne Valley.

(a) Longnon, *Sens*, 252 (late XIV c.). (b) Quantin, *Rép.*, 43; Philippe 69.

SEMUR EN AUXOIS (Côte d'Or) (73)

Notre Dame, Benedictine priory of Flavigny, in the diocese of Autun.

See pp. 66–68, 75, Fig. 18 and Plates 21 and 22b.

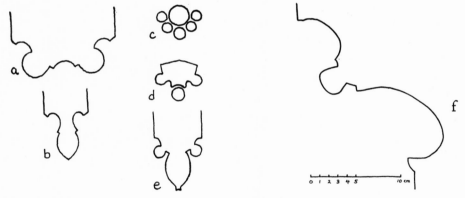

Fig. 90. Semur en Auxois, rib profiles and supports: a. transverse arch; b. aisle ogive; c. triforium respond in the choir; d. clerestory respond in the hemicycle; e. main ogive; f. base of hemicycle pier.

The Gothic edifice was begun about 1220–1225. The first campaign, comprising the chevet and lower walls of the transept, was divided into normal phases: the the peripheral wall; the piers and lower vaults; the triforium in the chevet and including the eastern walls and terminals of the transept, and finally the clerestory over these portions. Both triforium and clerestory were first erected in the hemicycle and then the choir and transept. The XIII c. portions of the nave were built in three phases from about 1235 on: the outer walls, including the responds at the western side of the fourth aisle bay, and six main piers; the triforium and clerestory of the transept, together with the next pair of piers and one more bay of the south aisle; and finally the triforium and clerestory over these portions. The western bays of the nave and the porch are from the early XIV c.

Severe damage was inflicted on the church during the Hundred Years' War, and restorations were made in the XV c. (Courtépée: 1403? and 1450), for which see de Truchis. The latter's suggestion that the triforium of the nave was suppressed about 1370 seems to be incorrect. On the west wall of the south transept, this story was obviously removed at a later date, but there are no signs of a passage running through the supports at the original clerestory level. On the west wall of the north transept, the remains of such a passage are still evident at the intermediary support and behind the north-western crossing pier. Such remains are not to be found behind the south-western crossing pier, but the masonry in this area is all new. It would seem as if the clerestory passage were first abandoned and then the triforium suppressed, all during the original campaign of construction. The entire building was thoroughly restored in the XIX c.

The vaults are constructed *en tas-de-charge*. The supports in the triforium are all detached shafts, the core-colonnettes having a diameter of less than 30 cm. The chevet may have been planned with a very low aisle roof, since the supports for the flying buttresses consist, in the hemicycle bay, of heavy detached shafts resting on moulded bases and socles, with sculpted capitals above, the whole obviously designed to be uncovered. The present slope seems to have been planned only with the construction of the bay adjacent to the transept, where the normal pilaster makes its appearance, although the aisle roofs of the nave were also intended to be low, as is indicated by the water conduits. The clerestory supports are also *en délit*, excepting only those above the third piers of the nave, in the XIII c. work.

The north transept portal (Portail des Bleds) is sculpted. There are extensive remains of the cloister, known to Viollet-le-Duc (*Dictionnaire*, 3, 441).

(a) Courtépée 3, 469–474; Petit 6, 197. (b) Maillard de Chambure, "Histoire et description de l'église Notre-Dame de Semur-en-Auxois", *Mém. com. C.-d'Or*, (s. 1), 1, 1832–1833, 48–84; P. de Truchis, "Semur-en-Auxois", *Cong. arch.* (Avallon), 74, 1907, 64–79; Cl. Contant, "Le tympan de la porte des Bleds", *Bulletin mensuel de la Société des sciences historiques et naturelles de Semur-en-Auxois*, 1932, xlviii–li; Jantzen, 25–27. (c) Cottineau (2) 3002.

SENS (Yonne) (11)

A. St Etienne, cathedral of the metropolitan see.

See pp. 30, 88–90, Figs. 25, 26 and Plates 8a, 12b and 45a.

The edifice was begun under Archbishop Henri le Sanglier (1122–1142), possibly between 1124 and 1128 (Salet), but it is doubtful if much was accomplished at this time beyond the laying of the foundations of the chevet and the erection of part of the peripheral wall. The project seems to have included groined-vaults in the ambulatory (remains of the departures are visible alongside two of the respond capitals, as noted by de Maillé) and simple columnar piers in the hemicycle (cf. one unrestored impost above the weak pier to the north of the axis, which is composed of two stones, one of which was originally made to surmount a single hemicycle capital, and the fact that all the twin capitals are cut in separate stones which were often recut to permit their closer juxtaposition [Plate 45a.]). It is possible that the

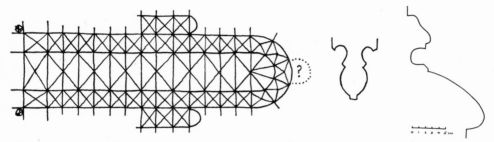

Fig. 91. Sens Cathedral, plan, ogive profile from XIII c. chapel and base from south-eastern pier of the north tower.

hemicycle was to have been covered by a half-dome, although the diameter is large (15 m. 25; cf. 12 m. 34 [interior] at Langres). The revision of this project, about 1140, included raising and ribbing the ambulatory vaults and doubling the hemicycle columns. The heavy composed piers of the hemicycle may have been planned only at this time. The clerestory seems originally to have had twin lancets in each bay, with an exterior decoration of four arcades, the outer two of which were blind (the design used in the transept tribunes at Arras, probably about 1170). Construction proceeded rather uniformly and with remarkably few changes of plan from this time on. The chevet was ready in 1164, and work continued on the nave (in 1165 alms were solicited, and in 1168, when Archbishop Hugues de Torcy died, it was said, "[ecclesiam] . . . fere perfecit"). A fire of 1184 is thought to have interrupted work and caused some destruction, but it certainly was not responsible for the alteration of the main vaults, which was not effected before the 1230's, when the lateral webs were raised and new clerestory windows created. It is uncertain whether the axial chapel, which also dates from this period, replaced an older one or not. By 1195–1200, the west façade and towers were under construction, and altars were established in the upper chambers here in 1214 and 1221. The south tower fell in 1268 and was rebuilt at once, together with the south lateral chapel and the adjacent bays, although this work was not finished for several centuries.

The Synodal Hall, or Officialité, was part of the archiepiscopal palace built by Gautier Cornut (1222–1241), probably during the last years of his administration. The vast, open hall of the upper story is supported by several rows of piers and vaults beneath. The most distinctive characteristics are the complex window forms, derived from central Champagne (perhaps the clerestory of the chevet of the cathedral at Châlons sur Marne), and the Laonnois passage along the western wall, for which see Bony (1958). The edifice was severely damaged by the fall of the cathedral tower in 1268 and repaired at once. In view of this restoration, and another very thorough one by Viollet-le-Duc, it is impossible to draw any definite conclusions as to the shop or master.

(b) E. Chartraire, *La cathédrale de Sens (PM)*, Paris, (1921); L. Bégule, *La cathédrale de Sens*, Lyon, 1929; de Maillé, *Provins*, Paris, 1939, I, 86, n. 1; R. Hamann, sen., "Ottonische Kapitelle im Chor der Kathedrale von Sens", *Festschrift für Hans Jantzen*, Berlin, 1951, 92–96 (the dating of the capitals is hardly acceptable); R. Fourrey, *Sens. Ville d'art et d'histoire*, Lyon, 1953; Salet in *Comptes-rendus, Académie des inscriptions et belles-lettres*, 1955, 182–187. (c) Besse 6 (1913), 15, n. 1.

B. St Jean l'Evangéliste, Augustinian abbey founded in 1111 by the provost of the metropolitan chapter.

See p. 69 and Plate 23b.

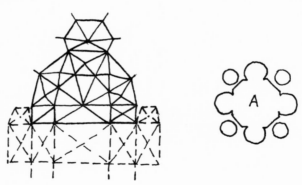

Fig. 92. Sens, St Jean, plan and pier.

The church and conventual buildings are said to have been first built in 1127, with materials taken from the church of St Sauveur des Vignes. The present chevet was begun about 1230. The destroyed nave dated from the XV c., but this may have replaced an earlier one. The clerestory and vaults of the chevet were in ruins in the XVII c. (see Paris, *Bibl. Nat., Est.*, Va 16) and were restored in the XIX c. The axial chapel was inspired by Auxerre cathedral and possibly by the cathedral of Sens, if, in fact, there was a XII c. chapel there, but the transept suggests a different order of sources. The elevation at present contains a normal clerestory and a section of plain wall above the main arcades. The Rémois passage in the aisle wall is limited to the chapel and the two adjoining bays of the ambulatory on each side; it may, before the XIX c. restorations, have existed further to the west. The responds in the chapel passage consist of three detached shafts in a cluster.

St Jean is the best extant evidence for an active Burgundian milieu at Sens in the 1220's and 1230's. It is related to Nevers cathedral and to nearby Villeneuve sur Yonne.

(b) V. Petit in *Ann. Yonne*, 1843, 144 and 1847, 122; C. Porée in *Cong. arch.* (Avallon), 74, 1907, 227–228; R. Fourrey, *Sens*, Lyon, 1953, 115; Y. Bruand in *Cong. arch.* (Auxerre), 116, 1958, 383–391. (c) Cottineau (2) 3007.

C. St Paul sur Vanne, founded in 1192 as a priory of Dilo and promoted to the status of abbey in 1221.

See p. 69.

The church was begun about 1230 and is destroyed. One bay of the aisle wall has been reconstructed in the Museum. It is very close to the ambulatory of St Jean, having a Rémois passage, triplet windows and an inner screen.

(c) Cottineau (2) 3008.

D. St Pierre le Rond, parish church under the patronage of the abbot of St Rémi.

The apse was reconstructed about 1230–1240. The vaults are not extant.

The edifice is small and has a single story of windows above a dado. There is a triplet in the axial bay, and in the others twin lancets with nearly round-headed arches surmounted by an oculus. The embrasures are deep, but there is no passage.

(a) Longnon, *Sens*, 5 (about 1350). (b) R. Fourrey, *Sens*, Lyon, 1953, 115–116.

[E. St Pierre le Vif, Benedictine abbey.]

See p. 69.

St Pierre is famous as having had one of the late Carolingian eastern rotundae (before 1015). The entire church is now destroyed. A campaign was inaugurated under Abbot Hugh (in office about 1215–1221; his epitaph is quoted by Bouvier, 126) in 1219 (in 1218, the edifice "minabatur ruinam et dissipata fuit", undoubtedly in order to give place for the new work; there was an exhibition of relics in this year, probably to raise funds for the campaign). Under Abbot Geffroy (1240–1282), work was carried out on the refectory, infirmary, *basse-cour* and so on, suggesting that the fabric of the church had been terminated, perhaps before the May, 1255, transfer of relics for a visit of the archbishop. Bouvier also attributes the monks' choir to Geffroy (130).

The church is known from a 1656 plan (Paris, *Arch. Nat.*, N III 4, reproduced in J. Hubert, *L'art préroman*, Paris, 1938, pl. 1d and Bouvier, pl. iv); and from a view of the exterior northern elevation in the *Monasticon Gallicanum*, pl. 137 (also Bouvier, pl. 1). Another northern elevation can be found in the bird's-eye view of the city, in Paris, *Bibl. Nat., Est.*, Va 416. The view contained in Claude Chastillon's *Topographie françoise* (ed. Boisseau, Paris, 1641, p. 203) and identified as St Pierre only by the table of contents (it was probably made not by Chastillon himself), seems entirely imaginary.

The dimensions and a brief, archaeologically almost useless description, are given by Dom Cotron (Auxerre, *Bibl. mun.*, ms. 156, pp. 658–659): length, about 80 m.; width, about 24 m.; length of transept, about 36 m.; height, about 32 m. The 1656 plan indicates: height of the western part of the nave, with a wooden roof, 16 m. 58; of the aisles here, 7 m. 80; of the crossing (in ruins), 13 m. 16; of the eastern aisles of the nave (also in ruins), 8 m. 78; of the buttresses on the north side here, 17 m. 55. The plan also says that the eastern bays of the nave were in ruins and that the six piers here were new and rose to a height of 5 m. 85. The elevation of the nave is very uncertain.

(a) Geoffroi de Courlon, *Chronique de l'abbaye de Saint-Pierre-le-Vif de Sens*, ed. Julliot, Sens, 1876, 508–510; Abbé Bouvier, "Histoire de Saint-Pierre-le-Vif", *Bull. Soc. Yonne*, 45, 1891, 5–212. (b) F. Salet in *Bull. mon.* 92, 1933, 140–141; J. Hubert, *L'art préroman*, Paris, 1938, 32–33 (where the erroneous date of 1118 (for 1218) is reproduced from Bouvier, 122), and *id.* (1952), no. 92.

SERRIGNY (Côte d'Or) (97)

St Marcel, parish and, sometime after 1134, priory, at the presentation of the abbot of St Seine, in the diocese of Autun.

About 1200 were constructed a small, rectangular apse, single, projecting transept bays, and a crossing to support a tower. All have four-part vaults. The responds are similar to those at Epoisses. The nave of three aisles (totally restored) has a pointed barrel vault and XVI c. groined vaults over the aisles. The vaults over the eastern parts are probably not authentic.

An interesting, if minor, extension of style from the west of Burgundy.

(a) Courtépée 2, 353–355; Longnon, *Lyon*, 79 (XIV c.); Roserot 378. (b) Foisset, 179; Guillaume 81. (c) Cottineau (2) 3018.

TALANT (Côte d'Or) (82)

Notre Dame, priory of St Bénigne at Dijon.

The priory was founded in 1209, but the present church was not built until about 1240–1245 ff.

The apse is rectangular, with a four-part vault resting on corbels. The next bay is six-part, and a tower surmounts the eastern half. The nine-bay nave has irregular alternation and six-part vaults, the weak ogives on corbels. The elevation has two stories with a small lancet above unornamented wall. The ogives have simple chamfers.

An example of the monastic style, but with evidence of frequent changes of plan.

(a) Roserot 384. (b) Garnier, "Monographie . . .", *Mém. com. C.-d'Or*, 3, 1847–1852, 213–311; Foisset 64–65; Guillaume 54–56, with interior view. (c) Laurent-Claudon (1941), 610 and n.

TANNAY (Nièvre) (108)

St Léger, collegiate church in the diocese of Nevers.

The apse was erected about 1230, the transept about 1240–1250. A dedication is said to have been performed in 1313.

The edifice is small. The crossing is low and the tower planned above it was never executed. The responds in the apse are detached shafts. The eastern terminal wall has a triplet and oculus in an unornamented wall; the south transept has a triplet. The eastern crossing piers have three contiguous colonnettes set forward of the wall at the entrances to the chapels; the western pair are cruciform with colonnettes on the faces and in the angles, and rounded pilasters. The minor rib of the apse is corbelled, and one ogive of the north transept rests on a corbelled, detached shaft. The rib of the north chapel is similar to the oldest one at Clamecy (St Martin).

Perhaps related to the later Clamecy shops, this church represents the diffusion of Gothic designs into the country.

(b) J. J. Bourassé, *Esquisse archéologique . . . de Nevers*, Nevers, 1844, 122; Soultrait, *Rép.*, 65–66.

TONNERRE (Yonne) (24)

Notre Dame, collegiate church shortly before 1219 (it had been a branch of St Aignan from 1164), dissolved 1224–1225, and thereafter a parish in the diocese of Langres.

The eastern portion was probably begun about 1230; the transept and nave were recognized in 1855 as dating from the XVI c., although they are now imitation-XIII c. The edifice burned in 1359 and 1414, and was restored after 1878 and again after the last war.

The apse has seven bays, the choir two, each covered by a four-part vault. The transept does not project, and this feature conceivably reflects the original XIII c. disposition. There are two stories, each with windows, the upper set lacking capitals on the framing rolls. The ribs are ultimately related to those at Pontigny and the departures are *en tas-de-charge*.

(a) Longnon, *Lyon*, 148 (1436). (b) Cotteau-Petit in *Ann. Yonne*, 1855, 469–470; Quantin, *Rép.*, 273; figure in *Bull. mon.* s.2, v.8 (18), 1852, 237. (c) Laurent-Claudon (1941), 177–178.

TOUCHES (Saône et Loire) (114)

St Symphorien, parish in the diocese of Chalon sur Saône, under the patronage of the cathedral chapter.

Built in the second quarter of the XIII c., the church is small. There is a tower over the third bay from the west. The elevation consists of a single, low story, and the ribs, with concave chamfers, rest on corbels. The nave is only slightly taller than the aisles, and the vault lunettes are blind.

(a) Longnon, *Lyon*, 183 (XIV c.). (b) J. Ancelin, "L'église de Touches", *Mémoires, Société d'histoire et d'archéologie de Chalon-sur-Saône*, s.2, v.14 (22), 1926–1927, 35–46; mentioned in Y. Fernillot, "Les églises gothiques de l'ancien diocèse de Chalon", *Positions de thèses de l'école des chartes*, 1946, 55–61.

TROYES (Aube) (2)

[A. St Etienne, collegiate church in the château of the counts of Champagne, enlarged in 1157 by Henri I from a chapel (St André) with two chaplains, to a full chapter possessing no less than 72 prebends at a slightly later date. A loge opening onto the western end of the building formed part of the *corps de logis* of the château. Destroyed in 1791.]

See p. 22 and Plates 38b and 39c.

The edifice seems to have been begun shortly after 1157, perhaps at the eastern end. It was affected by the fire of 1188 and restored and completed by Thibault III and Henri II. The 1769 plan suggests that there were at least three campaigns of construction, excluding the north tower. The only known extant fragment is a large capital in the *Musée de la Ville (St Loup)* (Pl. 39c), but a late XVIII c. view, perhaps made shortly after the destruction, is in the *Musée Historique de Troyes et de la Champagne* (Pl. 38b and Roserot, p. 1655).

According to Roserot, there were fourteen bays but only seven keystones in the main vessel, suggesting six-part vaults that would match the alternating piers of the plan. In fact there must have been another keystone, on the transverse arch of the hemicycle. According to de Maillé, the axial chapel was original and there was a non-projecting transept. In the XVIII c. view, the corbel table and windows of the chapel resemble those of the ambulatory, although in the original plan the chapel bends so far to the north of the axis of the church that it seems to have been added at a later date. The view shows clearly that there was no transept of

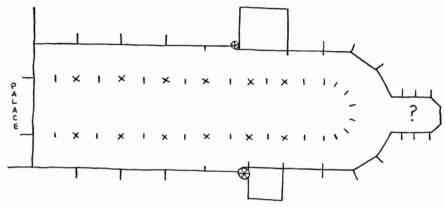

Fig. 93. Troyes, St Etienne, regularized plan.

any sort. The ambulatory may have borne a certain resemblance to Arras, for the twin windows undoubtedly indicated five-part vaults here and in the eastern bays of the collaterals. The general plan may belong to the series with alternating piers but no transept, of which Sens and Senlis are better-known examples. De Maillé also says the elevation had three stories with a "false" triforium, such as at Sens and St Germain des Prés in Paris, and this may be confirmed by the slope of the roof. The corbel table and the series of tall lancets in the clerestory, while not undebatable, bear a strong relationship to the XII c. work at Sens as I see it (the flying buttresses were obviously added later in both cases). The disposition of the western end is unclear: the count's loge lay upstairs – but within the church, according to the view – while the ground story here formed part of the palace.

(a) The 1188 fire is recorded in *Monumenta Germaniae Historica, Scriptorum, 26, 253* (Robert de St Marien). (b) the plan is freely taken from A. F. Arnaud, *Voyage archéologique et pittoresque dans le département de l'Aube*, Troyes, 1837, pl. IV (see also pp. 27–33) and ultimately from the 1769 city plan now in the Museum; A. Roserot, *Dictionnaire historique de la Champagne méridionale (Aube) des origines à 1790*, v. 3, Troyes, 1948, 1600–1601 and fig., p. 1655; the capital is described by Arnaud, "Notice sur quelques fragments de sculpture . . .", *Mémoires, Société d'agriculture, des sciences et arts du département de l'Aube*, 7, 1834–1835, 2, 11–19; see also de Maillé, *Provins*, Paris, 1939, 1, 71, n. 6. (c) Besse 6 (1913), 129–130.

B. Madeleine, branch of the parish of St Remy.

See pp. 34–35 and Plate 12a.

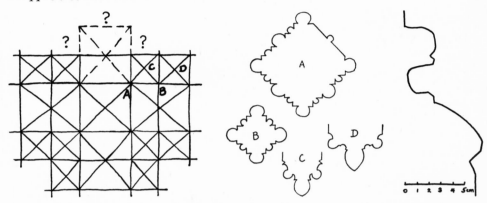

Fig. 94. Troyes, Madeleine, XII c. plan, piers, ogive and base profiles.

Begun at the end of the XII c., the first campaign included the ground-story, the triforium and clerestory in the chevet and the south transept and perhaps also the nave. About 1230 ff., the north side of the church was completed. The present chevet was begun in 1501. The whole edifice is very restored and is undergoing further reparations at the present time.

The plan is cruciform, although the form of the original eastern end is unknown. The aisle vaults are very domed. The triforium passage was not introduced until the second campaign, in the northern bays of the north transept (eastern side; see *Cong. arch.* (Troyes), 69, 1902, fig. following p. 288); the clerestory in the northern terminal here is screened, with small ribbed vaults in each of five bays, as at Coutances and Lyon (*ibid.*, fig. following p. 292).

(b) F. Salet, in *Cong. arch.* (Troyes), 113, 1955, 139–152, with bibliography.

VAL DES CHOUX (Côte d'Or) (54)

[Notre Dame (St Jean Baptiste), Trappist priory in the diocese of Langres, founded in 1193–1196 by Duke Eudes III. Destroyed.]

The nave, probably under construction in the 1230's, had eight bays and alternating piers with six-part vaults. The weak ribs rested on corbels at the base of the vault-zone, the strong ones were supported by colonnettes corbelled at the spandrels of the main arcades. The piers were alternately columnar and rectangular, the latter probably with shafts engaged on the aisle-side and beneath the arcades. The elevation had two stories, with a large expanse of plain wall between the low arcades and the short clerestory. There were flying buttresses on the exterior, and the aisle roof had a very steep slope.

In the monastic style.

(a) Courtépée 4, 235–237; Roserot 402. (b) Mignard in *Mém. com. C.-d'Or*, 6, 1861–1864, 412–483, with general plan of the abbey, pp. 412–413; Petit 6, pl. 4, with view of cloister in 1830; E. Nesle, *Album pittoresque de l'arrondissement de Châtillon-sur-Seine*, Châtillon sur Seine, 1853, 416–417, with interior and exterior views; Guillaume 340–341. (c) Laurent-Claudon (1941), 425–429.

VANDENESSE (Côte d'Or) (87)

Notre Dame, parish in the diocese of Autun, under the patronage of the chapter of Marrigny le Cahouet.

The edifice is small. In the mid-XIII c., the nave of the barrel-vaulted edifice (of which the transepts are extant) may have been replaced by two simple bays with four-part vaults, the whole now totally rebuilt (it is possibly even fictitious). There is a single story, and the ribs, with chamfered angles, rest on corbels, as in the apse of La Bussière. The rectangular chapels flanking the small apse and choir may be from this period. In the late XIII c., certainly after the donation of Anséric de Vergy for a "balustrade" (Courtépée: 1270), and perhaps in the early XIV c., the apse and choir were rebuilt with four-part vaults, and the vault beneath the crossing tower was remade.

A provincial design.

(a) Courtépée 4, 88; Longnon, *Lyon*, 84 (XIV c.); Roserot 404. (b) Foisset 251–252; Guillaume 144.

VARZY (Nièvre) (107)

[A. Ste Eugénie, collegiate church in the diocese of Auxerre. Now in ruins.]

The chapel of St Roche, on the north side of the choir and over a spring said to have healing powers, was reconstructed in the early XIII c. It had two bays covered by four-part vaults. The north-east and south-east responds have three colonnettes each, with rectangular socles and bases with feet. The capitals have crockets. The vaults measured 6 m. 45 to the keystone.

(b) Soultrait, *Rép.*, 72; R. Lussier–J. Palet, "La collégiale Sainte-Eugénie de Varzy", *Bulletin, Société nivernaise des lettres, sciences et arts*, v. 28 (29), 1930–1933, 547–566 (fundamental); M. Anfray, *L'architecture religieuse du Nivernais*, Paris, 1951, p. 118. (c) Besse 6 (1913), 77 and n.

B. St Pierre, parish under the patronage of Ste Eugénie.

See p. 8 and Plate 36b.

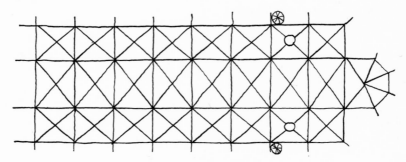

Fig. 95. Varzy, plan.

Probably begun about 1250, the eastern end seems to have been dedicated in 1280, despite Lebeuf's and Serbat's refusal to admit the latter date because it was preserved on a tablet of a later period. The nave was in the works in the last twenty years of the century and the early ones of the XIV c.

The plan bears a certain resemblance to the type of the Saône River Valley, because of the towers over the transept arms (cf. Lyon). The chevet has tall lancets over a Rémois passage; there are deep niches in the eastern walls of the chapels, but no passage, that is, the adaptation of the Burgundian parti to small edifices as at Bèze. The rounded pilaster is also present, and the shop may ultimately have come from Auxerre cathedral. The nave was begun about 1280, the campaign starting with the completion of the upper portions of the transept.

(a) Lebeuf 1, 467. (b) Soultrait, *Rép.*, 72–73; L. Serbat in *Cong. arch.* (Moulins-Nevers), 80, 1913, pp. 401–415; L. Schürenberg, *Die kirchliche Baukunst in Frankreich*, Berlin, 1934, 167–169.

VAUX (Yonne) (27)

St Loup, parish in the diocese of Auxerre, at the presentation of St Julien lès Auxerre.

See p. 18, n. 14 and Fig. 2g.

About 1170–1180, a small, rectangular apse with a four-part vault was built onto the older church (now much more recent). There are single, plain lancets in the walls and the responds have alternately large and small engaged colonnettes separated by half-pilasters. The capitals have crockets on a tall core, some with patterns of leaves. There are wall-ribs.

The apse represents the continuation of the earliest ribbed-vault style in the Yonne Valley. The capitals look forward to those in the chevet of Pontigny and possibly at the Madeleine at Troyes.

(a) Longnon, *Sens*, 257 (late XIV c.). (b) Cotteau-Petit in *Ann. Yonne*, 1852, 416; Quantin, *Rép.*, 21–22; Philippe, *passim*.

VERMENTON (Yonne) (32)

Notre Dame, parish in the diocese of Auxerre, under the patronage of the bishop.

See pp. 20–23, Fig. 3 and Plate 4b.

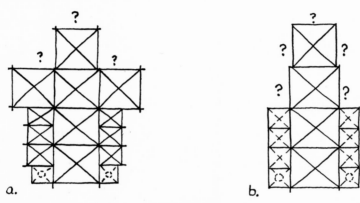

Fig. 96. Vermenton, plans: a. suggested XIII c. plan; b. suggested XII c. plan.

A tower was said to have been built in 1158 (Courtépée), but there is no extant portion of the edifice corresponding to this date. Mathilda, wife of Guy, Count of Nevers, is said to have founded the building "around the middle of the XII c." (Courtépée), but probably not before about 1170. The church may have attracted attention about 1200 when the well-known preacher, Etienne de Cudot, nephew of the Blessed Alpaix, resigned the archdeaconship of Auxerre and a prebend at Paris, to become parish priest. In 1213, the bishop gave part of the parish revenue to the new cathedral wardens (Lebeuf 4, 77). Built from east to west, the work of a new shop (predominantly sculptors) is noticeable in the west bay, about 1190. The eastern end was rebuilt and the aisles enlarged about 1230; further enlargements were made in the east in the late XIII c. or early XIV c.

First plan: the form of the XII c. chevet cannot be determined without excavation; only parts of the piers and the vault ribs in the third and fourth bays from the west are intact. The supports and the elevation were probably the same here as in the western bays, and it is likely that the aisles were narrower and groin-vaulted, as in the extant bays beneath the western towers (only one of these is completed). The weak pier on the south side of the west bay forms a rectangle with detached shafts set into the angles (chamfered); the shafts are made to resemble tree-trunks and evince the vivid sculptural imagination of this shop. The edifice is now covered by a single roof over nave and aisles. There are important remains of a sculpted western portal, with statue-columns.

Second plan: The reconstruction or enlargement of the chevet consisted in removing the walls of the two eastern bays and adding square transept bays. The terminals have triplet windows in the lunette and twin windows below the string-course. The form of the eastern walls of the transept is unknown. The nave aisles were also enlarged, and the roof perhaps altered to the present disposition at this time. The imposts and socles are circular, the piers contain rounded pilasters between the colonnettes.

Third plan: the chevet was converted into a hall-church by the addition of similar rectangular bays around the old sanctuary, terminating in a flat wall.

The second plan was executed by a sophisticated Burgundian shop in a simple and inexpensive manner.

(a) Lebeuf 4, 77; Courtépée 4, 373–378; A. Lecoy de la Marche, *Anecdotes historiques . . . d'Etienne de Bourbon* (*Société de l'histoire de France*), Paris, 1877, 27, 29. (b) A. Philippe in *Cong. arch.* (Avallon), 74, 1907, 148–154, where the (correct) analysis of the campaigns of construction is misrepresented in the chronological indications of the plan; views of the interior of the chevet in Hautecœur (2), pls. 103–104; M. Aubert in *Cong. arch.* (Auxerre), 116, 1958, 275–281.

VERONNES LES GRANDES (Côte d'Or) (71)

St Hilaire, parish in the diocese of Langres, under the patronage of the bishop.

The apse was built about 1220 and the nave in the late XIII c., perhaps at the time Philippe le Bel enfranchised the hamlet (Courtépée: 1294). The church was formerly part of the château and was fortified with it in 1369.

The edifice is small. The rectangular apse has a four-part vault; the responds are colonnettes engaged into two half-pilasters fitted into the corner. The imposts are polygonal, the ogive has an almond torus flanked by two cyma recta mouldings. The nave has three aisles and five bays, with a tower above the eastern one and four-part vaults. The ribs here have simple chamfered angles.

(a) Courtépée 2, 262–263; Longnon, *Lyon*, 156 (1436); Roserot 414. (b) Foisset 135–136; Guillaume 365.

VEZELAY (Yonne) (39)

Ste Madeleine, Benedictine abbey in the diocese of Autun.

See pp. 17, 30–34, Fig. 2f and Plates 9b and 42b.

The narthex, planned about 1120, was not executed until the 1150's, and the two ribbed vaults in the tribunes here were constructed about 1155. The capitular hall was probably built between 1161 and 1164. The Gothic chevet was begun about 1185, a year or two before Pontigny, and probably terminated about 1205–1210.

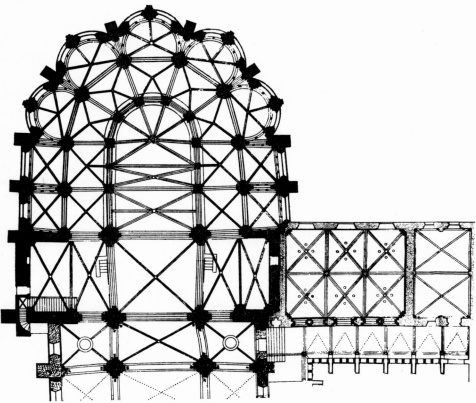

Fig. 97. Vézelay, plan of chevet, transept and chapter house (after Salet).

There is considerable difficulty in determining the details of the original plan of the Gothic chevet. The eight columns of the hemicycle undoubtedly supported a single vault, and this must have been preceded by a single four-part vault resting, on the west, on the present (eastern) crossing piers. Following M. Salet's discerning analysis of these crossing piers, it would appear that the transept was an afterthought. It is possible that the present crossing was intended to contain two bays and two four-part vaults, or perhaps a single six-part vault. It seems unlikely, however, that the lateral chapels were meant to be prolonged to the Romanesque nave: construction began at the west side of the present north-western chapel, and there is no indication that another chapel was to have been placed on the opposite side of the wall here; and the capitular hall on the south impinges on the site for chapels on this side.

The verso of the narthex façade was reworked about 1230, when the present interior passages and lancets were added. The arcading and sculpture at the base of the passage were probably executed by someone intimately familiar with the cathedral of Auxerre.

(b) F. Salet, *La Madeleine de Vézelay*, Melun, 1949, with bibliography.

VILLENAUXE (Aube) (1)

St Pierre & St Paul, Augustinian priory of St Quentin at Beauvais, in the diocese of Troyes.

The chevet was begun about 1235.

Five niche-like chapels surround the ambulatory, and there is no passage between them. The peripheral wall has an arcaded dado and a window with an oculus above two lancets. The respond, across the small face of the trapezoidal pier, has three thin engaged colonnettes; the capitals and imposts are *à bec*, continuing across the lateral faces of the pier as a frieze. Some of the bases here have denticulations in place of the normal cavetto. The main piers are columnar with octagonal imposts. The wall-respond has three shafts, with side ones with capitals and, above them, rings, supporting an extra arch of the main arcade; the central shaft, only, rises to the string-course. The upper portions of the hemicycle are not extant.

The details of the chevet reveal the presence of an Ile de France shop, although the chapels seem like reduced versions of a Cistercian formula.

(b) d'Arbois, *Rép.*, 98–99; notice in *Cong. arch.* (Troyes), 69, 1902, 59–60.
(c) Cottineau (2) 3390.

VILLENEUVE L'ARCHEVEQUE (Yonne) (10)

Notre Dame, Augustinian priory of St Jean at Sens, founded in 1172 by Archbishop Guillaume de Champagne.

The westernmost bay of the nave was erected about 1240. The eastern portions have groined vaults over the aisles and perhaps the main vessel was to have been similarly covered. The western bay of the north aisle has a tower above it and a sculpted portal on the north flank. The pier beneath the tower has groups of three colonnettes on a rounded core, separated by detached shafts. A similar but smaller design is found in the south aisle. The vault beneath the tower is taller than those over the aisles.

The western bay represents a late extension of Burgundian details to the north.

(b) V. Petit in *Ann. Yonne* 1843, 2, 150–152; Quantin, *Rép.*, 230–231. (c) Cottineau (2) 3392.

VILLENEUVE SUR YONNE (Yonne) (12)

Notre Dame, parish in the diocese of Paris, under the patronage of the bishop. *See pp. 80–81 and Plates 26b and 27b.*

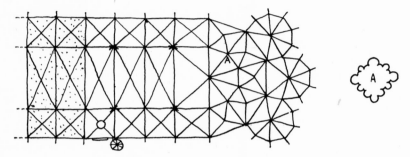

Fig. 98. Villeneuve sur Yonne, plan and pier.

The church was begun about 1245–1250, despite the presence of a stained-glass window dated, by Lafond, in the second quarter of the XIII c. The eastern periphery was erected first, including three of the straight aisle bays, and the hemicycle piers followed at once. About 1255–1260, one more aisle bay was put up, together with eight main piers, probably about the time the hemicycle clerestory was under construction. The next six piers and eight aisle bays were constructed about 1270, and the western end of the church was not terminated until the XVI c.

(a) Longnon, *Sens*, 351 (about 1205). (b) E. Lefèvre-Pontalis in *Cong. arch.* (Avallon), 74, 1907, 654–674; J. Lafond in *Cong. arch.* (Auxerre), 116, 1958, 378–382.

BIBLIOGRAPHICAL NOTE

The most recent and fundamental study for Gothic Burgundy is Jean Bony's "The resistance to Chartres in early thirteenth-century architecture", *Journal of the British Archaeological Association*, s. 3, vols. 21–22, 1957–1958, 35–52. Jantzen's *Burgundische Gotik*, Munich, 1948, is also of considerable interest, although the context is limited and the developments somewhat oversimplified. E. Lefèvre-Pontalis "'Les caractères distinctifs des églises gothiques de la Champagne et de la Bourgogne", *Congrès archéologique* (Avallon), 74, 1907, 546–558, while containing much useful information, is very old, and the same must be said of A. Philippe's "L'architecture religieuse aux XIe et XIIe siècles dans l'ancien diocèse d'Auxerre", *Bulletin monumental*, 68, 1904, 43–92. J. Carlet, "De l'origine de l'ogive et du style architectural des églises bourguignonnes du moyen âge", *Mémoires, Société d'histoire, d'archéologie et de littérature de l'arrondissement de Beaune*, 3, 1878, 171–218, and J. Calmette, "Les limites architectoniques du gothique bourguignon", *Mémoires, Commission des antiquités du département de la Côte-d'Or*, 16, 1909–1913, 73–86 (reprinted in his *Etudes médiévales*, Paris, 1946, 270–281), are almost useless. The various works of C. Oursel ("Une vieille question: comment l'art gothique a-t-il pénétré en Bourgogne?" *Bulletin, Société archéologique de Sens*, 37, 1929–1930, 117–132; "La place de la Bourgogne dans le développement de l'architecture religieuse du moyen âge", *Bulletin, Société des amis du Musée de Dijon*, 1942–1943, 17–20; *L'Art en Bourgogne* (*Art et paysages*, 14), Grenoble–Paris, 1953), are always stimulating and informative, as are his numerous monographs listed in the Catalogue. The most useful volumes of the *Congrès archéologique*, also monographic in nature, are Avallon (74, 1907), Moulins-Nevers (80, 1913), Dijon (90, 1928), Lyon-Mâcon (98, 1935), Troyes (113, 1955) and Auxerre (116, 1958), the latter with a general review of mediaeval architecture in the Yonne Valley by J. Vallery-Radot ("Aspects et tendances de l'architecture religieuse dans les pays de l'Yonne", 9–25).

The archaeological repertories of the various departments of France have served in two particular ways: the notices often indicate older states of edifices that have since been restored, rebuilt or destroyed, and they sometimes form virtually the only bibliography on the smaller churches. Likewise, A. Guillaume's *La Côte-d'Or. Guide du touriste . . .*, composed for the casual tourist and extremely weak historically, is nonetheless informative and covers the department of the Côte d'Or, for which there is no complete archaeological repertory. The *pouillés* and the topographical dictionaries have served largely to identify the mediaeval patrons and votive saints of the churches.

For the Templars and Hospitallers in Burgundy, see Mignard, "Statistique des possessions de la milice du Temple en Bourgogne", *Congrès archéologique* (Dijon), 19, 1852, 205–216; C. Lavirotte, "Mémoire statistique sur les établissements des Templiers et des Hospitaliers de Saint-Jean de Jérusalem en Bourgogne", *ibid.*, 224–291; M. Quantin, "Histoire des ordres religieux et militaires du Temple et de Saint-Jean de Jérusalem dans le département de l'Yonne", *Annuaire historique du département de l'Yonne*, s. 2, vol. 21 (46), 1882, 39–118 and J. Vallery-Radot, "L'ancienne chapelle de la commanderie des Templiers du Saulce d'Islande", *Congrès archéologique* (Auxerre), 116, 1958, 298–301. H. Drouot ("Petites églises des vallées de la Montagne", *Annales de Bourgogne*, 24, 1952, 218–219) concludes that the Templars did not have a specific form of architecture in the Commandery of Châtillon and, by implication, in Burgundy at large.

THE PLATES

1. Auxerre Cathedral, the interior of the chevet.

2a. Anzy le Duc, the nave.

2b. Paray le Monial, the nave.

3b. Pontigny, the nave.

3a. Fontenay, the nave.

4a. Fontenay, the chapter house.

4b. Vermenton, detail of the nave.

5a. Bar sur Aube, St Pierre, the exterior of the chevet.

5b. Bar sur Aube, St Maclou, detail of the nave.

6b. Montréal, the crossing and apse.

6a. Chablis, St Pierre, the nave.

7b. Bar sur Aube, St Maclou, the nave.

7a. Langres Cathedral, the interior.

8b. Chablis, St Martin, the hemicycle.

8a. Sens Cathedral, the interior of the chevet.

9b. Vézelay, the interior of the chevet.

9a. Auxerre, St Eusèbe, the nave.

10. Pontigny, the interior of the chevet.

11a. Canterbury, a detail of Trinity Chapel.

11b. Geneva, former Cathedral, a detail of the choir.

12b. Sens Cathedral, a detail of the north tower wall.

12a. Troyes, Madeleine, a detail of the choir.

13b. Clamecy, St Martin, the ambulatory wall.

13a. Auxerre Cathedral, the north aisle of the chevet.

14. Auxerre Cathedral, an exterior detail of the hemicycle clerestory.

15. Auxerre Cathedral, a detail of the clerestory and triforium.

16b. Troyes, St Urbain, a detail of the choir.

16a. Dijon, Notre Dame, a detail of the choir.

17b. Reims, St Remi, a detail of the inner face of the west façade.

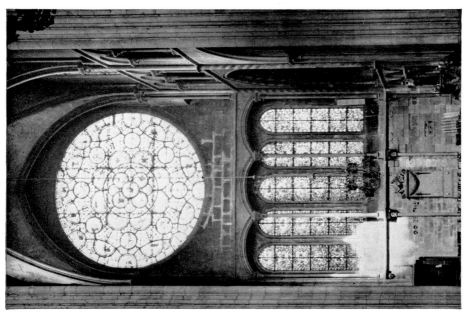

17a. Dijon, Notre Dame, the north transept.

18. Dijon, Notre Dame, the interior.

19. Dijon, Notre Dame, the porch.

20. Chalon sur Saône, Cathedral, the interior of the chevet.

21. Semur en Auxois, Notre Dame, the interior.

22b. Semur en Auxois, Notre Dame, a detail of the north transept.

22a. Nevers Cathedral, part of the nave.

23b. Sens, St Jean, the ambulatory and chapel.

23a. Auxonne, the apse.

24c. St Seine, the nave from the east.

24b. Bourges, St Pierre, the pier at the entrance to the southern chapel.

24a. Bourges, St Pierre, the interior.

25b. Cluny, Notre Dame, the nave from the east.

25a. Rougemont, a detail of the nave.

26b. Villeneuve sur Yonne, the interior of the chevet.

26a. St Père sous Vézelay, the interior.

27b. Villeneuve sur Yonne, the ambulatory.

27a. St Julien du Sault, the ambulatory.

28b. St Julien du Sault, the south aisle of the nave from the east.

28a. Auxonne, a detail of the eastern bays of the nave.

29b. Lyon Cathedral, the interior.

29a. Lyon Cathedral, a detail of the triforium passage in the north transept.

Vue de la façade de l'Église cathédrale de Mâcon

30a. Mâcon, former Cathedral, a view from the west by J. B. Lallemand (Paris, *Bibliothèque Nationale, Estampes*, Ve 26 p. 218).

30b. St Thibault, a detail of the St Gilles chapel.

30c. Mâcon, former Cathedral, a detail of the north aisle wall of the nave.

31. St Thibault, the apse.

32. Auxerre, St Germain, the interior.

33. Auxerre, St Germain, the ambulatory and chapel.

34. Dijon, St Bénigne, the interior.

35. Mussy sur Seine, the apse.

36b. Varzy, St Pierre, a detail of the nave.

36a. Chalon sur Saône Cathedral, the nave.

37b. Nevers Cathedral, the interior of the chevet.

37a. St Satur, the hemicycle.

38a. Flavigny, St Pierre, anonymous view of the nave in the XIX c. (Paris, *Bibliothèque Nationale, Estampes*, Ve 26 p. 145 r°).

38b. Troyes, St Etienne, anonymous view in the late XVIII c. (Troyes, *Musée Historique de Troyes et de la Champagne*).

39a. Flavigny, St Pierre, a detail of the nave.

39b. Flavigny, St Pierre, a detail of the narthex.

39c. Troyes, St Etienne, capital (Troyes, *Musée de la Ville* [*St Loup*]).

39d. Flavigny, St Pierre, a detail of the trumeau (now at Seigny).

40a. Boiscommun, the nave.

40b. Blécourt, the nave.

40c. L'Epau, the north transept and part of the north aisle from the west.

41c. Petit Ouges, the apse.

41b. Aignay le Duc, the nave.

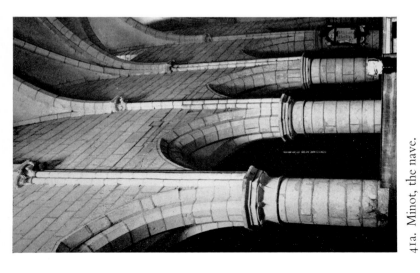

41a. Minot, the nave.

42a. Chalon sur Saône Cathedral, a detail of the intermediate respond in the choir.

42b. Vézelay, a detail of the passage running across the western wall of the narthex.

43a. Nevers Cathedral, a detail of the north arm of the west transept.

43b. Nevers Cathedral, a detail of an ambulatory respond.

44a. Aignay le Duc, a detail of the nave.

44b. L'Epau, a detail of the nave.

45a. Sens Cathedral, the capitals of the south weak pier of the ambulatory.

45b. Ste Colombe lès Sens, the capital unearthed by Brullée (now in the garden).

INDEX